What the Experts Are Saying .
Combatting Cult Mind Control

"*Combatting Cult Mind Control* combines superb research with authentic personal experience. The result is a remarkable achievement."

Rabbi A. James Rudin, Director
National Interreligious Affairs, The American Jewish Committee
Co-author of *Prison or Paradise:The New Religious Cults*

"*Combatting Cult Mind Control* puts everything into proper perspective. [Hassan] explains the differences between coercion and freedom. He plunges right into the intricacies of mind manipulation to produce a clear understanding of the process and its dangers."

Rev. James J. LeBar
Consultant on Cults
Archdiocese of New York

"A major contribution....For the first time, a skilled and ethical exit counselor has spelled out the details of the complicated yet understandable process of helping free a human being from the bondage of mental manipulation....Steve Hassan has written a 'how to do something about it' book."

Margaret Singer, Ph.D.
Department of Psychology
University of California, Berkeley

"Steve Hassan has demonstrated his openness and ability to bring a broad range of knowledge and scholarship to bear on vexing questions of cult methods and alternatives for intervention. The result is a significant contribution to public understanding of the modern reality of mind control and the widening dimensions of the cult experience."

Flo Conway and Jim Siegelman
Authors of *Snapping* and *Holy Terror*

"I strongly recommend *Combatting Cult Mind Control*. Cults are a major problem that affects more than a few people....Steve Hassan is a bright and superior person who has authored an important book. Go to a bookstore to buy it....Really try to get it!"

Steve Allen, Entertainer, Comedian, Songwriter
Creator of the original *Tonight* Show
Parent of an ex-cult member
Author of Beloved Son: A Story of the Jesus Cults

"A valuable, well-written book on a topic of genuine importance. Steve Hassan explains precisely how cults operate to control minds and, in the process, he provides sharp insights into how the influence process works in everyday situations as well."

Robert B. Cialdini, Ph.D.
Author of *Influence*

"...It is my hope that *Combatting Cult Mind Control* will reach many readers, including parents of children in cults, ex-members, and the public at large. A result of Hassan's experience and laborious research, this work is a most crucial contribution to the understanding of cults and the prevention of their further destructive influence on our society."

Dr. Phillip Abramowitz, Director
Interfaith Coalition of Concern About Cults

"Hassan is a master in the difficult task of opening closed minds. Anything he writes is on my booklist concerning destructive religious practices."

Robert Watts Thornburg
Dean of Marsh Chapel
Chaplain to Boston University

"... the serious clinician will find Hassan's book a challenge to the ignorance and prejudice that tragically surrounds the cult phenomenon."

Paul Martin, Ph.D.
Director of Wellspring Retreat and Resource Center
Rehabilitation facility for ex-cult members

"His book is well worth reading by professionals in mental health, particularly those involved with students, because early recognition and appropriate intervention depend on greater awareness of this menace."

Peter Tyrer, M.D.
"Review of Books"
The Lancet (Medical journal of Great Britain)

"Anyone who has witnessed a loved one rapidly slip into the emotionally insulated and distant world of a cult, knows the extent and swiftness of its catastrohic effects. Few people understand the mechanisms by which these devastating seductions are systematically engineered by cult leaders. Steve Hassan knows from experience. Through his examples and analyses, we finally witness how cults work and learn how we can protect ourselves and our loved ones from them."

Stephen Josephs, Ed.D.
Psychologist
Founder of Massachusetts Instutute of Neuro-Linguistic Programming

Combatting CULT MIND CONTROL

STEVEN HASSAN

Park Street Press
ROCHESTER·VERMONT

Park Street Press
One Park Street
Rochester, VT 05767

Library of Congress Cataloging-in-Publication Data

Hassan, Steven.
    Combatting cult mind control / Steven Hassan.
        p.   cm.
    Includes bibliographical references and index.
    ISBN 0-89281-311-3
    1. Cults—Controversial literature.   2. Cults—Psychological
aspects.   3. Hassan, Steven.   I. Title.
BP603.H375   1990
306'.1—dc20   90-43697
                                                   CIP

Printed and bound in the United States

10   9   8   7   6   5   4   3   2

Park Street Press is a division of Inner Traditions International, Ltd.

Distributed to the book trade in Canada by Book Center, Inc., Montreal, Quebec

I dedicate this book to people all over the world who have ever experienced the loss of their personal freedom, in the hope that it might help ease their suffering.

Contents

Acknowledgments

With heartfelt gratitude, I thank my parents, Milton and Estelle Hassan, for all their love and support. Whenever I needed them, they were there for me. They risked everything to rescue me from the Moonies and I will be forever grateful that they did.

I wish to thank my sisters, Thea and Stephanie, as well as my brothers-in-law, Doug and Ken, for all they have done throughout the years. My aunt and uncle, Phyllis and Mort Slotnick, have always been a strong support.

In addition I wish to thank Gary Rosenberg, Michael Strom, Nestor Garcia, and Gladys Rodriguez for their willingness to spend five very difficult days in 1976 counseling me back to reality. Without their help, I might have spent many more years in the Moonies.

Special acknowledgments go to Aureet Bar-Yam who for more than seven years has put up with the incredible demands that my work has required. Her parents, Drs. Zvi and Miriam Bar-Yam, have been a source of much love, inspiration, and help in ways too numerous to recount.

I would also like to thank just a few special friends: Gary Birns, Marc and Elyse Hirschorn, Monica Weiss, Lenny Harris, Dr. Karen Magarian, Joan Lebach, Michael Lisman, Russell Backer and Susan Mayer, Michael Stone, Chris and Lee Benton, Steve and Nell Morse, and others too numerous to mention here. They know who they are.

Some individuals have been my teachers and, at times, my inspiration. I would like to thank Robert Jay Lifton, M.D.; Milton H. Erickson, M.D.; Margaret Singer, Ph.D.; Flo Conway and Jim Siegelman; John Grinder, Ph.D.; and Richard Bandler, Bill and Lorna Goldberg, David Gordon, and Stephen Lankton.

Warm thanks go to those people who were instrumental in making this book happen. My best friend Chris Kilham helped me find my publisher, Ehud Sperling, who had the boldness, vision, and integrity to bring out this book. I also wish to thank Leslie Colket, managing editor, who believed in this book, made innumerable contributions, and oversaw its development from infancy to completion.

I would like to acknowledge Ed Conroy for his editorial contribution, reworking my manuscript. He approached this project with vigor and insight and made it a much stronger book.

My thanks also to Susan Davidson and Anna Congdon for their valuable assistance refining the book into its present form.

Many other people have helped me substantially along the way, providing me with information, insight, and editorial comments. I would also like to thank Alan MacRobert, Herb Rosedale, Betty and Kate Kilham, Fred Clarkson, James and Marcia Rudin, Priscilla Coates, David Rich, Carol Turnbull, Carol and Noel Giambalvo, Chip Berlet, and Ford Greene.

Some people mentioned here—friends, colleagues, former clients—were willing to share their stories of cult involvement and thereby enriched this book. I am most grateful for their assistance and their encouragement. In the many years I have been involved in the cult field, I have met some of the most talented, most caring, and best people in the world.

Foreword

The phone was frighteningly loud. The clock read 4:30 A.M. It was difficult to take in what a reporter from *The Berkeley Gazette* was saying on the phone: "Margaret, I hate to bother you this early, but we have just learned that Jim Jones has decided to pull the trigger down in Guyana. I've been here all night at a house in Berkeley talking with ex-members of People's Temple and with relatives of persons down in Jonestown. There's a mother here whose husband and twelve-year-old son are down there and she is desperate. It is not known if everyone's dead, or if there are survivors. I know I've told you not to work with ex-members of People's Temple because of the dangerous harassment that Jones' so-called 'Angels' direct against former members. But these people need to talk with you and get some help with what has happened."

As daylight was breaking, I passed up the steps guarded by somber Berkeley police, as it was feared that Jones had left "hit orders" for members still in the area to wipe out defectors when he ordered the final "White Night," his term for the often rehearsed moment when he would have all his followers drink poison.

The reporter, my son (also a reporter), and a few police officers had warned me not to give my usual gratis consultation services to ex-People's Temple members, even though I had long given these services to former cultists. Jones allegedly used his "angels" to wreak vengeance against members who left and against their supporters as well.

The woman whose husband and young son were eventually identified as dead in Jonestown was only one of many. I spent hours and days meeting and talking with various survivors as they returned from Guyana to the Bay Area and attempted to get their lives going again after the Guyanese holocaust. There were attorney Tim Stoen and his wife Grace, whose young son had been held captive by Jones and died in Jonestown. There were the members of the basketball team who missed the mass suicide-murder. There was a nine-year-old girl who had survived having had her throat slit by a woman who then killed herself in Georgetown, Guyana, as part of Jones' mass death orders. There was Larry Layton, who faced courts in two countries for allegedly carrying out Jones' orders at the airport in Guyana where Rep. Leo J. Ryan and others died.

I began to work with ex-cultists about six years before Jonestown and continue to do so to this day. I have provided psychological counseling to more than three thousand persons who have been in cults. I have written about some of this work and have talked with lay and professional groups in many countries about thought reform programs, intense indoctrination programs, cults, and related topics.

My interest in the effects of thought reform programs began when I worked at the Walter Reed Army Institute of Research after the Korean War. At that point I met and worked with Edgar H. Schein, Ph.D., Robert J. Lifton, M.D., and Louis J. West, M.D., pioneers in the study of the effects of intense indoctrination programs. I was involved in the follow-up studies of former prisoners of war, interviewed long-term prisoners of the Chinese, and participated over the years in much of the work on conceptualizing thought reform programs. As Steve Hassan does in this volume, I have repeatedly described the specific needs of persons who have been subjected to such and have emphasized the lack of knowledge that most citizens as well as mental health professionals have about the processes, effects, and aftermath of being subjected to thought reform programs.

Steve Hassan has clearly and convincingly described how mind control is induced. He integrates his personal experience in a cult, and his practical skills developed in twelve years of exit-counseling of persons who have been in mind control situations, with theories and concepts in the scientific literature. The book comes alive with real-life examples.

For the first time, an experienced exit-counselor outlines step by step the actual methods, sequence, and framework of what he does and how he works with families and the persons under mind control. He draws on the various scholarly works in the fields of thought reform, persuasion, social psychology, and hypnosis to offer theoretical frameworks for how mind control is achieved.

Exit-counseling is a new profession, and Steve Hassan has spelled out here a type of ethical, educational counseling which he and others have developed. He has devoted the time and has the literary skill and educational background to make this volume a major contribution. The reader is taken from Steve's first telephone contacts with desperate families to the final outcome of his interventions. These counseling techniques and tactics are socially and psychologically well worked out. They are ethical and growth-enhancing. While the need is great, there are few really adequately prepared and experienced exit-counselors. They do not offer what psychologists and psychiatrists offer, nor can they be replaced by these or other mental health professionals. Exit-counseling is a special field, one that demands specific knowledge, special techniques and methods, and a high level of skill.

This book should have a wide appeal. Anyone with a relative or friend who has become involved with a group using mind control procedures will find it useful. Any citizen can profit from seeing how vulnerable to influence we all are and learning that mind control exists—that it is not a myth.

We must heed the potentially destructive and frightening impact that the use of mind control by selfishly motivated groups can have on the very fabric of a society. This book fills a need and deserves a wide audience.

Margaret T. Singer, Ph.D.
Adjunct Professor, Department of Psychology
University of California, Berkeley, California
Recipient of the Leo J. Ryan Memorial Award

Preface to the Paperback Edition

Since the publication of *Combatting Cult Mind Control* in the fall of 1988, I have heard from hundreds of people who have told me about the positive impact this book has had on their lives. Lawyers, educators, mental health professionals, and clergy have let me know how valuable it has been in their work. Families have told me incredible stories of how reading it led to a series of phone calls, meetings, and ultimately a successful intervention with a loved one. Yet, nothing gratifies me more than to hear from individuals involved with a destructive cult for many years, who felt that reading this book helped them open a door to freedom.

For those of you who might be considered to be either a current or former member of an organization that is "controversial," or to those who are friends or relatives of someone involved with such a group, I have some special words of advice.

■ **If you are currently a member (or a former member) of a group or organization that has been alleged to be a cult:**

You may find that it takes a great deal of strength, courage, and integrity to make the effort to learn about this phenomenon. But as difficult as it is, keep in mind what you stand to gain by reading this book in its entirety. Knowledge is power. You may even discover that although the public views your group as a cult, there in fact is no mind control being used by the group. I have been thanked countless times by members of unorthodox organizations who were able to, once and for all, discuss with their families and friends the criteria I have outlined here and to demonstrate that they *are* exercising their own free will with their affiliation.

If you are questioning the ethics, policies, or practices of your group, approach this book with an open mind. However, please be careful about letting other group members know you are reading it, as this might invoke unwanted attention and disciplinary measures from the group's leadership. If it is at all possible to take some time off and get some distance from other members, I urge you to do so. Find a place where you have minimal pressure and few distractions.

I also strongly suggest reading the book at least two times. When reading it for the first time, do so with the perspective that it is describing *other* groups (preferably one's that you do believe are destructive), and really allow yourself the opportunity to understand the process of mind control and the characteristics of destructive cults. Be sure to make notes as you read, writing down everything you agree with or disagree with, as well as things you will want to research further. Then do all the follow-up research necessary to fully answer the questions!

Once you have finished the book, give yourself at least a few days before reading it again. When you pick it up a second time, read it objectively, as though it may or may not apply to your own personal situation. Make a new set of notes on what you agree with, what you disagree with, and what you need to research further. On completing this second reading, go find the answers to the issues that are raised pertaining to your group! Take some time off (if possible, a minimum of a few weeks) and go to a restful place away from other group members and gather more information from other sources. *Remember, if the group is a legitimate, valid organization, it will stand up to any scrutiny.* It is far better to find out the truth now than to invest more time, money, energy, and resources only to discover years later that the group is very different from it's idealized image.

Truth is stronger than lies, and love is stronger than fear. If you are involved with a religious organization, keep in mind that God created us with free will and that no truly spiritual organization would *ever* use deception or mind control or take away that freedom.

- **If you are a family member or friend of a loved one who is involved in what you suspect is a destructive cult:**

It is best to approach the problem in a systematic and methodical manner. Avoid overreacting and getting hysterical! Don't jump the gun and tell the individual that you have bought this book or are reading this book. Wait until you and other significant people in your family have had a chance to read and get prepared before planning an intervention strategy. Unfortunately, there have been cases in which people have bought the book and impulsively mailed it to the cult member only to find that it increased that person's mistrust of the outside world.

Most cult groups fear exit-counseling, and this book may tip them off that you are thinking about taking some action. Instead of sounding the alarm, adopt a curious yet concerned posture. Try to avoid confrontations and ultimatums. Read the book as many times as you need to in order to clearly explain to others the characteristics of mind control, the criteria of a destructive cult, and the basics of cult psychology. Get as many concerned friends and relatives involved as you can. A strong first step will be for them to read this book too. If everyone is prepared you will not be caught off guard!

Although this book is meant as a resource, there is no substitute for professional advice geared to your own unique situation. Do not hesitate to seek such help from those who are qualified and informed.

Chapter 1

Exit-Counseling: The Background

Finally: a chance to relax, forget about work, and enjoy some social time off with my friends. Maybe meet some new people at this party.

"Hi. My name is Steve Hassan. Nice to meet you." *(I just hope no one asks me to talk about work.)*

The question: "So, what do you do?" *(Oh no, not again!)*

The dodge: "I'm self-employed."

"Doing what?" *(No escape.)*

"I'm a cult exit-counselor." *(Here come the fifty questions.)*

"Oh really? That's interesting. How did you get into that? Can you tell me why. . . ."

Since February 1974, I have been involved with the problems caused by destructive cults. That was when I was recruited into the "One World Crusade,"[1] a front group for the Unification Church, also known as the "Moonies." After two and a half years as a member of that cult, I was deprogrammed after suffering a serious injury in a van accident.

Ever since then, I have been actively involved in fighting destructive cults. I have become a professionally trained therapist and fly anywhere my help is genuinely needed. My phone rings at all hours of the day. My clients are people who, for one reason or another, have been damaged emotionally, socially, and sometimes even physically by their involvement with destructive cults. I help these people recover and start their lives over. My approach to counseling enables them to make that transition in a way which avoids most of the trauma associated with the more forceful technique known as "deprogramming."

I prefer to call my work "exit-counseling" to distinguish it from "deprogramming" and other forms of counseling being practiced today. The work is intensive, totally involving me with a person and his or her family, sometimes for days at a time. I call these intensive periods "interventions." Usually I am able to assist a person in making a dramatic recovery to his original identity. Since only a handful of people in the world do similar work with members of destructive cults, this book reveals, for the first time, most of the significant aspects of this unique profession.

Having seen that destructive cults deliberately undermine the democratic way of life, I am also an activist to protect people's rights. I am especially concerned with everyone's right to know about the highly sophisticated techniques used by destructive cults to recruit, keep, and exploit highly talented, productive people. For the past twelve years, my activism and work as a therapist have been focused on these problems.

My life as a cult exit-counselor often makes me feel as though I'm in the middle of a war zone. In the seven years we've been together, Aureet has had to put up with all sorts of incredible situations blowing through our household. Even though I try to regulate my case load, see only a reasonable number of clients each week, and plan one or two interventions a month, my careful plans are always disrupted by unexpected events.

Aureet and I came home late one Friday night with friends. I checked the answering machine. There were four calls. When I played back the messages, they were all from the same family in Minnesota. "Call us any time of night, please," said a woman's voice on the tape. "Our son has gotten involved with the Moonies. He's going on a three-week workshop with them in Pennsylvania on Monday. He's a doctoral student in physics at MIT. Please call us back."

I called right away and talked with the mother and father for about an hour. The parents had heard that their son had become a member of an organization called C.A.R.P. (Collegiate Association for the Research of Principles). They had done some investigation and found out that C.A.R.P. was the international student recruiting arm of the Unification Church.[2] We agreed there was no time to lose.

I discussed the situation with his parents and we decided on a course of action. They would take a 6:45 A.M. flight to Boston the next day. They would go to his apartment, take him out to a restaurant, and assess his situation. Success or failure depended on how close Bruce was to his mother and father and how far the Moonies had already indoctrinated him. Had they gotten to the point where they could make him reject his family as "satanic"? His mother and father assured me they would be able to talk to him. I wasn't so sure, but agreed it would be well worth the attempt. From my experience with the Moonies, I felt that if Bruce went to the three-week indoctrination, he could be locked into the group's mindset thereafter.

The next step would be for the parents to persuade Bruce to talk to me. I was worried about whether they could. The Moonies do a very thorough job of convincing people that former members are satanic and that even being in their presence could be dangerous.[3] For the moment, then, all I could do was wait.

The next morning I taped a television show on cults, something I do frequently in various parts of the country. After the taping, I canceled all my appointments for the day. Bruce's parents called from the Boston airport. They had arrived and were about to leave for their son's house. We reviewed our strategy one more time. I crossed my fingers.

Two hours later the phone rang. They had managed to bring Bruce to a Chinese restaurant not far from my house. Bruce had agreed to meet me. I grabbed whatever I thought I might need to show him—file folders, photocopies of articles, and books—and threw them into the car and drove to the restaurant.

When I arrived and met the family, the parents' faces were full of worry and concern. Bruce tried to smile at first and shook my hand. But it was clear to me that he was thinking, "Can I trust this guy? Who *is* he?"

I sat down with them in the booth. I asked Bruce about himself and why he thought his parents were so concerned that they flew from Minneapolis. Within an hour, after asking him enough questions to get a good handle on his state of mind, I decided to risk a big question.

"Did they tell you about pledge service yet?" I asked.

He shook his head and looked surprised. "What's that?"

"Oh, that's a very important ceremony members do every Sunday, on the first day of every month, and on four holy days the group observes," I started. "Members bow three times with their face touching the floor before an altar with Sun Myung Moon's picture on it and recite a six-point pledge to be faithful to God, to Moon, and to the fatherland—Korea."

"You're kidding."

At that moment I knew Bruce would be all right. Because I could see that he was not yet fully under the group's mind control, I knew he would respond well to hearing more information about the group's leader, multimillionaire Korean industrialist Sun Myung Moon. I began telling him facts about the Moonies unrelated to mind control—Moon's tax-conspiracy conviction, the Congressional report on the Moonies' connections to the Korean CIA, and their suspected illegal activities.

"You know, I've been looking for someone like you for a few months," Bruce said after hearing me out. "I went to the priest at MIT to ask him for information. He didn't have anything."

Bruce was still thinking for himself, but in my opinion he had been on the verge of being recruited. The three-day and seven-day workshops he'd been through had set him up for the twenty-one-day program. When I was a member, it was common practice after this latter program to ask recruits to donate their bank accounts, move into the Moonie house, and become full members.[4]

Bruce and I spent the next couple of days going over more information, watching videotapes, and talking about mind control and destructive cults. Much to his parents' relief, he finally announced he wasn't going to the workshop. He spent a lot of time photocopying stacks of documents and wanted to try to talk to the other students being recruited at MIT. He went back to the priest and told him about his close call. A week later the priest called to see if I would conduct a briefing session for college administrators.

That case was an easy one with a happy ending. The family had been quick to spot their son's changing personality, discover that C.A.R.P. is a front for the Moonies, and locate people who could refer them to me. Their fast action enabled them to help their son easily and quickly.

The phone calls I receive are usually variations of the same plea for help. A son or daughter, sister or brother, husband or wife, mother or father, boyfriend or girlfriend is in trouble. Sometimes he or she is just being recruited; other times the call is about someone who has been in a cult for many years.

It is relatively easy to deal with someone not yet fully indoctrinated, like Bruce. Most people who call me, though, have had a longer-term problem. Some cases are emergencies; others require a slower, more methodical approach. Emergencies like Bruce's are tricky because there is little or no time to prepare. Nonetheless, I have learned that fast action is often necessary. If someone is being worked upon in a mind control environment, sometimes the difference of even a few hours can be crucial.

For some unknown reason, the calls for help seem to come in waves: only a few a day for a while, then suddenly ten or fifteen calls. Although I have gone overseas to help people in cults, I spend most of my time traveling all over the United States and Canada. More than once I have found myself on a train or plane sitting next to a dissatisfied member of a destructive cult. During the encounter I have discovered that the person wanted more information about how to change his or her life. I freely offer this information. These encounters are "mini-interventions;" I employ the same listening and counseling skills as for major interventions—I just spend less time.

My work entails two parts: counseling individuals and alerting the public to the cult phenomenon. I believe that sensitizing the public to the problem of mind control is the only way to slow the growth of these groups. It is fairly easy to warn people what to watch out for even if they're just listening to the radio with half an ear while washing the dishes. It is much harder and more compli-cated to get someone out of a cult who is already in it. For every person I counsel out of a cult group, it seems as though a thousand new members are recruited in.

I believe the only solution to the damage done to people in destructive cults is to "immunize" the general population against mind control groups. The most effective way to do so is to expose people to information about how the groups work. A person's resistance then becomes higher because he'll know what to watch out for if he encounters a recruiter. To this end, I give lectures and seminars and appear on television and radio shows wherever possible. It is also the reason why I'm writing this book.

CULTS: A NIGHTMARE REALITY

Had someone told me when I was in high school that at the age of 36 I would be a cult expert, I would have thought the idea bizarre. I wanted to be a poet and writer, and thought that one day I might become an English professor. If that person had gone on to say that my clients would be people who had been systematically lied to, physically abused, encouraged to lose contact with family and friends, and induced to work at jobs which offered them little or no significant opportunities for real personal or professional growth, I would have laughed in his face and might even have thought that he was conjuring up an image of totalitarianism from George Orwell's *Nineteen Eighty-Four.*

The world at large has not become the nightmare reality that Orwell depicted—a place where the "thought police" maintained the state's complete control of people's mental and emotional lives, and where it was a crime to act and think independently or even to fall in love. Yet, in an increasing number of organizations in our world, *Nineteen Eighty-Four* has come true: basic respect for the individual simply doesn't exist, and people are gradually led to think and behave in very similar ways through a process of mind control. As a result, they become totally dependent on the group; they lose the ability to act on their own and are often exploited for the sake of the group's economic or political ends. Any group that engages in outright deception to pursue its ends, whether religious or secular in its apparent orientation, I define as a destructive cult.

The world of *Nineteen Eighty-Four* was a far cry from the typically middle-class American world of my childhood. I grew up in a conservative Jewish family in Flushing, Queens, New York, the youngest of three children and the only son. I vividly remember helping my father in his hardware store in Ozone Park. My mother, a junior high school art teacher, raised me in a warm, loving, unconditionally supportive way. I look back on my childhood and remember myself more as a loner than a joiner. While I always had a few close friends, I never felt comfortable in school cliques. The only group I really belonged to was my synagogue's basketball team. After high school I decided to pursue a liberal arts education at Queens College, which is where I first encountered the Moonie recruiters. Before I even knew what was happening, my world altered dramatically.

WHO ARE THE MOONIES?

The Unification Church (whose formal name is The Holy Spirit Association for the Unification of World Christianity) is one of the largest, and certainly most visible destructive cults in the United States. The organization is completely dominated by its absolute leader, Sun Myung Moon,[5] a Korean-born business-man who in 1982 was convicted of tax fraud and served thirteen months in the federal penitentiary in Danbury, Connecticut.[6]

During the 1970s, members of this group became a regular feature in most American cities. They stood on street corners selling flowers, candy, puppets, and other small items, and actively recruited young people in colleges and universities. Generally clean-cut, courteous, and persistent, the Moonies pro-liferated for years and gained unfavorable media attention almost everywhere. As far as the media were concerned, though, the Unification Church and its followers faded away in the 1980s. The truth, however, is that the Moon organization became even more sophisticated, expanding its numerous reli-gious, political, cultural, and economic front groups. Because the Unification Church keeps its vital statistics as secret as possible, it is impossible to give a reliable figure representing the total number of church members in the United States. Even though Church officials claim to have thirty thousand members here (and some three million in the world), I estimate that the numbers are much lower. There are probably some four thousand Americans and another four thousand foreigners (many married to American members) working in the United States today.[7]

Another aspect of the Unification Church, still insufficiently recognized, is that members justify the use of deception[8] to recruit individuals. When I was a Moonie recruiter, we also used psychological pressure to convince members to turn over all their personal possessions and wealth to the church.[9] Members are subjected to workshops that thoroughly indoctrinate them in church beliefs,[10] and typically undergo a conversion experience in which they surrender to the group. As a result, they become totally dependent upon the group for financial and emotional support, and lose the ability to act independently of it. Under these conditions, members are required to work long hours; exist on little sleep; eat boring junk food, sometimes for weeks on end; and endure innumerable hardships for the sake of their "spiritual growth." They are discouraged from forming close relationships with members of the opposite sex,[11] and may be married only under arrangements made by Sun Myung Moon himself or his proxy.[12] They are sometimes asked to participate in political demonstrations and other activities which aid causes, candidates, and public office holders supported by Moon and his organization.[13] If they snap from the pressure and begin to challenge their leaders' authority or otherwise fall out of line, they are accused of being influenced by Satan and are subjected to even greater pressure in the form of re-indoctrination. I know these things are true. I was a leader in the Moon cult.

WHAT IS MIND CONTROL?

There are many different forms of mind control, and most people think of brainwashing almost as soon as they hear the term. But for the purpose of this book—which is to help you recognize it and protect yourself and others from groups that use it—"mind control" may be understood as a *system* of influences that disrupts an individual's identity (beliefs, behavior, thinking, and emotions) and replaces it with a new identity. In most cases, that new identity is one that the original identity would strongly object to if it knew in advance what was in store.

In this book, I will be referring to the *negative* uses of mind control. Not all mind control techniques are inherently bad or unethical; for some, the manner in which they are used is what is important. The locus of control should always remain within the individual. It is fine to use hypnosis to stop smoking, for example, as long as the hypnotist leaves the desire and control to stop with the client and doesn't try to move them towards himself.

Today, many techniques of mind control exist that are far more sophisticated than the brainwashing techniques used in World War II and the Korean War. Some involve covert forms of hypnosis, while others are implemented through the highly rigid, controlled social environment of the destructive cult. Above all, it should be recognized that mind control is a very subtle process. I have included more information about mind control in chapter 4, including some basic guidelines for recognizing the signs of mind control when it is practiced in a group. All the groups mentioned in this book as being destructive cults using mind control techniques are so identified only after thorough research. It would be unfair to accuse an unusual group as being a practitioner of unethical mind control without a basis for doing so. I have no qualms about referring to the Unification Church as a destructive cult.[14] That group's record speaks for itself, for it is a highly controversial political group that has already been the center of one major Congressional investigation.[15]

THE MANY FACES OF THE UNIFICATION CHURCH

How did this group start out? One of the best summaries of the story of the early years of the Unification Church is in the Fraser Report, published on

October 31, 1978, by the U.S. House of Representatives' Subcommittee on International Organizations of the Committee on International Relations. Chaired by Rep. Donald Fraser, a Democrat from Minnesota, the committee conducted the investigation which unearthed many previously unreported facts about the Moon organization, among them the Unification Church's links to the Korean Central Intelligence Agency (KCIA). That investigation brought to public attention the fact that the Unification Church is not only a body of believers but also a political organization with an active political agenda. The Fraser Report tells the story of the Moon organization's beginnings:

> "In the late 1950s, Moon's message was favorably received by four young, English-speaking Korean Army officers, all of whom were later to provide important contacts with the post-1961 Korean government. One was Bo Hi Pak, who had joined the ROK (Republic of Korea) army in 1950. Han Sang Keuk . . . became a personal assistant to Kim Jong Pil, the architect of the 1961 coup and founder of the KCIA. Kim Sang In retired from the ROK army in May, 1961, joined the KCIA and became an interpreter for Kim Jong Pil until 1966. At that time, [Kim Sang In] returned to his position as KCIA officer, later to become the KCIA's chief of station in Mexico City. He was a close friend of Bo Hi Pak and a supporter of the Unification Church. The fourth, Han Sang Kil, was a military attache at the ROK embassy in Washington in the late 1960s. Executive branch reports also link him to the KCIA. On leaving the service of the ROK government, Han became Moon's personal secretary and tutor to his children.
>
> Immediately after the coup, Kim Jong Pil founded the KCIA and supervised the building of a political base for the new regime. A February 1963 unevaluated CIA report stated that Kim Jong Pil had 'organized' the Unification Church while he was KCIA director and has been using the Unification Church as a 'political tool.' "[16]

Fred Clarkson, who quotes this report in the Spring 1987 issue of *Covert Action Information Bulletin,* a magazine which covers the politics of intelligence-gathering organizations and extremist political groups, goes on to say:

> "Though the Fraser Report noted that 'organized' is not to be confused with 'founded,' since the Unification Church was 'founded' in 1954, [the Fraser Report goes on to state that] '. . . there was a great deal of independent corroboration for the suggestion in this and later intelligence reports that Kim Jong Pil and the Moon organization had a mutually supportive relationship, as well as for the statement that Kim used the Unification Church for political purposes.' "[17]

It is remarkable that so many people become involved with the church while knowing absolutely nothing about it or about Moon's background. Certainly, if I had learned that it was connected with the KCIA or that in 1967 Moon had forged an organizational link with Yoshi Kodama, a leader of the *Yakuza,* the Japanese organized crime network,[18] I would have never become involved. While the story of the Unification Church's theology is too involved to detail here, the most important feature of it is the church's position that Sun Myung Moon is the new Messiah and that his mission is to establish a new "kingdom" on Earth. Yet, many ex-members like myself have observed that Moon's vision of that kingdom has a distinctly Korean character. During my two-and-a-half-year period in the church, I understood that the highest positions of membership (closest to Moon) were available only to Koreans, with the Japanese coming in a close second. American members like me were third down on the ladder. Members believe, as I did, that their donation of time, money, and effort is contributing to the salvation of the world. What they do not realize is that they are the victims of mind control.[19]

It is impossible to gain a full picture of Moon and his influence in the United States, however, by looking only at the Unification Church, although there is plenty there to see. In fact, Moon has developed a complex organization, which embraces both businesses and non-profit organizations in his native Korea, here in the United States, and in many other countries, with a special emphasis on Latin America. Moon has founded enterprises ranging from ginseng exportation to the manufacture of M-16 rifles,[20] and in the United States has started several think tanks and organizations to promote a variety of conferences and cultural interchange programs (scientific, academic, and religious as well as legal). Perhaps the most visible Moon-connected enterprise in the United States is *The Washington Times,* a newspaper with a respectable circulation of about 100,000 and considerable clout in Washington.[21] President Ronald Reagan has repeatedly said it is his favorite newspaper and that he reads it every day.[22] Han Sang Keuk and Bo Hi Pak are both top executives of the *Times.*

The thread running through all the activities of the Moon organization, both within and without the Unification church, is Moon's strong anti-Communist position. To put it simply, the Moonies believe that Christians and the citizens of the non-Communist world are locked in a mortal struggle with the satanic forces of materialistic Communism. To the extent that America and other countries do not fight Communism, they will grow weak and fall. The world's only salvation lies in Moon and in the establishment of a theocratic form of government which will replace secular democracies.

Had it not been for the Congressional Subcommittee Investigation and the work of Rep. Donald Fraser, Moon would very likely have recruited even more Americans in recent years and would have increased his power even faster. I was glad to give staff members of Fraser's subcommittee a copy of *Master Speaks,* a set of private speeches by Moon reserved for Unification Church leaders and members, which was submitted as evidence in the Investigation. One speech which entered the record quoted Moon as saying, in 1973, that "when it comes to our age, we must have an automatic theocracy to rule the world. So we cannot separate the political field from the religious. . . . Separation between religion and politics is what Satan likes most."[23]

Moon's stated belief in the necessary fusion of religion and politics underscores his organization's involvement, over the years, in a wide variety of extreme right-wing groups. Currently, his chief political arm is an organization known as CAUSA,[24] which was founded in 1980 after a tour of Latin America by Moon's right-hand man, Bo Hi Pak. A North American branch was formed in 1983, and CAUSA has since moved to every continent of the globe, providing seminars for people in leadership positions. According to Fred Clarkson, "The general thrust of CAUSA is anti-communist education from a historical perspective. The CAUSA antidote to communism is 'Godism,' which is simply the Unification Church philosophy without Moonist mythology."[25]

In the late 1980s, the Moonies continue to expand their sphere of influence and power. Moon is apparently trying to buy his way into legitimacy, lending and giving millions of dollars to conservative causes.[26] His strategy, "serve and help people until they are dependent on you, then control them," seems to still be working for him.

However, things aren't entirely rosy for the group. According to Frank Greve's Knight-Ridder report,[27] "door-to-door Moonie salesmen (in Japan) using illegal high-pressure sales tactics bilked buyers of their cheaply-made religious artifacts, charms and talismans out of at least $165 million between 1980 and 1987. The figure is said to represent just the total money paid in 14,579 complaints made to government consumer centers and private attorneys. The report (from the Japanese bar association), which estimates that only 1 percent of consumer fraud victims complain, concludes that $165 million is only the 'tip of the iceberg.' "

According to Greve, the victims are predominantly "women who have had an accidental death or fatal illness in the family, are widowed or divorced, or have had a miscarriage." They reportedly sometimes paid more than $100,000 for urns, pagodas, and other charms that would, Moonie salesmen persuaded them, "ward off the evil spirits affecting them."

It seems probable that at least some of this illegally obtained revenue was sent to the United States to finance *The Washington Times*, which is aimed at political conservatives. Some $200,000,000 has already been poured into this newspaper,[28] but the business has yet to show any profit. However, the newspaper has served its true purpose: enabling Moon to have access to the power brokers of American politics.

The Unification Church is a destructive cult *par excellence*. However, many other groups in this country also espouse strange theological doctrines and have members who engage in practices which, to many people, might seem downright bizarre. Are all these groups "destructive cults?"

Not by any means. The United States of America has always been a land where freedom of thought and tolerance of differing beliefs have flourished under the protection of the First Amendment of the Constitution. Our religious and political life is as diverse as that of any country in the world. The basis of that diversity is found in the principle of respect for individual rights which is written into our Constitution. Difficult as it may be to believe, in the past twenty-five years we have seen the rise of organizations in our society that systematically violate the rights of their members, subject them to many kinds of abuse, and make them less capable of acting and thinking as responsible adults. For people who stay in these organizations, the result is damage not only to their self-esteem, but often to their whole sense of identity. Their connection with others is also harmed; in some cases they completely lose contact with family and friends for long periods of time.

The damage from living in a cult may not be readily apparent to family members or friends or even—in the early stages—to someone casually meeting such a person for the first time. But many forms of violence, from the very gross to the very subtle, are the inevitable result. Some members of destructive cults suffer physical abuse during their involvement, in the form of beatings or rape, while others simply suffer the abuse of long hours of grueling, monotonous work—fifteen to eighteen hours a day, year in and year out. In essence, they become slaves with few or no resources, personal or financial, to leave the group, and the group does everything it can to keep them as long as they are productive. When they fall sick or are no longer productive, they are often kicked out.

Groups with such practices often appear, on the surface, to be respectable associations. Cults using mind control appeal to many different human impulses. Religious cults, the best known, are focused on religious dogma. Political cults, often in the news, are organized around a narrow political theory. Psychotherapy/educational cults, which have enjoyed great popularity, purport to give the participant "insight" and "enlightenment." Commercial cults play on people's desires for exciting and lucrative careers. None of these destructive cults deliver what they promise; all, in the long run, entrap their members and destroy their self-esteem.

Destructive cults do many kinds of damage to their members, and I will illustrate this with several case histories including my own. It is not easy to recover from the damage done by membership in a destructive cult, but it is possible. My experience proves that some definite steps can be taken to learn how to help either oneself or a friend return to a normal productive life. Cult mind control does not have to be permanent.

Chapter 2

My Life in the Unification Church

As a child I had always been very independent. I wanted to be a writer and poet, but during my college years I struggled to find a career path in which I could make enough money to pursue my dreams. My sense of struggling with life was increased by the depression I felt after I broke up with my girlfriend in January 1974. I wondered if I would ever find my true love. I had always been an avid reader; during that time I began to read a great deal of psychology and philosophy. Through the writings of G. I. Gurdjieff and P. D. Ouspensky I became interested in what was presented as ancient, esoteric knowledge. Much of what I read described man's natural condition as being "asleep" to the truth and in need of someone more spiritually advanced who could teach him about higher levels of consciousness. The suggestion that one should join a spiritual school was embedded in those books.

At age nineteen, I felt that I was never going to be happy as a businessman, living my life to pursue money. I wanted to know the answers to the deeper questions. Is there a God? If so, why does he allow so much suffering? What role am I to play in the world eventually? Can I do anything to make a difference? At that time I felt extreme pressure to make a big contribution to humankind. I had been told all my life how intelligent I was and how much I would accomplish when I grew up. I was going to graduate in another year, and time was running out.

I had already become a "foster parent" of a little girl in Chile to whom I sent money each month. I had decided that writing was probably my most important pursuit, and so I wrote. Still I felt it wasn't enough. I looked out at the world and saw so much in the way of social injustice, political corruption, and ecological problems that it seemed I could offer little. I knew that I wanted to change things, but I didn't know how to go about doing it.

One day, as I was reading a book in the student union cafeteria, three attractive women of Japanese background and an Italian-American man approached me. They were dressed like students and carried books. They asked if they could share the table. I nodded, and was engaged in a friendly conversation within minutes. Since I had a three-hour break between classes, I stayed and talked. They told me they were students too, involved in a small community of "young people from all over the world." They invited me to visit them.

The semester had just started and I wanted to make new friends, so I drove to their house that night after class. When I arrived I found a lively group of about thirty people from a half dozen countries. I asked if they were a religious group. "Oh, no, not at all," they laughed. They told me they were part of something called the One World Crusade, dedicated to overcoming cultural differences between people and combatting just such major social problems as the ones I was concerned about.

"One world where people treat each other with love and respect," I thought to myself. "What idealists these people are!"

I enjoyed the stimulating conversations and energetic atmosphere at the meeting. These people related to each other as easily as brothers and sisters and clearly felt they were part of one global family. They seemed very happy with their lives. After my depression of the previous month, I was invigorated by all that positive energy. I went home that night feeling lucky to have met such nice people.

The next day I ran into Tony, the man who had approached me in the cafeteria. "Did you enjoy the evening?" he asked. I answered that I had. "Well, listen," Tony said. "This afternoon Adri, who's from Holland, is going to give a short lecture on some interesting principles of life. Why don't you come over?"

I listened to Adri's lecture a few hours later. It seemed vague and a bit simplistic but pleasing, and I could agree with nearly everything he said. However, the content of his speech didn't explain why everyone in this group seemed so happy all the time. I felt there must be either something wrong with me or something exceptional about them. My curiosity was fully engaged.

I wound up going back the next day, too, and this time another person gave a talk about the origin of all the problems that humankind has had to face. This lecture had a decidedly religious tone; it dealt with Adam and Eve and how they were corrupted by a misuse of love in the Garden of Eden. At that point I didn't notice that my questions were never answered, and didn't suspect I was being deliberately strung along. However, I did feel a bit confused and said I didn't think I'd be coming back.

When I said this, a silent alarm seemed to go off among the people in the house. As I walked out and got into my car, a dozen people came running out into the icy February air in their stocking feet (it was the custom to remove shoes in the house) and surrounded my car. They said they wouldn't let me leave until I *promised* to come back the following night. "These people are crazy," I thought, "standing outside in the freezing cold without shoes, without jackets, holding me hostage because they like me so much." After a few minutes I relented, mostly because I didn't want to feel guilty if one of them caught a cold. Once I had given my word, I wouldn't think of not following through, even though I didn't really want to go back.

When I returned on Thursday night, I was barraged with flattery from all sides all evening. This practice, I would later learn, is called "love bombing." I was told over and over what a nice person I was, what a good person I was, how smart I was, how dynamic I was, and so forth. No fewer than thirty times they invited me to go with them for a "weekend away from the city for a retreat in a beautiful place upstate."

Over and over I told them that I had to work as a waiter on weekends and could not go. Before I left, I was pressured to promise that if I was ever free on a weekend, I would go. I had not had a free weekend for a year and a half, so I was certain not to have to keep my promise.

The next day I phoned my boss at the Holiday Inn banquet office to get my schedule for the weekend. He said, "Steve, you're not going to believe this, but the wedding was called off this afternoon. Take the weekend off!" I was flabbergasted. Was this a sign that I was *supposed* to go to this weekend outing? I asked myself what Gurdjieff or Ouspensky would have done in my situation. They had spent years searching for greater knowledge. I called the people at the house, and off I went that Friday night.

MY INDOCTRINATION: HOW I BECAME A MOONIE

As we drove through the tall, black, wrought-iron gates of a multimillion-dollar estate in Tarrytown, New York, someone leaned over and told me, "This weekend we'll be having a joint workshop with the Unification Church." My mental reaction was an immediate series of questions, which at the time I didn't verbalize. "Workshop? Church? What is going on here? Why didn't anyone tell me this before? How can I get back to Queens?"

We were herded from the van into a small wooden structure nestled in some large trees. I had a feeling of dread. "Listen, I really think I would like to go back to Queens," I told one of the members, a smiling young man with blond hair and a smile pasted to his face.

"Oh, come on, you'll have a good time!" he said patting me on the back. "Anyway, there's no one driving back to the city tonight." I decided to make the most of the situation and avoid creating a scene. We climbed the stairs and entered a room that I later learned had once been an artist's studio. A large blackboard was at the other end of the room. Metal folding chairs were stacked neatly in a corner.

Within a few minutes we were divided up into small groups. The leaders handed us sheets of paper and crayons and asked us to draw a picture with a house, a tree, a mountain, a river, the sun, and a snake. Nobody asked why; everyone just obeyed. (Much later I learned that the excercise was a form of projective personality testing used to probe people's inner thoughts.)

We took turns introducing ourselves while seated cross-legged on the floor of the handsome wooden structure, all part of a large estate with an enormous mansion which I later learned had been purchased from the Seagram family. We were led in singing folk songs while sitting on the floor. I was embarrassed by the childishness of it all, but no one else seemed to mind. The atmosphere of the event, with lots of enthusiastic young people all together, brought back warm memories of summer camp. That night we were escorted to bunk beds above a converted garage, and the men and women were put in separate rooms. As it turned out, getting a good night's sleep was nearly impossible. Not only was it crowded, but there were two loud snorers! So much for imagining I was at summer camp. The other newcomers and I spent a wakeful night.

When morning came, an intense young man from the group house in Queens sat down and talked with me. He told me that he too had been put off at first by some of the strange things he had heard and seen at his first workshop. He begged me not to have a closed mind but to give "them" a chance to present what he called the Divine Principle. "Please don't judge them until you've had a chance to hear the whole thing," he pleaded. He told me that if I left now, I would regret it for the rest of my life.

His voice was so full of mystery and intrigue that it offset my suspicions and engaged my curiosity. "Now," I said to myself, "I'll finally get all my questions answered." Or so I thought.

In the morning we were led in calisthenics before breakfast. Afterward, we sang more songs. As we sat on the floor a charismatic man with ice-blue eyes and a penetrating voice introduced himself and the ground rules for the weekend. He was the workshop director. We were told we had to spend all of our time together in the small groups to which we were assigned. There was to be no walking around the estate alone. Questions were to be asked only after a lecture was over, when we were back in our small group. He then introduced the lecturer, Wayne Miller.

An American in his late twenties, dressed in a blue suit, white shirt, and red tie, Mr. Miller exuded the charm and confidence of a family doctor. As he lectured for hour after hour, I became very uncomfortable. The workshop was all too weird. I liked almost everyone there as people: they were bright, good-hearted college students like myself. But I disliked the overly structured environment, the childishly religious atmosphere, and having been misled about the nature of this weekend retreat. Whenever I started to object, however, I was told to save my questions until after the lecture. In the small group I was always told, "That is a very good question. Hold onto it because it will be answered in the next lecture." Again and again I was told not to judge what I was hearing until I had heard it all. Meanwhile, I was listening to an enormous amount of material about mankind, history, the purpose of creation, the spiritual world versus the physical world, and so forth, much of which presumed an acceptance of what had been said earlier.

The entire weekend was structured from morning until night. There was no free time. There was no possibility of being alone. Members outnumbered newcomers three to one and kept us surrounded. We newcomers were never permitted to talk among ourselves unchaperoned. Day one came and went, leaving my sense of reality more or less intact. Before we went to bed we were asked to fill out "reflection" sheets to reveal all we were thinking and feeling. Naively, I filled them out. I had another restless night but was so exhausted emotionally and physically that I did manage to get a few hours' sleep.

Day two, Sunday, began in exactly the same way. But now we had all been in this crazy, intense environment for thirty-six hours, which felt more like a week. I started asking myself, "Is something wrong with me? Why do *I* seem to be the only person questioning this stuff? Is it more profound than I am able to grasp? Am I not spiritual enough to understand what they are teaching?" I started listening to Mr. Miller more seriously and began to take notes.

By Sunday evening I was more than ready for the ride back home. But it grew later and later, and nobody made any move to depart. Finally I spoke up and said I had to leave now. "Oh, *please* don't go!" several people pleaded. "Tomorrow is the most important day!"

"Tomorrow? I have classes on Monday!" I explained that it was impossible for me to stay another day.

The workshop director took me aside and told me that everybody else had decided to stay for the third day. "No one told you this was a three-day workshop?" he asked.

"No," I responded. "I never would have come if I'd known it would make me miss a day of school."

"Well, since you've heard the first two-thirds, don't you want to know the conclusion?" he asked, intriguingly. Tomorrow, he promised, everything would become clear.

Part of me was really curious to hear the whole thing. But also I was dependent on these people for transportation. I didn't want to bother my friends or family with an emergency call to drive all that way to get me, or worse, start hitchhiking in a strange part of the state at night in the middle of winter.

On the third day, we were lifted up to an unprecedented emotional high. The most powerful of Mr. Miller's lectures that day was called "The History of

Restoration." It claimed to be a precise and accurate map of God's method for directing mankind back to His original intention. "It is scientifically proven that there is a pattern of recurring cycles in history," Mr. Miller declared. Throughout hours of lecturing, these cycles all pointed to an incredible conclusion: God had sent His second Messiah to the earth between 1917 and 1930.

Who was this new Messiah? No one at the workshop would say.

By the time we were ready to drive back to the city, I was not only exhausted but very confused. I was elated to consider the bare possibility that God had been working all of my life to prepare me for this historic moment. At other moments, I thought the whole thing was preposterous—a bad joke. Yet, no one was laughing. An atmosphere of earnest seriousness filled the crowded studio. I remembered the final moments of Mr. Miller's lecture.

"What if?. . . what if?. . . what if. . . it is true? Could you betray the Son of God?" Mr. Miller had questioned with passion in his voice, his eyes moving slowly upward as he concluded. Finally, the workshop director had stepped up and prayed a very emotional prayer about how we were God's lost children and needed to be open-minded to follow what God wanted in our lives. On and on he went, praying that all of mankind would stop living such selfish materialistic lives and return to Him. He apologized over and over for all the times in history that God called people to do His will and was forsaken. He pledged himself to a higher level of commitment and dedication. His sincerity was overpowering. One couldn't help but be moved.

When the van finally returned late that night to the One World Crusade house, I was completely exhausted and wanted only to go home and sleep. But I was still not permitted to leave. Jaap Van Rossum, the house director, insisted that I stay and talk with him for a while. I wanted desperately to go. He was emphatic. He sat me down in front of a crackling fire and read me the biography of a humble Korean man I had never heard of before, Sun Myung Moon. The story was that Moon had suffered through tremendous hardships and tribulations to proclaim the truth of God and to fight Satan and communism. When he had finished, Jaap begged me to pray about what I had just heard. He told me that I was now responsible for the great truth I had been taught. If I turned my back on it, I would never forgive myself. He then tried to persuade me to stay in the house overnight.

My insides were screaming at me, "Get out! Get out! Get the hell away from these people! You need time to think." In order to escape I yelled, "No! Get off my case!" and charged out into the night. Nevertheless, I felt guilty for being rude to those sincere and wonderful people. I drove home, almost in tears.

When I arrived home, my parents (as they told me later) thought I had been drugged. They said I looked awful: my eyes were glassy, and I was obviously very confused. I tried to explain to them what had just happened. I was exhausted and incoherent. When I told them the workshop was affiliated with the Unification Church, my parents became upset and thought I was going to become a Christian. Their immediate response was "Let's go talk with the rabbi tomorrow."

Unfortunately my rabbi had never heard of the Unification Church, nor had he ever dealt with anyone involved with a cult. He thought I was interested in becoming a Christian. He didn't know what to say or do. I came away telling myself, "The only way I can get to the bottom of this thing is investigate it myself." Still, I was afraid. I wished I could speak with someone who knew about this group but wasn't a devoted member. In February 1974, no one I knew had heard of the Moonies.

Ceaseless questions ran through my mind. Had God been preparing me throughout my life for the mission of setting up the Kingdom of Heaven on earth? Was Sun Myung Moon the Messiah? I prayed earnestly to God for Him to show me a sign. Was the Divine Principle the new truth? What should I do?

It didn't dawn on me in my agitated state of confusion that I had been subjected to mind control[1]—that whereas one week earlier, I had had no belief in Satan, now I was afraid that he was influencing my thoughts.

My parents told me to stay away from the group. They didn't want me to abandon Judaism. I didn't want to abandon Judaism either; I wanted to do the right thing. If Moon is the Messiah, I reasoned, then I will be fulfilling my Jewish heritage by following him. Even though my parents opposed the group, I believed that as an independent nineteen-year-old person, I was capable of making my own decision in this matter. I wanted to do what was right. In doing so, I had been told by members of the group, I could later intervene on my parents' behalf and save them spiritually.

After several earnest days of prayer, I received what I thought was the "sign." Unable to concentrate on my schoolwork, I was sitting on the edge of my bed. I reached down, picked up one of my philosophy books, and opened it to a paragraph at random, which said that history goes through certain cycles to help human beings evolve to a higher plane. At that moment I thought I had had a spiritual experience. How could I have chanced to open the book to that paragraph? I thought that God was surely signaling me to heed Mr. Miller's lectures. I felt I had to go back and learn more about this movement.

TYING THE KNOT: I BECOME AN "INSIDER"

As soon as I called the center, I was whisked off to another three-day workshop. When I asked a member why I hadn't been told the truth about the religious quality of the movement, he asked, "If you knew in advance, would you have come?" I admitted that I probably wouldn't have. He explained that the world was controlled by Satan after he had deceived Adam and Eve into disobeying

God. Now God's children had to deceive Satan's children into following God's will. He said, "Stop thinking from fallen man's viewpoint. Think about God's viewpoint. He wants to see his creation restored to His original ideal—the Garden of Eden. That's all that matters!" Later, it became evident that this "heavenly deception" was used in all aspects of the organization—recruiting, fundraising, public relations. Since members are so focused on meeting their assigned goals, there is no room for the "old morality." The group even uses the Bible to "show" that God condoned deception several times in history in order to see His plan accomplished.[2] By accepting the way in which I was deceived, I set myself up to begin deceiving others.

Although the workshop was almost identical in content to the one I had taken the previous week, I felt that I needed to listen this time with an open mind and take notes. "Last weekend I was too cynical," I thought.

This time Miller gave a lecture on Communism. He explained that Communism was Satan's version of God's ideal plan, yet it denied the existence of God. It was therefore Satan's own religion on earth and must be vehemently opposed. He said the final world war would be fought within the next three years between Communism and democracy (at that time, by 1977), and that if members of the movement didn't work hard enough, incredible suffering would result.

By the end of those three days the Steve Hassan who had walked into the first workshop was gone, replaced by a new "Steve Hassan." I was elated at the thought that I was "chosen" by God and that my life's path was now on the only "true track." I experienced a wide range of other feelings too: I was shocked and honored that I had been singled out for leadership, scared at how much responsibility rested on my shoulders, and emotionally high on the thought that God was actively working to bring about the Garden of Eden. No more war, no more poverty, no more ecological destruction. Just love, truth, beauty, and goodness. Still, a muffled voice deep within was telling me to watch out, to keep questioning everything.

After that workshop, I returned to Queens. I decided to move into the local Moonie house for a few months to get a feel for the lifestyle and to study the Divine Principle before I made a lifetime commitment. Within the first few weeks of my residence there, I met a powerful leader, Takeru Kamiyama,[3] a Japanese man in charge of the Unification Church throughout New York City. I was instantly drawn to him. He struck me as having a very spiritual, humble character. I wanted to learn everything I could from him.

In retrospect, I realize that Mr. Kamiyama appealed to me because he had qualities different from those I had been exposed to as a child. He was a visionary. He had a great deal of power and status. My father, a simple businessman, had repeatedly told me that no one person could ever change the world. Kamiyama very much believed that one person could make a big difference. He was very religious and emotionally expressive. My father, though a sincere man in his own quiet way, was not. In looking back and analyzing the relationship, I see that I allowed Kamiyama to take the place of my father. The kind of verbal approval and physical affection I sought from my father was given to me by this man, who used this emotional leverage to motivate and control me.

As it turned out, I had been the first new person to join the center in Queens. Just a month earlier, the big center in Manhattan had been divided into eight satellite centers spread out in different boroughs. Since I was the first, Mr. Kamiyama said it was a sign that I was meant to become a great leader. He made me one of his twelve American disciples and oversaw everything I did.

Although I had never liked being in groups before, my elite status in this group made me feel special. Because of my relationship with Kamiyama, I had access to the Messiah himself—Sun Myung Moon—who was the ultimate father figure.

LIFE WITH "FATHER": I GET CLOSER TO MOON

Sun Myung Moon is a short stocky man who has more than an average share of charisma. He was born in 1920 in what is now North Korea. He carries himself like a small sumo wrestler in a $1,000 business suit. He is a shrewd manipulator and an effective communicator, particularly with those who are indoctrinated to believe he is the greatest man ever to walk the face of the earth. Moon usually spoke either Korean or Japanese and used a translator. I was told he did so for "spiritual" reasons. During my membership, I was present at more than one hundred of his lectures, and participated in approximately twenty-five leadership meetings with him.

Mr. Moon and Mr. Kamiyama knew how to cultivate their disciples to be loyal and well disciplined. Members of the core leadership were trained to follow his orders without question or hesitation. Once I had become totally indoctrinated, all I wanted to do was to follow my central figure's instructions. I was so committed that I had suppressed the real me with my new identity. Whenever I look back now, I am amazed at how I was manipulated and how I manipulated others "in the name of God." I can also see very clearly that the higher I rose in the hierarchy, the more corrupt I became: Moon was making us over in his image. Once he actually told the leaders that if we remained faithful and carried out our missions well, we would each be President of our own country one day. We too would have Mercedes Benz automobiles, personal secretaries, and bodyguards.

I learned how to present the introductory lectures of the Divine Principle within the first three months of my membership. By that time I had recruited two more people, who became my "spiritual children," and was instructed to drop out of school, quit my job, and move into the center. My hair was cut short and I started to wear a suit and tie. At the request of an older member I had performed a forty-day "condition," a self-sacrificing penance exercise, giving up my friends and family for forty days—not seeing them or communicating with them in any way.

I donated my bank account to the center and would have given my car except that my parents had the title. I had to abandon my Chilean foster child because I had no way to earn money to send her. I was asked to sacrifice my "Isaac," a term used by the Moonies for something the members hold very dear. In my case it was my poetry. I threw out everything I had written—some four hundred pieces.

Once I had officially dropped out of college, I was sent back onto the campus to recruit new members. The leaders told me I could go back to finish my degree the following year. When I told them about my desire to teach, they informed me that the "Family," as members refer to the movement, was planning to start its own university in a few years and I could be an instructor there.

I was ordered to set up an official student club at Queens College even though I was no longer a student. The club was to be called Collegiate Association for the Research of Principles, or C.A.R.P. Within a couple of weeks I had done so and was made C.A.R.P. director. Although I told students that C.A.R.P. had no affiliation with another group, I received all of my instructions and funding from the director of the Unification Church in Queens. We put on free lectures, poetry readings, anti-Communist political rallies, and free movies, all the while seeking to meet potential converts. We were then the most successful C.A.R.P. chapter in the country.

I was in a high-speed daze of exhaustion, zeal, and emotional overload. I generally slept between three and four hours a night. Almost all my time that first year was spent recruiting and lecturing. Occasionally I went out with others "fundraising"—selling flowers or other items on the street for donations—to support the house and the operations of the New York Church. I learned how to fast for three days only drinking water. Later I was to do three separate seven-day fasts on water, having been told it was part of the purifying process.

During my time in the group, I was directly involved in numerous political demonstrations, although they were usually organized under the names of front groups. (The Moon organization has, over the years, used hundreds of such groups.[4]) For example, in July 1974 I was sent to the Capitol steps with several hundred Moonies under the name "National Prayer and Fast for the Watergate Crisis" to demonstrate on behalf of Richard Nixon.

Before joining the Moonies I had had long debates with my father at the dinner table about Nixon. My father, a businessman, was at that time a die-hard Nixon supporter. I had always felt strongly that Nixon was not to be trusted and in fact had often referred to him at dinner as a crook. Now, in the heat of my Moon-inspired prayer vigil *for* Nixon, I called my parents from Washington to tell them about the fast. Because my father had always been so staunchly behind Nixon, I thought he would be pleased.

When I told him the news, my father said to me, "Steven, you were right. Nixon's a crook!"

"But Dad, you don't understand; God wants Nixon to be President!" I exclaimed.

"Now I *know* you are brainwashed," my father said, exasperated. "The guy's a crook."

It was only when I left the group that I laughed at the irony in this sudden role reversal.

Later in 1974, I was part of a seven-day fast[5] in front of the United Nations the week the U.N. voted on whether to withdraw its troops from South Korea because of human rights violations. We were personally instructed by Sun Myung Moon not to tell anyone that we were members of the Unification Church or had any political motivation. We established a front group called The American Committee for Human Rights for Japanese Wives of North Korean Repatriates, and successfully shifted the delegates' focus from human rights abuses in South Korea to those perpetrated by North Korea. The vote to withdraw was defeated. The Moonies claimed a victory and we were told the South Korean government was pleased.[6]

Being so close to the "Messiah" was exhilarating. I felt incredibly fortunate to be part of this movement and took myself very seriously because of the spiritual repercussions of everything I did. I thought my every action had monumental and historical implications. I strived to be the perfect "son" of the "True Parents"[7]—obedient and loyal (these two virtues were valued above all else). I always did what I was told, and then some. I wanted to prove my loyalty, and I was tested many times by Kamiyama and other leaders.

As a leader, I was able to see and hear things that rank-and-file members never could. Once, in late 1974, Moon took a few of us to inspect some new real estate he had acquired in Tarrytown. As usual, he gave an impromptu talk. However, this one stuck in my mind. "When we take power in America," he said, "we will have to amend the Constitution and make it a capital offense for anyone to have sexual relations with anyone other than the person assigned to him." He went on to explain that sex that was not God-centered was the greatest sin a person could commit; therefore, if a person couldn't overcome temptation, it would be better to take away his physical body. In that way we would be doing him a favor and making it easier to restore him to righteousness in the spirit world. I thought of all the married people not in the movement who were destroying their spiritual bodies by having intercourse. I never stopped to think of the mass genocide that might result if we took over America.

Leadership had other benefits, too. On one occasion Moon gave me an Italian hand-blown glass figurine and $300 in cash as a present. I was often permitted to play softball with his son and heir apparent, Hyo Jin Moon (now head of C.A.R.P.). Twice I ate with Moon at his lavish dinner table. I came to love the feeling of getting up in front of hundreds of people and giving a Sunday service or a Divine Principle lecture, of having members look up to me as a wonderful and spiritual person.

There were even "miracles" in my life. At one point I learned that all American members had been ordered by Moon to undergo a 120-day leadership training. Much to my surprise, Kamiyama interceded with Moon to keep me from being sent to that training session. I was brought before Moon—referred to by members as "Father"—and before I knew what had happened, he put his hand over my head and announced that I had just graduated from the 120-day program! When I asked Kamiyama why he had requested my exemption from the training, he told me that I was too important where I was in New York and that he didn't want to lose me. I had gotten the approval of a man who, I thought, was God's representative on Earth.

Moon had a novel style of motivating leaders. He would be nice to us at first, buying us gifts and taking us out for dinner or a movie. Then he would bring us back to his estate and yell and scream about how poorly we were performing.

Moon also liked to stimulate the highest degree of competition between leaders in order to maximize productivity. He would single out someone who was very successful at recruiting or fundraising (he did this with me), and present that person as a model of excellence, shaming the others into being more successful. It is ironic that whereas Moon's stated goal is to unify the world, many of his strategies foster jealousy and spite among leaders, virtually insuring a lack of unity.

When I knew him, Moon was a movie junkie. One of his favorite movies was *Rocky,* which he watched repeatedly, he told us. On one memorable occasion he told us that we had to have the same determination as Rocky Balboa to defeat our enemy. Later he was to spend $48 million in making a film of his own, *Inchon,* about General Douglas MacArthur's landing in Korea to stop the Communist invasion. Even though Moon bought top talent in Laurence Olivier and Jacqueline Bisset, *Inchon* was a failure. It was the most expensive movie ever made at the time, and received roundly bad reviews from the critics.[8]

Looking back on it all now, I believe one of Moon's major problems as a leader was his shortsightedness. He seemed always to be more concerned with immediate results than with the future. For example, his disregard for legal and accounting advice eventually landed him in jail.[9] His use of deception in order to buy real estate and businesses caused great enmity in many communities. His use of political shortcuts, like supporting Nixon, brought him into the national spotlight, but also alerted people to his background and unethical practices. This lack of foresight has caused his organization tremendous problems over the years.

Eventually I became the main lecturer in Manhattan and experienced a strange twist in my relationship with another American in the group. I was made assistant director of the Unification Church at national headquarters and was told to work with Neil Salonen, then president of the Unification Church of America. Mr. Kamiyama told me that Salonen needed to learn how to submit to the Korean and Japanese leadership in the church, and that I had been placed in the headquarters to teach him the "Japanese standard." That month the headquarters had been moved from Washington, D.C., to New York to bring the American staff under stricter Oriental control.

In my new position, it was my job to recruit newcomers to workshops. There had been a good deal of public exposure to the group's activities, and we felt the full brunt of public "persecution." We truly identified with the early Christians: the more people opposed us, the more committed we felt. At that time the media carried some sensational articles and television shows about the Moonies, which reinforced our fears that Communists were now taking control of America. Re-motivated by our increased level of fear, we continued our recruiting activities at a blinding pace. We all felt a great deal of pressure to recruit a minimum of one new person per member per month, and all members had to report their activities each night to their central figure. It was as if we were God's army in the middle of a spiritual war—the only ones who could go to the front lines and fight Satan each day.

When Moon decided to give a lecture at Yankee Stadium in 1976, he needed to raise several million dollars for the publicity campaign. At this point I was sent out with other American leaders as part of a model fundraising team in Manhattan. We fundraised twenty-one hours a day. We were constantly out on the streets, in the worst places imaginable. Once I was almost mugged in Harlem by someone with a garotte who saw me selling candles at night. Another time a man demanded my money and threatened me with a knife near my stomach. As a loyal, dedicated Moonie I would never let anyone steal God's money and refused. Both times, I narrowly escaped.

FALLING ASLEEP AT THE WHEEL

One irony of my experience in the Moonies is that the higher I rose in the organization, the closer I got to the total burn-out and exhaustion that eventually led to my exit from the group. Because I was so successful at fundraising, I pressed myself to the limit again and again. I had little concern for my overall well-being during those days. The most important thing was to work as hard as

I could for "Father." Fortunately for me, though, my family had not forgotten about me and was greatly concerned for my welfare.

After my time on the model fundraising team in Manhattan, I was told that my family was trying to kidnap and deprogram me. I was sent "underground" to Pennsylvania. I was instructed not to tell my family my whereabouts and to have all my mail forwarded through another city. Years later, after I left the group, I suspected I had been sent out of town as a distraction. The Moonies wanted to keep me from pursuing some disturbing questions about the validity of the "time parallels" used in the "History of Restoration" lecture. I had discovered some glaring inconsistencies. It was dangerous for someone in my position in the organization to ask questions that couldn't be answered. The other group leaders filled me with so much fear about deprogrammers that my questions simply disappeared. I believed my spiritual survival was at stake.

I had been repeatedly told horror stories about deprogramming. I had come to believe that group members were brutally kidnapped, beaten, and tortured by deprogrammers—Satan's elite soldiers committed to breaking people down and destroying their faith in God.[10] A couple of members were sent around to different centers to tell us about their deprogramming experiences. Fear of the outside world, particularly of parents, was drilled into our minds. Although I didn't realize it then, each successive deprogramming story became more and more exaggerated.

After a couple of months of fundraising on a model team in Pennsylvania, I was put in charge of all fundraising in Baltimore. My regional commander had ordered me to have each member make a minimum of $100 a day even if it meant staying up all night to reach that goal. I had a "young" team of eight inexperienced fundraisers. As a good leader I had to set an example and stay up with them.

I drove my team hard, and they averaged over $1,000 a day total profit—hard, tax-exempt cash. It was my responsibility to feed, clothe, and shelter my team, as well as to order, buy, and pick up product—the items we pushed on people for donations—and to collect the cash nightly and wire it to New York twice a week. We sold things like chocolate mints, sour balls, chocolate bars, roses, carnations, and candles. The markups were enormous. A box of mints that cost thirty cents was sold for two dollars. A ten-cent flower was sold for a minimum of a dollar and usually went for two dollars.

People would buy these items from us because they thought they were donating to a charitable cause. Our consciences had been reprogrammed by Moon's value system. We told people we were sponsoring Christian youth programs: a lie. We told them we operated drug rehabilitation houses: another lie. We told them that we were helping orphaned kids: another lie. On the spur of the moment we told them anything that we thought would work.[11] Since we thought saving the world from evil and establishing God's kingdom on earth was the most important effort on earth, we didn't look at it as "real" lying.

After all, every person but us was being controlled by Satan, and it was up to the "Heavenly Children" to claim money back from Satan for God's Messiah, Sun Myung Moon. We truly believed that we were saving the world from Satan and Communism by selling those products, and that we were giving people the opportunity to help the Messiah create the Garden of Eden on earth.

At about 5:30 A.M. on April 23, 1976, I was driving the van to pick up the last member of my group who had been out all night fundraising in front of a twenty-four-hour convenience store. I hadn't slept at all in the previous two days and was driving alone. Usually I had someone ride "shotgun" position to protect me from being attacked by evil forces, the "sleep spirits." As ridiculous as it seems now, I actually believed that spiritual entities were all around me, waiting to invade me and possess me. This was all part of the mind control indoctrination. Staying focused on the True Parents was the only way to ward off the evil spirits. If my attention wavered, I could be taken over. Phobias such as this kept me and other members dependent and compliant.

This time I was overconfident. I fell asleep and awoke abruptly. All I could see was the red back end of the eighteen-wheeler I was driving into at high speed. I hit the brakes, but it was too late. The impact was awful. The van was crushed and I was pinned. The pain was excruciating, but I could do nothing— I was trapped. The door had to be sawed off. It took an emergency team about thirty minutes to set up a winch and pull the steering column forward to make enough room to free me.

All I could think then was "Father, forgive me" and "Crush Satan." Over and over I chanted those lines to try to focus my mind on God and beg His forgiveness. I thought what had happened was "spiritual"—that I had been tested by Satan in the spirit world and had been defeated, and that this was what caused the accident, not the fact that I hadn't slept in days. Like any dedicated cult member I blamed myself for not being "pure" enough. It didn't dawn on me that I should have been sleeping at least my normal three or four hours a night. I felt that I had been chosen by God for this holy mission but had failed.

DEPROGRAMMING: HOW I FOUND MY WAY BACK TO MYSELF

After two weeks in the hospital and an operation for my broken leg, I got permission from my Moonie superiors to visit my sister Thea. I was able to do this for two reasons: Thea had never openly criticized my involvement in the Moonies, and I had been a trusted leader—someone whose faith in God and in the group was believed to be absolute.

The accident, however, subtly began breaking the Moonies' hold over me in several ways. First, I could sleep, eat, and rest. Second, I could finally see my family. My parents and my other sister Stephanie had been judged "satanic" by the Moonies, but I still loved them and wanted to convert them. Third, I could slow down and think, being away from the group's constant reinforcement. Fourth, my parents decided to have me deprogrammed. Fifth, I had a cast on my right leg from my toes to my pelvis, so I couldn't move without crutches. I could neither fight nor run away.

I was sitting on the living room couch at my sister's home when my father appeared unexpectedly. He sat down next to me and asked me how I was doing. When I said "fine," he stood up. He took my crutches to the other side of the room and said, "That's great!" Then seven more people appeared and announced that they had come to "talk to me about my affiliation with the Unification Church." I was shocked, and realized I was trapped.

By now I was thoroughly programmed and immediately "knew" that the deprogramming team had been sent directly by Satan. In my terror, their faces looked like images of demons. It was very surprising to me, then, when they turned out to be warm and friendly. They spent several hours talking to me about what they knew to be wrong with the Moonies. As a committed member, I fought to keep from hearing their words. After all, I had been told all about deprogramming by leaders of the group. I wasn't going to allow my faith in God to be broken by Satan.

The next morning my father said that we were going to go for a drive to see my mother. What had actually happened, I learned later, was that the Moonies had called to see why I hadn't reported in and were on their way to rescue me. Believing that my mother would be sympathetic and put an end to the deprogramming, I eagerly hobbled on my crutches and got into the back seat of the car, with my broken leg outstretched. My father was driving, and two of the deprogrammers sat next to him. I became angry, though, as my father passed the exit from the Long Island Expressway to my parents' home. While it might seem hard to believe, my first impulse was to escape by reaching over and snapping my father's neck. I actually thought it was better to do that than betray the Messiah! As a member I had been told many times that it was better to die or kill than to leave the church.[12]

At that point, however, I was still confident that they could never break me. I knew I would have other chances to escape, so I decided not to kill my father. When we arrived at the apartment in which the deprogramming was scheduled to continue, I refused to get out of the car without a fight. I threatened my father with extreme violence and told him that I would break my leg again and let it bleed until I died.

My father turned around from the driver's seat and started to cry. I had seen my father cry only once before: when I was fifteen and my grandmother died. Then, as now, I felt a big lump in my throat and an ache in my heart. "This is crazy," he pleaded. "Tell me, what would you do, if your son, your only son, went away for a weekend workshop and all of sudden disappeared, dropped out of college, quit work, and got involved with such a controversial organization?"

That was the first time since I had joined that—for even a moment—I allowed myself to think from his perspective. I felt his pain and anger, as well as his parental love. But I still believed he had been brainwashed by the Communist media.

I answered, "Probably the same thing that you're doing now." I meant it. "What do you want me to do?" I asked.

"Just talk to these people," he replied. "Listen to what they have to say. I can't sleep at night as your parent, knowing that you haven't heard both sides."

"For how long?" I asked.

"For five days." he said.

"Then what—can I go back if I want to?"

"Yes, and if you want to come out, that will be your choice."

I thought about the proposition. I *knew* that what I had been doing was right. I *knew* that God wanted me to remain in the group. I *knew* the Messiah personally, in the flesh. I *knew* the Divine Principle by heart. What did I have to fear? Besides, I believed that I could prove to my parents once and for all that I wasn't brainwashed. Also, I knew that if I remained with my parents involuntarily and then escaped, I could be ordered to press kidnapping charges against them. I didn't want to do that.

The bargain was struck. I would not contact the Moonies for five more days. Also, I would make no effort to escape. I would talk to the ex-members in the apartment and listen to what they wanted to say, taking breaks as often as I wished.

The former members were not at all what I expected. I assumed, because of my training, that they would be cold, calculating, unspiritual, money-hungry, and abusive. They were warm, caring, idealistic, and spiritually minded, and they treated me with respect. As former members, they should have been miserable and guilt-ridden. They weren't. They were very happy that they were out and free to lead their lives as they were doing. All of this was very perplexing.

I was a very difficult person to deprogram. I fought the process with prayer and chanting and threw up expert barricades of denial, rationalizations, justifications, and wishful thinking. The former members brought out psychiatrist Robert Jay Lifton's book *Thought Reform and the Psychology of Totalism* and discussed the techniques and processes used by the Communist Chinese (the enemy!) to brainwash prisoners during the 1950s. It became obvious to me that the processes we used in the Moonies were almost identical. The big question for me became "Does God have to use the same tactics as Satan in order to make an ideal world?" Thinking and reasoning for me at that time felt like wading through waist-high mud.

On the fourth day they discussed Hitler and the Nazi movement, comparing Moon and his philosophy of world theocracy to Hitler's global goals for German National Socialism. At one point I remember saying, "I don't care if

Moon is like Hitler! I've chosen to follow him and I'll follow him 'til the very end!" When I heard myself say that, an eerie chill went down my spine. I quickly suppressed it.

On the morning of the last day of deprogramming, I had the indescribable experience of my mind suddenly opening up, as if a light switch had been thrown. The former members were reading to me from one of Moon's speeches to members of Congress.[13] I thought "what a snake" when they read me Moon's hypocritical words. He was talking about how Americans were too smart to allow themselves to be brainwashed by a Korean, and how he respected Americans very much. I had listened to him say, on at least a dozen occasions, how stupid, lazy, and corrupt Americans were, particularly politicians. Also, three Americans, former members, were sitting in front of me, and they each took turns telling me that they had been brainwashed by Moon. I asked everybody to leave the room. In comparison with the pain of the accident, I felt much worse. I cried for a long time. Someone returned and gave me a cold compress for my forehead. My head pounded, and I felt like a large open wound. That night was the most painful time of my whole life.

RECOVERY: RETURNING TO A NORMAL LIFE

After rediscovering myself, I had a whole new string of questions in my mind. How could I have ever believed that the Messiah was a multimillionaire industrialist from Korea? How could I have turned my back on virtually every moral and ethical principle I had? How could I have done so many cruel things to so many people? The fantasy I had used to inspire myself day after day and month after month was gone. What was left was a frightened, confused, yet proud person. I felt as though I had awakened from a dream and wasn't sure what was reality, or as though I had stepped off a skyscraper and was headed toward the earth but never crashed.

I was overwhelmed by many emotions. I was sad and missed my friends in the group, particularly my "spiritual children," the people I recruited. I missed the excitement of feeling that what I was doing was cosmically important. I missed the feeling of power that singlemindedness brought. Now, all I knew was that my leg was broken. I was broken. I felt tremendous embarrassment about having fallen for a cult. My parents had told me it was a cult. Why hadn't I listened to them? Why hadn't I trusted them? It was weeks before I could thank my parents for helping me. It was months before I could even refer to the Moonies as a cult.

I read for months. For me, the burning issue was how the Moonies had ever managed to convert me and indoctrinate me so thoroughly that I could no longer think for myself. I read everything I could get my hands on. At first, the act of reading itself was extremely difficult. I had read only Moon literature for more than two years. I had difficulty concentrating and was sometimes spaced out for long periods, not comprehending what I was reading.

Living at home was difficult. I was very depressed. Since I still had a full cast on my leg, I needed help to move about, to eat, even to go to the bathroom. I was unaccustomed to being so dependent. I had been running a house and controlling the lives of eight people. Now I was a captain with no one to lead. I felt terrible for what I had put my family through. They were wonderful to me, but I still felt a tremendous sense of guilt.

I felt even more guilt for what I had done as a Moonie. I had lied to people, manipulated them, tricked them, and induced them to abandon their families, education, and relationships to follow a would-be dictator.[14] The guilt turned to anger the more I studied mind control.

I tracked down Robert Jay Lifton and arranged a meeting at his apartment in Manhattan. He was curious to know why I was so interested in a book about Chinese brainwashing he had written 15 years earlier, in 1961. He was amazed when I described to him, in detail, what the Moonies do to recruit members and how they run their three-day workshops, their seven-day workshops, and their twenty-one-day, forty-day, and 120-day workshops. He said, "What you are telling me is so much more sophisticated than what the Chinese did in the '50s. It's like a hybrid mutation of a virulent virus strain!"

Lifton shifted my entire perspective on myself when he said, "Steve, you know more about this than I do, because you've lived it. You know it instrumentally. I only know it theoretically and second-hand. You must study psychology and take what you know through your experience and tell others about it." He later asked me to coauthor a book with him on mind control, something that was never to be. I was flattered by his offer and intended to take him up on it, but the timing wasn't right for me.

I DECIDE TO GO PUBLIC

Meeting Lifton changed my life. Instead of looking at myself and seeing a college dropout, a poet with no poetry (I sorely regretted throwing those four hundred poems away when I joined), and a former cult member, I saw that perhaps there was a higher purpose for me. At that time, although I was no longer a Moonie, I was still thinking somewhat in black and white terms: good versus evil, us versus them. The world's most renowned expert on brainwashing thought that I had an important contribution to make, that what I had experienced could be useful in helping people. By this time I had started attending cult awareness meetings of people affected by the problem and was approached by many parents of people in the Moonies. They asked me if I would talk to their children. I agreed.

It was then (1976) that I seriously began taking steps to become a professional counselor. At first I had my work cut out for me; there were then no alternatives to forcible deprogramming. I had undergone a little training as a peer counselor at college before joining the Moonies. I myself had been deprogrammed. Most helpful of all in talking to members was that I had been a Moonie at a high level, and I knew what made members tick inside and out. I was involved with deprogramming for about a year. A couple of the cases may have involved abduction by parents or people they hired; most were cases in which members came home to visit and weren't allowed to leave. Some of these were legal conservatorship cases, in which the family received legal custody of its adult child. Such conservatorship laws are now unusable in the courts. In my opinion, it is likely they were lobbied out of existence by cult lawyers.

Fortunately, I was never sued. Most of my cases were successful. However, I did not enjoy the stress of forcible deprogramming and wanted to find some other way to help members of destructive cults.

After a year of going public, giving lectures, and giving television and radio interviews, I decided that I needed to find out who I was again. I went back to college and dropped out of my life as a cult fighter. I wrote poetry, played basketball, went out on dates, volunteered to be a counselor in two student counseling agencies at Boston University, and got in touch with myself again.

During this time, though, Moon was making new and bigger waves. In Congress, the House Subcommittee on International Relations held a lengthy investigation into Korean CIA activities in the United States and other efforts by Korean agents to influence United States government decisions. I agreed to help the investigation as much as the committee wanted, provided they not ask me to testify publicly. I didn't really follow the "Koreagate" investigation, except when I read an occasional article. I was absolutely confident that the government would expose the Moon group and it would be destroyed.

The final report of the investigation[15] had an eighty-page section on the Moonies. The report found that the Moon organization "systematically violated U.S. tax, immigration, banking, currency, and Foreign Agents Registration Act laws, as well as state and local laws relating to charity fraud." It called for an interagency task force to continue to gather evidence and to prosecute Moon and other Unification Church leaders for their criminal violations. The subcommittee's Republican minority included its own statement, reading in part, "It is difficult to understand why the appropriate agencies of the Executive Branch have not long since taken action against those activities of the Moon organization that are illegal." Little did I know that events would soon induce me to take a more visible position.

The report was released October 31, 1978. Three weeks later, California Congressman Leo J. Ryan, a member of the Koreagate investigation, was gunned downed at an airstrip near Jonestown, Guyana, while trying to help members of another cult, the People's Temple, escape the horrors of Jim Jones' camp. I watched the news bulletins about the nine hundred people who were dead because a cult leader had gone insane. Chills went down my spine. I had never heard of the People's Temple before, but I completely identified with the mindset of its members. I remembered listening to Moon harangue us and ask if we were willing to follow him to our deaths. I remembered hearing Moon say that if North Korea invaded South Korea, he would send American Unification members to die on the front lines, so that Americans would get inspired to fight another land war in Asia.

I spent days thinking about the cult problem. More than anything else, the Jonestown massacre motivated me to become a public activist again. I accepted several invitations to appear on television. I was asked to speak at Senator Robert Dole's public hearing on cults on Capitol Hill in 1979. But at the last moment, all the ex-cult members who had been invited to speak were taken off the program. The hearing was a disaster.

After that, Moon's political influence began to grow. When Ronald Reagan became president, Moon-controlled groups began funding the New Right political movement in Washington. When it was clear the federal government would do nothing about the Moonies, I decided to organize. I started a group called Ex-Members Against Moon, later Ex-Moon, Inc. I sponsored press conferences, edited a monthly newsletter, and gave numerous interviews. I had considered starting a group of former members from many different cult groups, but I decided that with the release of the Congressional investigation, it would be more effective for me to focus on the Moonies. I filed a Freedom of Information Act request with the Department of Defense, asking why a Moon-owned company, Tong Il Industries, was permitted to make American M-16 rifles in Korea when only the South Korean government had legal permission to do so. Was the Moon organization part of the Korean government? Was the Department of Defense giving it favored treatment? The request was turned down on the grounds that revealing the information I asked for would compromise the security of the United States. To this day I do not know the truth.

I knew that I didn't want to do any more deprogrammings. I had to find a way to help people out of cults that would be less traumatic and less expensive, and would not violate the law. I had read dozens of books and thousands of pages—everything I could get my hands on—about thought reform, brainwashing, attitude change, persuasion, and CIA recruitment and indoctrination. The next and most important area to research was the field of hypnosis.

In 1980, I attended a seminar by Richard Bandler on hypnosis that was based on a model he and John Grinder had developed, called Neuro-Linguistic Programming (NLP). I was impressed by what I learned, because it gave me a handle on techniques of mind control and how to combat them. I spent nearly two years studying NLP with everyone involved in its formulation and presentation. At one point I moved to Santa Cruz, California, to undergo an apprenticeship with John Grinder. By this time, too, I had fallen in love and gotten married. I moved back to Massachusetts when my wife, Aureet, was given a scholarship to work for her master's degree at Harvard.

However, I became concerned about the ethics of what seemed to me to be a mass-market campaign to promote NLP as a tool for power enhancement. I eventually left my association with Grinder and began to study the works of Milton Erickson, Virginia Satir, and Gregory Bateson on which NLP is based. I learned a great deal about how the mind functions as well as how to communicate with a person more effectively. These studies gave me a way to move forward and apply what I had learned to help people trapped in cults. It was possible, I discovered, to analyze and create a model for the process of change that occurs when a person goes into a cult group and then successfully leaves it.

What individual factors make a person able to move away from the mind-controlled psyche? Why are certain interventions successful and others not? What goes on in the thought processes of people who simply walk out of cults? Patterns began to appear. I found that "walk-aways" were people who had been able to maintain contact with people outside the destructive cult. It was clear that if such people could maintain communication with outsiders, valuable information that could change a person's life could penetrate cult-controlled mental walls.

I knew how important my father's tears had been for me. More importantly, I realized that he had been able to invite me to *look at myself from his perspective* and re-sort my information from his viewpoint. In analyzing my own experience, I recognized that what helped me the most was my own internal voice and my own first-hand experiences, buried beneath all of the thought-stopping rituals of chanting and praying and all the emotional repression. Underneath, the real me wasn't dead. Maybe it had been bound and gagged, but I was very much alive. The accident and deprogramming had helped move me physically and psychologically to a place where I was able to get in touch with myself. Indeed, it was my ideals and my own fantasy of an ideal world that had lured me into the Moonies. Those ideals ultimately enabled me to walk out and publicy condemn cult mind control.

Since receiving my master's degree in counseling psychology from Cambridge College in 1985, I have begun a new phase of my life. While practicing psychotherapy and conducting my public education activities, I have also worked as the national coordinator for FOCUS, a support group of former cult members who want to help each other. Above all, I have worked to increase public awareness of the fact that the problem of destructive cults did not go away as the idealistic youth of the 1970s became the young professionals of the 1980s. Destructive cults are going after many different kinds of people and gaining many more members, as I will show.

Yet, while destructive cults continue to grow, so too does our understanding of the process of unethical mind control. The field of exit counseling is expanding as more mental health professionals, social workers, doctors, lawyers, and people from all walks of life, many of them people who have lost family members to destructive cults, become aware of the dynamics of mind control. There *are* some basic ways to identify destructive cults, protect yourself from mind control, and help others shake free of its influence. Giving you the keys to that knowledge is what this book is all about.

Chapter 3

The Threat: Mind Control
Cults Today

IMAGINE, if you will, the following scenes.

Saffron-robed men on street corners dancing and chanting with cymbals and drums. Bedraggled teenagers running from car to car selling flowers in the pouring rain. High-strung men in suits and ties confronting people in airport lobbies for money to quarantine AIDS victims and build particle-beam weapons. Over nine hundred people—men, women, and children; white and black—lying face down in the mud at Jonestown, Guyana.

Mention "cults" to someone and these are the images you'll evoke. Many of us have seen such images ourselves, either through personal experience or through the mass media.

Yet these images do not represent the overall destructive cult phenomenon as it has become today. They are only its most visible aspect.

Imagine, then, a different set of images.

Business executives in three-piece suits sitting in hotel ballrooms for company-sponsored "awareness" training, unable to get up to go to the bathroom. Housewives attending "psych-up rallies" so they can recruit friends and neighbors into a pyramid sales organization. Hundreds of students gathering at an accredited university being told they can levitate and "fly" through the air if they only meditate hard enough. High-school students practicing satanic rituals involving blood and urine directed by an older leader who claims he will develop their personal power. Hundreds of people of every description paying huge sums to learn cosmic truths from a "channeled" spirit.

These are some of the forms the destructive cult phenomenon is taking today.

Do you know anyone who has undergone a radical personality change because of an involvement with such a group? The odds are that someone you know—someone in your family, one of your friends, someone from work or school—has been affected by contact with a destructive cult. If not, it is probably just a matter of time before this happens.

In the past twenty years, the destructive cult phenomenon has mushroomed into a problem of tremendous social and political importance. It is estimated that there are now approximately three thousand destructive cults in the United States, involving as many as three million people.[1] They come in many different types and sizes. Some cults have hundreds of millions of dollars, while others are quite poor. Some, however, are clearly more dangerous than others. Not content to exercise their power simply over the lives of their members, they have an agenda to gain political power and use it to reshape American society— and, in the case of some of them, even the world.

Considering how well destructive cults have been able to shield themselves from public scrutiny in the past few years, it might seem alarmist to regard them as a threat to individual liberty and society as a whole. Yet, they are influencing the political landscape by extensive lobbying efforts and elec-tioneering for candidates.[2] Some are attempting to influence United States foreign policy by lobbying covertly for foreign powers.[3] The Moonies have been found to be a major supplier of money and guns to the contra forces in Nicaragua.[4] They also invested between $70 and $100 million in Uruguay,[5] perhaps in an attempt to turn that country into the cult's first theocratic state—a springboard from which to pursue its declared goal "to conquer and subjugate the world."[6]

In the United States, cults exert tremendous economic clout by buying up huge blocks of real estate and taking over hundreds of businesses. Some enter corporations under the pretense of offering executive leadership training, while harboring a covert agenda to take over the company. Some seek to influence the judicial system by spending millions of dollars annually on top attorneys to try to bend the law to their will.

Since all destructive cults believe that the ends justify the means, they believe themselves to be above the law. As long as they believe that what they are doing is "right" and "just," many of them think nothing of lying, stealing, cheating, or unethically using mind control to accomplish their ends. They violate, in the most profound and fundamental way, the civil liberties of the people they recruit. They turn unsuspecting people into slaves.

What right do I have to call a group a destructive cult, anyway? My right to freely express my opinion short of libeling someone is, of course, guaranteed by the United States Constitution. Yet, when I call a cult "destructive" I do so because it meets the criteria described in more detail in chapter 6. In brief, it is a group which violates the rights of its members and damages them through the abusive techniques of unethical mind control. Not all groups which might be called "cults" because they appear to incorporate strange beliefs and practices are necessarily destructive. A destructive cult distinguishes itself from a normal social or religious group by subjecting its members to persuasion or other damaging influences to keep them in the group.

If I had not personally suffered from being under mind control for two and a half years, I would probably be a staunch defender of the rights of such groups to practice freely, unhindered by public scrutiny. I am a strong civil libertarian, concerned about protecting personal liberty and defending the Constitution's guarantees of religious freedom. I fully support people's rights to believe as they choose, no matter how bizarre or unorthodox their beliefs. If people want to believe that Mr. Moon is the Messiah, that is their right. However—and this is a crucial point—people should be protected from processes that *make* them believe Mr. Moon is the Messiah.

The purpose of this chapter is to demonstrate the prevalence of unethical, coercive mind control by describing the different areas of society in which cults arise and the techniques used for recruitment. Methods of operation are what make cults destructive. How a group recruits and what happens during membership determine whether or not it respects people's rights to *choose for themselves what they want to believe.* If deception, hypnosis, and other mind control techniques are used to recruit and control followers, then people's rights are being infringed upon.

"Cults" are not new. Throughout history, groups of enthusiasts have sprung up around charismatic leaders of every possible description. But in recent years, something has been added: the systematic use of modern psychological techniques to reduce a person's will and gain control over his or her thoughts, feelings, and behavior.

While we usually think of "cults" as being religious (the first definition of "cult" in *Webster's Third New International Dictionary* is "religious practice: worship"), actually they are often completely secular. *Webster's* also defines "cult" as "a usually small or narrow circle of persons united by devotion or allegiance to some artistic or intellectual program, tendency, or figure (as one of limited popular appeal)." That second definition begins to come close to the meaning of a modern cult but falls a bit short. Modern cults have *virtually unlimited* popular appeal. For the sake of brevity, I will refer to many groups from now on as simply "cults." You may assume, though, that I use that term only for groups which fit the criteria for being destructive.

In times past, cult or sect leaders could be very compelling, often abusively so. Charges of mind control against them have a long history. But the leaders gained their dominance over followers in a relatively hit-or-miss way, learning as they went along. Cult leadership was an art practiced by a very few. In some cases, groups which were originally considered cults in their earliest days have grown to become respected, mainline religions, such as Christian Science, which came into prominence around the turn of the century. Yet even mainline religious organizations can have destructive aspects and can have elements shared by newer destructive cults.

In our time, mind control is becoming more of a science. Since World War II, intelligence agencies around the world have been aggressively engaged in mind control research and development. The CIA admits to having performed drug, electroshock, and hypnosis experiments since the early 1950s under the code name MK-ULTRA.[7] Research has expanded into other areas since then.

A generation ago, the human potential movement in psychology began to experiment with procedures to direct individual and group dynamics. These techniques were developed with the best of motives: to force people out of debilitating mental ruts and show them how truly different they could become. During the late 1960s, a form of group therapy known as a sensitivity session became popular. In such a meeting, people were encouraged to speak about their most intimate personal matters with other people in a group setting. One technique widely popular at that time was the "hot seat," whereby a member of the group sat in the center of the circle while other members confronted him with what they considered to be his shortcomings or problems. Needless to say, without the supervision of an experienced therapist, such a technique opens up considerable possiblities for abuse.

Another development which began to affect many people was the popularization of hypnosis, in particular through the system known as Neuro-Linguistic Programming (NLP) (mentioned in chapter 2). Increasing numbers of people were introduced to certain techniques for inducing hypnotic trance, but often without adequate consideration of the ethical aspects of working with the subconscious mind.

Originally these group process methods were used only on willing participants, and positive experiences were reported by many of them. Soon, though, some of these techniques percolated out into the general culture of pop psychology, where they became available for anyone to abuse. Unscrupulous persons began using them to gain money and power by manipulating a coterie of followers. The "hot seat," in particular, is used in a number of destructive cults, according to former cult members.

Many members of pop psychology groups drifted from one organization to another, carrying the styles of group dynamics with them. Sect leaders of all types began to realize the success that the new methods of cult management could bring. The modern cult phenomenon was underway.

Because of increased media coverage, people in the United States began to become aware of the new cults in the middle to late 1970s. Who can forget the spectacle of Patty Hearst,[8] the daughter of one of the country's most powerful newspaper publishers, William Randolph Hearst III, transformed into "Tania," a member of the Symbionese Liberation Army, a left-wing terrorist cult?

As public awareness of the destructive potential of cult membership began to grow, we saw the birth of deprogramming. Professional deprogrammers like Ted Patrick hired by a cult member's family would forcibly abduct the person and, often in a secluded motel room, try to reverse the cult's "brainwashing."[9] Thousands of cult members, like myself, were indeed "de-brainwashed" permanently, and they gave dramatic public testimony of how cult mind control worked. Many other deprogrammings failed, and members and cults sometimes brought lawsuits against families and deprogrammers.

Many families with members in destructive cults found kidnapping repugnant, the financial burden great, and the threat of lawsuits intimidating. If they didn't want to try a forcible deprogramming, they had no choice but to be patient and wait for something to happen. The family members or friends of many people remained in cults throughout the mid-1970s. Then something happened to change the way the whole nation perceived destructive cults: the massacre at Jonestown.

Above Jones's throne was affixed a sign which read "Those who do not remember the past are condemned to repeat it." While no one can explain why Jones chose that saying from George Santayana as his motto, the truth in that message, ironically, is relevant to us today as we examine the recent history of cults and think about the implications.

THE FOUR MAIN TYPES OF CULTS

While news of the Jonestown massacre temporarily shocked the world, there was little general understanding in the late 1970s of the role of unethical mind control or of how widespread its use had already become in society at large. In the decade following that massacre, cult groups have continued to grow unabated. New cults appear and older ones grow more sophisticated. Currently, there are groups using mind control in several different areas of society. These organizations include religious cults, political cults, psychotherapy/educational cults, and commercial cults.

Religious cults are the best known and most numerous. These groups are focused on religious dogma. Some are Bible-based, some are eastern-religion-based, others draw on occult lore, and some are purely the inventions of their leaders. Although most claim to be of the spiritual realm, all one has to do to see their true colors is examine how much emphasis is placed on the "material" world—the luxurious lifestyle of the leaders, millions of dollars of real estate, extensive business enterprises, and so forth. One example, already examined in some detail, is the Unification Church. Others include the Church of Scientology,[10] Church Universal and Triumphant,[11] The Way International,[12] and Rajneesh.[13]

Political cults often make the news, usually with the word "fringe" or "extremist" attached, but most people do not hear about the deceptive recruitment and mind control practices that distinguish them from run-of-the-mill fanatics. These groups are organized around a particular political dogma. One such group's leader, Lyndon LaRouche, has run for President in the past three elections and claims to advise top government and business leaders.[14] Another group, known as "Move," was bombed by police in Philadelphia after holing up with an arsenal of weapons.[15] Another, The Aryan Nation, runs "survivalist" training camps to uphold a white supremacy doctrine, with plans to take over the United States or die trying.[16] It would be possible also to point to the now-defunct Democratic Workers' Party of California as an example of an extreme left-wing cult.[17]

Psychotherapy/educational cults hold workshops and seminars for hundreds of dollars to provide "insight" and "enlightenment," usually in a hotel meeting-room environment. These cults use many basic mind control techniques to provide participants with a "peak" experience. That experience may be all that happens to most customers, but others will be manipulated to sign up for the more expensive advanced courses. Graduates of the advanced courses may then become enmeshed in the group. Once committed to the group, members are told to bring in friends, relatives, and co-workers, or cut them off. But recruiters are not allowed to disclose much about the program. Many of these groups have caused nervous breakdowns, broken marriages, and business failures, not to mention some well-documented suicides and deaths by reckless accidents. The people who run these groups sometimes have questionable personal backgrounds and often few or no credentials.

Commercial cults believe in the dogma of greed. They deceive and manipulate people to work for little or no pay in the hope of getting rich. There are many pyramid-style or multi-level marketing organizations that promise big money but fleece their victims. They then destroy their victims' self-esteem so that they will not complain. Success depends on recruiting new people who in turn recruit others. Other commercial cults include those that browbeat people into hawking magazine subscriptions or other items door to door. These cults take out ads in local newspapers promising exciting travel and lucrative careers. Cult recruiters set up "interviews" inside their hotel rooms, preying on high school and college students. When people are "accepted," they usually have to pay money to be "trained" and then are sent in vans far away to sell merchandise. Salespeople are manipulated through fear and guilt and are sometimes physically and sexually abused. These people become slaves to the "company" and turn over their money in order to pay for "living expenses."

RECRUITMENT: HOW IT'S DONE

As you can see, there are many different ways people can be ensnared into a group which uses mind control. Since destructive groups deliberately seek out people who are intelligent, talented, and successful, the members themselves are powerfully persuasive and seductive to newcomers. Indeed, the sheer number of sincere, committed members whom a newcomer meets is probably far more attractive to a prospective convert than any doctrine or structure. The large cults prove that they know how to train their "salespeople" well. They indoctrinate members to show only the best sides of the organization. Members are taught to suppress any negative feelings they have about the group and always show a continually smiling, "happy" face.

Likewise, they are taught to size up the newcomer, and package the group in a form that will be easy to sell to him or her. In the Moonies, I was taught to use a four-part personality model to help recruit new members. People were categorized as thinkers, feelers, doers, or believers. Thinkers are people who approach life with their minds, like intellectuals. Feelers lead with their emotions. Doers are action-oriented and very physical. Believers are spiritually oriented.

If a person was categorized as a thinker, we would use an intellectual approach. We would show him pictures of Nobel Laureates at one of the group-sponsored science conferences, or philosophers discussing a variety of interesting topics. A deliberate misimpression was given that these giants of the scientific and academic communities were supporters of the movement. In fact, to my knowledge, none of them actually support the Moon cause. They were interested in meeting with professional colleagues and friends. Of course, their expense-paid trips and the thousands of dollars paid to them as honorariums were added incentives.

Feelers would always respond well to a loving, caring approach by cult members. With these people, my group would accent our emotional well-being, as well as the extended family aspect of the group. We would always talk about love with such people, and how there wasn't enough of the "real" kind of love in the world. Feelers automatically long to be accepted by others in group situations, so we would go out of our way to provide the person with a warm and enticing feeling of unconditional approval.

Doers tend to like challenges and strive to accomplish a great deal with their lives. They are action-oriented people. Perhaps they see poverty and suffering in the world and want to make it end. We would tell them how much we were doing along these lines. Perhaps they are concerned about war, or Communism. We would always make it sound as though we were the only organization with a plan of action that worked. (Even if it was objectively untrue, we believed it was true.) We would tell such people about all of the hundreds of programs we were sponsoring to fix and heal a "broken" world.

We saw believers as people searching for God, or looking for spiritual meaning in their lives. They typically would tell us about their spiritual experiences—dreams, visions, revelations. For the most part, these people were "wide open," and really recruited themselves. It was always amazing to me to realize how many people in this category told us they had just been praying to God to show them what He wanted them to do with their lives. Many believed they were "spiritually" led to meet one of our members. With them it was simply a matter of sharing our "testimonies" with them to convince them they had been led to us by God.

Contrary to public perception, most of the people we recruited did not fall into the believer category. Most were either feelers or doers. Many of the people who were so-called thinkers eventually became leaders within the organization.

With this personality model to guide recruiters, and hundreds of front groups to operate behind, the Moon organization casts a broad recruitment net that draws in a diversity of people.[18] Indeed, members regard themselves as "fishers of men," a term taken from Jesus' metaphor for his disciples in the New Testament.

The fishers' work, though, is made considerably easier by the fact that most people have no idea of the major destructive cults' considerable resources. Many of the larger ones have grown quite wealthy through public fundraising techniques and strategies as well as by tapping their own members' bank accounts and property. They reinvest a great part of their capital back into recruiting more members. Today, it is also quite common for some cult groups to spend huge sums of money on public relations firms. They pay top dollar to experts to help them make a positive "image" which will enable them to be more effective in pursuing their hidden agendas. They hire marketing specialists to design their recruitment campaigns. They will use anything that works.

The average person doesn't stand much chance. He doesn't understand mind control. He doesn't know how different cult groups operate. He doesn't know what questions to ask and what behaviors to watch out for. The average person assumes he could never be sucked in.

WHY DO THEY HAVE SO MUCH SUCCESS?

Why is there a pervasive complacency concerning the threat of mind control cults? First of all, accepting that unethical mind control can affect anybody challenges the age-old philosophical notion (the one on which our current laws are based) that *man is a rational being,* responsible for, and in control of, his every action. Such a world view does not allow for any concept of mind control. Second, we all have a *belief in our own invulnerability.* It is too scary to think that someone could take control of our mind. Third, influence processes start from the moment we are born, so it is easy to take the position that *everything is mind control.* It's easy, then, to simply say "Why worry about it?"

Let's start with the idea that man is a rational being. If people operate from such a viewpoint, they simply believe that members have rationally "chosen" to live a deviant lifestyle. If that person is an adult, goes the argument, then he or she has a right to live any way he or she chooses. That argument would be true if there were no deceptive techniques used to unduly influence a person's "choice."

Though it might be obvious, we human beings aren't totally "rational" creatures. Complete rationality denies our emotional and physical nature. We can't function without our emotions. We all need love, friendship, attention, and approval in our lives. Most of us would agree, for example, on the wonderfulness of falling in love. Neither would anyone argue that our bodies have a tremendous impact on the way we function. Have you ever gone for a few days with little or no sleep? If so, I doubt that without sleep you were functioning rationally and in total control of your every action. Have you ever fasted (no food) for days? The mind begins to hallucinate when the body doesn't have enough to eat. In such circumstances, our physiology undermines our rationality.

Then, of course, we have the problems that stem from our belief in our own invulnerability. We all need to feel that we are in control of our lives. We don't like feeling that events are out of control, so we put reality into an order that makes sense to us. When we hear that something bad has happened to someone (perhaps being mugged or raped), we usually try to find a reason to explain why that person was a victim. Was he or she walking at the "wrong" time in a "bad" neighborhood? People try to ascribe a direct cause-and-effect relationship to what happened: if something bad happened to her, then she must have done something wrong. This kind of behavior is called *blaming the victim.*

Although there is value in trying to assess possibly careless behavior (indeed, we must learn from life's tragedies), the reality is that the person just might have been in the wrong place at the wrong time. Blaming the victim plays an important psychological role in allowing us to distance ourselves from the person who was hurt. In this way, we say to ourselves, "Such a thing couldn't happen to me because I am different. I know better." Often people look at a cult victim and say mistakenly, "What a weak-minded person; he must have been looking for a way to escape responsibility and have someone control his life." In that way people deny the reality that the same thing could happen to them.

People believe that "it can never happen to them" because they want to believe they are stronger and better than the millions who have fallen victim to cult mind control. Our need to believe that we are invulnerable, though, is actually a weakness that can easily be played upon by cult recruiters. For example, a recruiter could say, "Now, Bill, you strike me as a very intelligent, worldly type of person. You would never allow anyone to force you to do something you wouldn't want to do. You like to make up your mind for yourself. So you won't let the biased media scare you with bizarre claims of mind control. You're too smart for that. So what time do you want to come over for that lecture?"

Last, what about the philosophical position that "everything is mind control?" Well, it is certainly true that we are influenced throughout our lives. Yet, there is a continuum of influence processes that starts at one end with benign influences (a friend suggesting that we see a particular movie) and ends at the other extreme with destructive influences such as indoctrinating a person to kill himself or harm others (Jonestown). Most of the groups I'm concerned with fall near this destructive end of the continuum.

What do I really mean by mind control? The term refers to a set of techniques that influences how a person thinks, feels, and acts. (See chapter 4.) Like most bodies of knowledge, it is inherently neither good nor evil. If mind control techniques are used to empower an individual to have more choice, and the authority for his life remains within himself, the effects can be very beneficial. For example, people have used hypnosis to enable them to quit smoking. However, if mind control is used to change a person's belief system *without informed consent* and make him *dependent on outside authority figures,* the effects can indeed be devastating.

Some destructive groups essentially make addicts out of their members. With alcoholism and substance abuse treatment so much in the national spotlight today, it is important that mental health professionals pay attention to this former cult member population. People indoctrinated to perform excessive (hours-long) meditation or chanting techniques daily can become psychologically and physiologically addicted to the mind control technique. Such mind-stilling generates strong releases of brain chemicals which cause not only a dissociated mental state but also a "high" similar to that created by illegal drugs. Some former members who have used these techniques for several years report a wide variety of deleterious side effects, including severe headaches, involuntary muscle spasms, and diminution of cognitive faculties like memory, concentration, and decision making ability.

PHOBIAS: THE FORCE THAT ROBS CULT MEMBERS' FREEDOM

Although I will go into great detail about the mind control process in chapter 4, one very important subject should be discussed on its own: phobias.[19] Do you know anyone who has ever had a phobia? Yourself, perhaps? The most common phobias include fears of flying in airplanes, public speaking, taking elevators, driving in tunnels or over bridges, and certain animals like snakes, spiders, and even dogs.

Basically, phobias are an intense fear reaction to someone or something. A phobic reaction can range from very mild to very severe. An intense phobic reaction can cause physical responses like racing heartbeat, dry mouth, sweating, and muscle tension. Phobias can immobilize people and keep them from doing the things they truly want to do. Indeed, phobias can rob people of free choice.

Ordinarily, people develop phobias as a result of a traumatic life experience. For example, a friend dies in a plane crash. An elevator someone is traveling in gets stuck for hours without light. Someone is bitten by a snake. We learn to associate extremely negative feelings with the object. After such an experience, our fears can then take on a life of their own and, in minutes or over several years, can become a full-blown phobia.

The structure of a phobia involves several internal components which interact and cause a vicious cycle. These components include worrisome thoughts, negative internal images, and feelings of dread and being out of control. Just thinking about the object can sometimes trigger the cycle into action. The person may say to himself, "Oh, I hope the teacher doesn't call on me to give my report," and that thought is enough to cause him to start getting tense and anxious. He sees (usually unconsciously) a picture of himself going to the front of the room and freezing up. In this vivid "motion picture," he sees himself sweating and fidgeting, and his mind becoming a blank slate. Everyone is laughing at him and the teacher starts yelling at him. This imagined ridicule causes him to feel even more upset and fearful that he will be the one called on, and he is well on the way toward having a fully developed phobia. People who were sexually abused as children often have crippling phobias about sex even as adults, unless they get proper therapy.

What do phobias have to do with cult groups and mind control? In some cults, *members are systematically made to be phobic about ever leaving the group.* Today's cults know how to effectively implant vivid negative images deep within members' unconscious minds, making it impossible for the member to even conceive of ever being happy and successful outside of the group. When the unconscious is programmed to accept the negative images, it behaves as though they were true. The unconscious mind is made to contain a substantial image-bank of all of the bad things that will occur if anyone should ever betray the group. Members are programmed either overtly or subtly (depending on the organization) to believe that if they ever leave, they will die of some horrible disease, be hit by a car, be killed in a plane crash, or perhaps even cause the death of loved ones. Some groups program members to believe that if they ever leave the group, planetary nuclear holocaust will be the result.

Of course, these thoughts are irrational and nonsensical. However, keep in mind that *most* phobias *are* irrational. Most planes don't crash, most elevators don't get stuck, and most dogs aren't rabid. In many ways, cult-induced phobias are so cleverly created and implanted that people don't even know they exist. Members are so conditioned to suppress their real selves that they aren't even aware of their desire to leave. They think they are so happy in the group that they would never want to leave. Such people can't generate positive images of themselves after leaving the group.

Imagine what it would be like if you believed that mysterious persons were determined to poison you. If this belief were implanted deep within your unconscious, do you think you would ever be able to go to restaurants and enjoy your meal? How long would it be before you ate only the food that you bought and prepared yourself? If, by chance, someone with whom you were eating in a restaurant suddenly became violently ill, how long would it be before you stopped eating altogether?

Such a belief would substantially limit your choices. Of course, you might try to cover it up or even rationalize your behavior by telling your friends that you don't like eating out because you are on a diet, or even by trying to convince them that restaurants are unsanitary and dangerous. Actually, your choices of ways to eat no longer include simply going to a restaurant and enjoying a good meal.

In the same way, cult phobias take away people's choices. Members truly believe they will be destroyed if they leave the safety of the group. They think there are no other ways for them to grow—spiritually, intellectually, or emotionally. They are virtually enslaved by this mind control technique.

THE UNCONSCIOUS MIND: THE KEY TO CREATIVITY—AND VULNERABILITY

What makes us all so vulnerable to these influence processes? The answer lies in the nature of the mind itself. The mind has been described as an unbelievably sophisticated biocomputer which is constructed for survival. It is remarkable in its ability to creatively adapt and respond to a person's needs as well as to the environment. Our mind filters out floods of information every second, so that we can cope with those things that we consider important.

Our minds are huge reservoirs of information, stored as images, sounds, feelings, tastes, and smells. Systematically, all this information is connected in meaningful ways. Our sense of self develops over years of life experience. As we grow and change, our beliefs about ourselves and the world change, too. Our beliefs serve as the major means of processing information as well as determining our behavior.

We have a certain degree of conscious control, but many more matters are controlled unconsciously. The conscious mind has a narrow range of attention. The unconscious does all the rest, including regulating all body functions. Imagine having to tell your heart to beat 72 times every minute. You would never have time for anything else. The unconscious mind is the primary manager of information.

It is our creative unconscious that allows us to make mental pictures and to experience them as "real." Try this experiment. Take a moment and allow your mind to transport you to a beautiful tropical paradise. Feel the warmth of the sun, a cool breeze, and the smell of the ocean. Even if you have never been to such a place, it is still possible to perform this experiment. Did you go somewhere else for that moment? Our imagination can be channeled in other ways too. For example, professional basketball players visualize the ball leaving their fingers and going through the net before they shoot. These capacities to fantasize and visualize exist within everyone and are an essential component of being human. We all have dreamed about happier times in our lives—perhaps meeting the "perfect" person, perhaps winning the lottery. But hypnosis can also be used to create in our unconscious minds a fantasy world that can be used to enslave us.

As we grow, the mind does not erase previous memories: it layers new experiences over them in a very systematic way. It is amazing how easily we can shift back into past memories. For example, try to remember playing with your favorite toy when you were a child, or eating your favorite food. Our memories of childhood form a vast storehouse which can be tapped and exploited by hypnotic techniques. It is not accidental that many destructive cults tell their members to "become like little children." Adults can easily be age-regressed to a time when they had little or no critical faculties. As children, we were helplessly dependent on our parents as the ultimate authority figures.

The mind, despite all of its strength and ability, has weaknesses too. It is dependent on a stream of coherent information for it to function properly. Put a person in a sensory deprivation chamber, and within hours he will start to hallucinate and become incredibly suggestible. Likewise, put a person into a situation where his senses are overloaded with noncoherent information, and the mind will go "numb" as a protective mechanism. It gets confused and overwhelmed, and critical faculties no longer work properly. It is in this weakened state that people become very suggestible to others.

The mind needs frames of reference in order to structure reality. Change the frame of reference, and the information coming in will be interpreted in a different way. Take, for example, the Jewish rite of circumcision. If you take away the cultural meaning and the medical advantages, it becomes an attack on a defenseless male child. Our belief system allows us to interpret information, make decisions, and act according to our beliefs. When people are subjected to a mind control process, most do not have any frame of reference for the experience, and consequently they often accept the frame of reference given to them by the group.

When we make decisions, we usually base them on information we believe to be true. We don't have the time to verify every piece of information that comes at us. When we shop, we tend to believe it when we are told that a particular item is cheaper here than at any other store. After all, why would the person lie, particularly if you could come back and complain? If we distrusted everything, we would be paranoid. If, at the other extreme, we were to trust everything and everybody, we would be naive and taken advantage of for the rest of our lives. Therefore, we strive to live our lives in a balance between skepticism and trust. A person with an open mind seeks to live within that healthy balance.

Con artists are professional liars. Their greatest assets are their looks and their ability to act. Most victims of con artists remark that they trusted the person because he (she) "didn't look like a criminal." The successful ones never do. They convey a "humanness" that allows a person's defenses to be bypassed. They are usually great talkers but do not appear to be too slick. "Slickness" would give them away. A criminal wants to size the "mark" up, make the con, get the money, and leave.

Cult recruiters use many of the same skills, but they want you to join. Almost all of them were victims themselves at one point. They believe that what they are doing is truly beneficial for you. However, they want something more valuable than your money. They want your mind! Of course, they'll take your money too, eventually. But they don't run away like common criminals. They want you to move in with them. Not only that, they want you to go out and do the same to others.

Everyone, like it or not, is vulnerable to mind control. Everyone wants to be happy. Everyone needs affection and attention. Everyone is looking for something better in life: more wisdom, more knowledge, more money, more status, more meaning, better relationships, or better health. These basic human qualities and needs are exactly what cult recruiters prey upon. It is important to remember that for the most part, people don't join cults. *Cults recruit people.*

BASIC CULT RECRUITMENT APPROACHES

How can one become more aware of cult recruitment? The best way is to be able to instantly recognize the ways in which cults make their appeals for membership. People are approached in three basic ways: by a friend or relative who is already a member, by a stranger who befriends them (often a member of the opposite sex), or through a cult-sponsored event, such as a lecture, symposium, or movie.

Very often an individual does not suspect he is being recruited. The friend or relative has just had some incredible insights and experiences and wants to share them, or says he or she "just needs your opinion," pretending he needs your help but intending to trick you into an indoctrination session. If the recruiter is a stranger, more often than not you think you've made a good friend.

Surveys of present and former cult members indicate that the majority of people recruited into destructive cults were approached at a *vulnerable time of stress in their lives.*[20] The stress is often due to some kind of major transition: moving to a new town, starting a new job, breaking off a relationship, experiencing financial instability, or losing a loved one. People in such situations tend to have defense mechanisms that are overloaded or weakened. If they don't know how to spot and avoid destructive cults, they are easy prey.

It is important to recognize that recruitment doesn't just happen. It is a process imposed on people by other people. High-powered business executives pressured by competition and driven by a need to succeed are recruited by *colleagues* who tell them about the incredible benefits to be obtained from taking the "course." College students pressured by academic work and a need for acceptance will make friends with a *professional cult recruiter,* or go to the group's lecture on some current social issue. A housewife driven by the need to "do something with her life" follows the example of a *friend* and buys into a pyramid-style home supplies company. A high school student is dared by *peers* into dabbling in satanic rituals.

Other people are initially brought into contact with a cult through an impersonal medium. Some people begin by buying a cult book advertised on TV as a best seller, while others receive in the mail an invitation to a seemingly harmless "Bible study" session. Some people answer a want ad. Some are recruited when they take a job with a cult-owned business.

Whatever the approach, the personal contact is eventually made. The recruiter starts to learn all about the potential recruit—his hopes, dreams, fears, relationships, job, interests. The more information the recruiter can elicit, the greater his chance of manipulating the person. The recruiter strategically plans how to bring him step by step into the group. The plan might include effusive praise and flattery, introducing the person to another member with similar interests and background, deliberate deception about the group, and evasive maneuvering to avoid answering questions.

Today, anyone can be recruited into a destructive cult. In the 1970s and early 1980s, the typical member was college-aged, but by the late 1980s it became commonplace for people of all ages to fall victim. An elderly person is also likely to be recruited.[21] Of course, most cults would not engage an elderly person in the same activities as the young or middle-aged. The elderly tend to be solicited for heavy financial contributions or public relations statements. Many middle-aged people are recruited for their professional expertise to set up or run a cult-owned business. Young people, for the most part, still represent the core workers. They can sleep less, eat less, and work more.

Although the white middle class is still the main target of recruitment, several groups are now actively seeking out blacks, Hispanics, and Asians. As they gather individuals from these communities, they use them to design programs that will bring in others. The big cults have already developed indoctrination programs in Spanish, for example. Another target population is made up of Europeans visiting or working in the United States. After a few years of training and indoctrination (usually with expired visas), they are sent back to recruit in their own countries.

It is of interest that cults generally avoid recruiting people who will burden them, such as those with severe emotional or psychological problems. They want people who will stand up to the grueling demands of cult life. If someone is recruited who uses drugs, he is told to either stop using them or leave. To my knowledge, there are almost no people with handicaps in cults, because it takes time, money, and effort to look after them.

CULT LIFE: ILLUSION AND ABUSE

Once a person joins a destructive cult, for the first few weeks or months he typically enjoys a honeymoon phase. He is treated as though he were royalty. He is made to feel very special as he embarks on a new life with the group. The new convert has yet to experience what life in the group is really going to be like.

Even though most cult members tell you they are "happier than they've ever been in their lives," the reality is sadly different. Life in a destructive cult is for the most part a life of sacrifice and pain. People involved full time in a destructive cult know what it is like to live under totalitarianism, but can't objectively see what is happening to them. They live in a fantasy world created by the group.

Cult members tend to spend all their time either recruiting more people, fundraising, or working on public relations projects. When people are fully hooked, they donate large amounts of their money and assets to the group, sometimes all they own. In exchange they are promised care and meaning for the rest of their lives. This transaction leaves the person dependent on the group for everything: food, clothing, shelter, and health care. In many of the groups, care is less than adequate. Medical neglect is rampant. People are made to feel that some personal or spiritual weakness is the cause of their medical problems. All they need to do is repent and work harder, and the problem will go away.

Few cults carry health insurance for their devotees, so when a person becomes critically ill, mentally or physically, he is often sent as an indigent to a hospital or free clinic. People who worked devotedly for years, sometimes making hundreds of thousands of dollars for the group, have been told that the group couldn't afford to pay their medical bills and were asked to leave the group until they were better. A person who requires expensive treatment will often be asked to go back to his family so that they will pay the bills. If the person doesn't have a family who will help, he may even be driven to a hospital and abandoned. These statements are based upon my personal experience and upon many reports of ex-cult members.

Some cults advocate faith healing as the sole treatment for medical problems. The outcome can be suffering and even death. People are told that their illness has a "spiritual" cause and are made to feel guilty for not totally devoting themselves to the group. Some cults tell members that going to a doctor proves their faithlessness and even threaten to excommunicate them if they do.

Along with medical neglect is the problem of child abuse. Many children have died or been scarred for life because of their parents' involvement in a destructive cult.[22] As a public, we have largely forgotten that nearly three hundred children were murdered during the Jonestown massacre. Those children had no choice but to drink the poisoned Kool-Aid mixture. The public also doesn't know that many of these children were the wards of the state of California and had been adopted by People's Temple members to provide more income as well as serve as an inexpensive work force.

Some groups advocate beating and even torturing children to enforce discipline. At Jonestown, children were put at night into dark pits which they were told were filled with snakes, while members dangled ropes from above in order to scare them. Although Jonestown was an extreme example, several groups do use rods and sticks to beat children, perhaps for hours and sometimes all over their bodies. Some groups subject children to sexual abuse. Because children are often kept out of school and away from other contact with society, the abuse goes unreported.

Children are often raised communally and allowed only infrequent visits with their parents. The children are taught to place their allegiance with the cult leader or the group as a whole, not their parents. Play time is limited or perhaps denied altogether. Children typically receive an inferior education, if any. Like their parents, they are taught that the world is a hostile, evil place, and are forced to depend on cult doctrine to understand reality. Although they may be regarded as the future of the group, they are usually seen as a hindrance to the immediate demands of the "work."

The casualties of cult mind control include not only the millions of cult members themselves, their children, and their friends and loved ones, but also our society as well. Our nation is being robbed of our greatest resource: bright, idealistic, ambitious people who are capable of making an enormous contribution to mankind. Many of the former members I know have become doctors, teachers, counselors, inventors, artists. Imagine what cult members could accomplish if they were all set free to develop their God-given talents and abilities! What if they channeled their energies into problem solving, rather than trying to undermine America's freedoms with some warped totalitarian vision?

In the meanwhile, destructive cult groups continue to grow more numerous and powerful, operating with virtual free license to enslave people. It is ironic that the United States, a country that cherishes freedom and liberty, does more to protect a person from sales pressure at a used-car lot than from organizations whose intent is to cripple a person's ability to act for himself. Until the law is able to set workable guidelines on such practices by individuals and organizations, and recognizes the existence of modern mind control techniques, people are left to protect themselves.

Perhaps the single most important thing to realize in dealing with destructive cults is that *we are all vulnerable.* The most we can do to protect ourselves is inform ourselves thoroughly about the ways in which destructive cults operate, and be "good consumers" when approaching any group we might be interested in joining. Friends or relatives of people seeking some kind of major group involvement or passing through times of unusual stress should remain alert to sudden personality changes in those people. If you do suspect that someone you know is beginning to come under the influence of a mind control organization, act quickly to seek competent help. Most medical problems respond better to early detection and treatment, and the same principle holds true for the problems of destructive cults.

Chapter 4

Understanding Mind Control

WHEN I lecture at colleges, I usually challenge my audience with the question "How would you *know* if you were under mind control?"

After some reflection, most people will realize that if one were under mind control, it would be impossible to determine it without some help from others. In addition, one would need to understand very clearly what mind control is.

When I was under mind control, I didn't really understand what it was all about. I assumed that mind control would involve being tortured in a dank basement somewhere, with a light bulb shining in my face. Of course, that never happened to me while I was in the Moonies. Whenever people yelled at me and called me a "brainwashed robot," I just took it as an expected persecution. It made me feel more committed to the group.

At that time, I didn't have a frame of reference for the phenomenon of mind control. It wasn't until my deprogramming that I was shown exactly what it is and how it is used. Since I was a member of the Moonies and we regarded Communism as the enemy, I was very interested in the techniques that the Chinese Communists used to convert their opponents during the 1950s. I didn't resist, then, when my counselors asked to read me parts of Dr. Robert Jay Lifton's book *Thought Reform and the Psychology of Totalism*.[1] Since the book had been published in 1961, I could not accuse Lifton of being anti-Moon.

That book had a major effect on my understanding of what had happened to me in the Moonies. I learned that Lifton had identified eight basic elements of the process of mind control as practiced by the Chinese Communists. My counselors pointed out that no matter how wonderful the cause, or how attractive the members, if any group employed all eight of Robert Jay Lifton's elements, then it was operating as mind control environment. I was eventually able to see that the Moon organization uses all eight of those elements: milieu control, mystical manipulation or planned spontaneity, the demand for purity, the cult of confession, sacred science, loading of the language, doctrine over person, and dispensing of existence. (A fuller description is given in the Appendix.)

Before I could leave the Moonies, though, I had to wrestle with several moral questions. Does the God I believe in need to use deception and mind control? Do the ends truly justify the means? I had to ask myself whether the means determine the ends. How could the world become a paradise if people's free wills were subverted? What would the world truly look like if Moon assumed total power? Through asking myself these questions, I decided I could no longer participate in an organization that used mind control practices. I left behind the fantasy world I had lived in for years.

Since leaving the group, I have come to believe that millions of people have actually been subjected to a mind control regimen but don't even know it. Hardly a week goes by that I don't talk with several people who are still experiencing negative side effects from their experience of mind control. Often, it is a great relief for them to hear that they are not alone and that their problems stem from their involvement with such a group.

Perhaps the biggest problem faced by people who have left destructive cults is the disruption of their own identity. There is a very good reason: they have lived for years inside an "artificial" identity given to them by the cult. While cult mind control can be talked about and defined in many different ways, I believe it is best understood as *a system which disrupts an individual's identity*. The identity is made up of elements such as beliefs, behavior, thought processes, and emotions that constitute a definite pattern. Under the influence of mind control, a person's original identity, as formed by family, education, friendships, and most importantly that person's own free choices, becomes replaced with another identity, often one that he would not have chosen for himself without tremendous social pressure.

Mind control practiced by destructive cults is a social process, often involving large groups of people who reinforce it. It is achieved by immersing a person in a social environment where, in order to function, he must shed his old identity and adhere to the new identity desired by the group. Any reality that might remind him of his previous identity—anything that might confirm his old sense of self—is pushed away and replaced by the group's reality. Even if he gets along by deliberate play-acting at first, the act eventually becomes real. He takes on a totalistic ideology that, when internalized, supersedes his prior belief system. The person usually shows a radical personality change and a drastic interruption of his life course. The process can be activated within a few hours but usually requires days or weeks to solidify.

Of course, we are all subjected to various social pressures every day, most noticeably in our work. The pressure to conform to certain standards of behavior exists in nearly every organization. Many kinds of influence are at work on us all the time, some of them obvious and benign (such as "Fasten Your Seat Belt" billboards) and others subtle and destructive. I cannot emphasize too strongly, then, that when I use the term "mind control," I am specifically referring to the destructive end of the spectrum. Therefore, as I have stressed before, the term "mind control" in this book will not apply to certain technologies (biofeedback, for example) that are used to enhance personal control and promote choice. It will refer to only those systems that *seek to undermine an individual's integrity in making his own decisions.* The essence of mind control is that it encourages dependence and conformity, and discourages autonomy and individuality.

Even so, it's worth noting, a mind control group's purpose may not be at all bad. For example, many drug rehabilitation and juvenile delinquency programs use some of these same methods to destroy a person's old identity as an addict or criminal. But such programs, successful as they may be, are fraught with danger. After the person is "broken" and given a new identity, he must have his autonomy and individuality restored—a process that depends entirely on the altruism and responsible behavior of the group's directors. One drug rehabilitation program, Synanon, has apparently conducted its activities in such a manner as to have drawn repeated allegations that it has abused the most basic rights of its members. [2]

MIND CONTROL VERSUS BRAINWASHING

While it is important to have a basic understanding of mind control, it is just as important to understand what mind control is not. Unfortunately, in popular discussions of the subject, the term "brainwashing" is often used as a synonym for "mind control." In actuality, though, the two processes are quite different and should not be confused. Mind control is not brainwashing.

"Brainwashing" is a term coined in 1951 by journalist Edward Hunter. He used it to describe how American servicemen captured in the Korean War suddenly reversed their values and allegiances and believed they had committed fictional war crimes. Hunter translated the term from the Chinese *hsi nao*, "wash brain."

Brainwashing is typically coercive. The person knows at the outset that he is in the hands of an enemy. It begins with a clear demarcation of the respective roles—who is prisoner and who is jailer—and the prisoner experiences an absolute minimum of choice. Abusive mistreatment, even torture, is usually involved.

Perhaps the most famous relatively recent case of brainwashing and mind control in the United States involved newspaper heiress Patty Hearst. She was kidnapped by the Symbionese Liberation Army (SLA), a small, political, terrorist cult, in 1974. She was locked in a dark closet for weeks and was starved and raped. Later she seemingly became an active member of the group. She passed up chances to escape and participated in a bank robbery, for which she was convicted and served a jail term.

Unfortunately, Hearst was the victim of an ignorant judge and jury.

The SLA may have succeeded in brainwashing Patty Hearst, but, on the whole, the coercive approach hasn't had an outstanding success rate. Once people are away from their controllers and back in familiar surroundings, the effects tend to dissipate. The SLA succeeded with Patty Hearst because they gave her a whole new identity as "Tania." They convinced her that the FBI was out to shoot her on sight. She was convinced her safety lay in remaining with the group rather than seeking rescue.

Brainwashing is effective in producing compliance to demands, such as signing a false confession or denouncing one's government. People are coerced into specific acts for self-preservation, and once they have acted, their beliefs change to rationalize what they have done. But these beliefs are usually not well internalized. When the prisoner escapes the field of influence (and fear), he is usually able to throw them off.

Mind control, also called "thought reform," is more subtle and sophisticated. Its perpetrators are regarded as friends or peers, so the person is much less defensive. He unwittingly participates by cooperating with his controllers and giving them private information that he does not know will be used against him. The new belief system is internalized into a new identity structure.

Mind control involves little or no overt physical abuse. Instead, *hypnotic processes* are combined with *group dynamics* to create a potent indoctrination effect. The individual is deceived and manipulated—not directly threatened—into making the prescribed choices. On the whole, he responds positively to what is done to him.

It is too bad that the word "brainwashing" is used so loosely by the news media. It evokes a picture of conversion by torture. Those inside a cult know they haven't been tortured, so they think critics are making up lies. When I was in the Moonies, I "knew" I hadn't been brainwashed. I do remember, however, Moon giving us a speech in which he said a popular magazine had accused him of brainwashing us. He declared, "Americans' minds are very dirty—full of selfish materialism and drugs—and they *need* a heavenly brainwashing!"[3] We all laughed.

A NOTE ON HYPNOTISM

If the term "brainwashing" is commonly confused with "mind control," the term "hypnotism" is often misused, also. The use of the term "hypnotism" in various forms is very common in our normal speech (we sometimes say such things as "She hypnotized him with her smile."). Actually, hypnosis is little understood by most people. When the term is mentioned, the first image that may come to mind is of a bearded doctor dangling an old pocket watch by its chain in front of a droopy-eyed person. While that image is certainly a stereotype, it does point to the central feature of hypnotism: the trance. People who are hypnotized enter a trance-like state which is fundamentally different from normal consciousness. The difference is this: whereas in normal consciousness the attention is focused outwards through the five senses, in a trance one's attention is focused *inwards*. One is hearing, seeing, and feeling internally. Of course, there are various degrees of trance, ranging from the mild and normal trance of daydreaming to deeper states in which one is much less aware of the outside world and extremely susceptible to suggestions which may be put into one's mind.

Hypnotism relates to the unethical mind control practices of destructive cults in a variety of ways. In many cults which claim to be religious, what is often called "meditation" is no more than a process by which the cult members enter a trance, during which time they may receive suggestions which make them more receptive to following the cult's doctrine. Non-religious cults use other forms of group or individual induction. In addition, being in a trance is usually a pleasant, relaxing experience, so that people wish to re-enter the trance as often as possible. Most importantly, it has been clinically established by psychological researchers that people's critical faculties are diminished in the trance state. One is less able to evaluate information received in a trance than when in a normal state of consciousness.

The power of hypnosis to affect people can be considerable. People can be put into a trance in minutes and perform remarkable feats. Perhaps the best-known example is that a hypnotized person may have a long needle inserted through thick muscle and register no pain. Hypnotic subjects have been made to dance like Fred Astaire, lie down between two chairs and assume a board-like rigidity, behave as though their hands were "glued" to their sides, and so forth. If they can be made to perform such feats, getting hypnotic subjects to believe that they are part of a "chosen few" is also easily achievable.

Destructive cults commonly induce trances in their members through lengthy indoctrination sessions. Repetition and forced attention are very conducive to the induction of a trance. Looking at a group in such a setting, it is easy to see when the trance has set in. The audience will exhibit retarded blink and swallow reflexes, and their facial expressions will relax into a blank, neutral state. With people in such a state, it is possible for unscrupulous leaders to implant irrational beliefs. I have seen many strong-willed people hypnotized and made to do things they would never normally do.

SOME BASIC PRINCIPLES OF SOCIAL PSYCHOLOGY AND GROUP DYNAMICS

The political experience of World War II, in which thousands of apparently normal people were involved in projects such as the operation of concentration camps where millions of Jews and others were killed, provoked considerable interest among psychologists.[4] How was it that people who had led ordinary lives prior to Adolf Hitler's rise to power in Germany became involved in a deliberate attempt to exterminate a whole group of people? Thousands of social psychological experiments have been conducted since World War II, yielding great insights into the various ways people are influenced, both as groups and as individuals. The net result of these studies has been the consistent demonstration of the remarkable power of *behavior modification techniques, group conformity,* and *obedience to authority.* These three factors are known in psychological terms as the "influence process." One of the most remarkable discoveries of social psychology is that in our attempts to find the most appropriate response to a social situation, we sometimes respond to information that we receive unconsciously.

For example, a class of psychology students once "conspired" to use behavior modification techniques on their teacher. As the professor lectured, the students would smile and act attentive when he moved toward the left of the room. When he moved to the right, the students appeared to be bored and listless. Before long, the professor began to drift to the left, and after a few classes he spent each lecture leaning against the left wall.

But here is the key point: when the students let the professor in on the joke, he insisted that nothing of the sort had happened at all—that they were just pulling his leg! He saw nothing odd about leaning against the wall, and angrily insisted that it was merely his personal lecturing style—something he had chosen to do of his own free will. He was clearly unconscious of how he had been influenced.

Of course, under ordinary circumstances, the people around us are not all secretly conspiring to make us do something. They simply act more or less as they have been culturally conditioned to act, which in turn conditions us. That is the way, after all, in which a culture perpetuates itself. In a destructive cult, however, the behavior modification process is stage-managed all around new recruits, who of course have no idea of what is going on.

If behavior modification techniques are powerful, so too are the influences of conformity and obedience to authority. A famous experiment in conformity by Dr. Solomon Asch[5] demonstrated that people will doubt their own perceptions if they are put in a social situation where it appears that the most confident people in the group are all giving the wrong answer to a question. Another psychologist, Stanley Milgram, tested people for obedience to authority and found that over 90 percent of his subjects would obey orders, even if they believed that doing so caused physical suffering to another person. Milgram wrote, "The essence of obedience consists in the fact that a person comes to view himself as the instrument for carrying out another person's wishes, and therefore no longer regards himself as responsible for his own actions."[6]

THE FOUR COMPONENTS OF MIND CONTROL

Clearly, one cannot begin to understand mind control without realizing the power of behavior modification techniques, as well as the influences of conformity and obedience to authority. If we take these insights from social psychology as a foundation, we may be able to identify the basic components of mind control. As I have come to see it, mind control may be largely understood by analysis of the three components described by Leon Festinger, a psychologist, in what has become known as the "cognitive dissonance theory."[7] These components are *control of behavior, control of thoughts,* and *control of emotions.*

Each component has a powerful effect on the other two: change one, and the others will tend to follow. Succeed in changing all three, and the individual will be swept away. However, from my experience in researching destructive cults, I have added one additional component which is vital: *control of information.* If you control the information someone receives, you restrict his free ability to think for himself. I call these factors the four components of mind control, and they serve as the basic reference points for understanding how mind control works.

Cognitive dissonance theory is not as forbidding as its name might sound. In 1950, Festinger summarized its basic principle thus: "If you change a person's behavior, his thoughts and feelings will change to minimize the dissonance."[8]

What did Festinger mean by "dissonance?" In basic terms, he was referring to the conflict which occurs when a thought, a feeling, or a behavior is altered in contradiction to the other two. A person can tolerate only a certain amount of discrepancy between his thoughts, feelings, and actions, which after all make up the different components of his identity. Festinger's theory states, and much research has since proved, that if any one of the three components changes, the other two will shift to reduce the dissonance.

How does this kind of "shift" apply to the behavior of people in cults? Festinger looked for a place to examine his ideas in the real world. In 1956, he wrote a book, *When Prophecy Fails,* about a Wisconsin flying saucer cult whose leader had predicted the end of the world. The cult leader claimed to be in mental contact with aliens from another planet. Followers sold their homes, gave away their money, and stood at the appointed date on a mountainside waiting all night to be picked up by flying saucers before a flood destroyed the world the next morning.

When morning came with no saucers and no flood (just a spate of satirical news stories about the group), the followers might have been expected to become disillusioned and angry. A few did—fringe members who had not invested much time or energy. But most members became more convinced than ever. The leader proclaimed that the aliens had witnessed their faithful vigil and decided to spare the Earth. Members wound up feeling *more* committed to the leader after they took a dramatic public stance that resulted in public humiliation.

Cognitive dissonance theory explains why this new commitment occurred. According to Festinger, a person needs to maintain order and meaning in his or her life. He needs to think he is acting according to his self-image and values. If his behavior changes for any reason, his self-image and values change to match. The important thing to recognize about cult groups is that they deliberately *create* dissonance in people this way and exploit it to control them.

Let's take a closer look at each one of these components of mind control.

Behavior Control

Behavior control is the regulation of an individual's physical reality. It includes the control of his environment—where he lives, what clothing he wears, what food he eats, how much sleep he gets—as well as of the jobs, rituals, and other actions he performs.

This need for behavior control is the reason most cults prescribe a very rigid schedule for their members. Each day a significant amount of time is devoted to cult rituals and indoctrination activities. Members are also typically assigned to accomplish specific goals and tasks, thus restricting their free time and their behavior. In destructive cults there is always something to do.

In some of the more restrictive groups, members have to ask permission from leaders to do almost anything. In some groups, a person is made so financially dependent that choices of behavior are narrowed automatically. A member must ask for bus fare, clothing money, or permission to seek health care, choices most of us take for granted. He must ask permission to call a friend or relative not in the group. Every hour of his day has to be accounted for. In these ways the group can keep a tight rein on behavior and therefore on thoughts and feelings.

Behavior is often controlled by the requirement that everyone act as a group. In many cults people eat together, work together, have group meetings, and sometimes sleep together in the same room. Individualism is discouraged. People may be assigned a constant "buddy" or be placed in a small unit of a half dozen members.

The chain of command in cults is usually authoritarian, flowing from the leader through his lieutenants to their sub-leaders down to the rank and file. In such a well-regulated environment, all behaviors can be either rewarded or punished. It serves the leadership to keep their members off balance. If a person performs well, he will be given public praise from higher-ups and sometimes gifts or a promotion. If the person performs poorly, he may be publicly singled out and criticized, and forced to do menial labor like cleaning toilets or polishing the other members' shoes.

Other forms of punishment may include "voluntary" fasting, taking cold showers, staying up for an all-night vigil, or doing remedial work. A person who actively participates in his own punishment will come to believe he deserves it.

Each particular group has its own distinctive set of ritual behaviors that help bind it together. These can include mannerisms of speech, posture, and facial expressions as well as the more traditional ways of representing group belief. In the Moonies, for instance, we followed many Oriental customs such as taking off our shoes when entering a Moonie center, sitting on our knees, and bowing when greeting older members. Doing these little things helped make us feel we were special.

If a person is not behaving "enthusiastically," he may be confronted by a leader and accused of being selfish or impure, or of not trying hard enough. He will be urged to become like an older group member, even to the extent of mimicking the tone of his voice. Obedience to a leader's command is the most important lesson to learn. The leaders cannot command someone's inner thoughts, but they know that if they command *behavior*, hearts and minds will follow.

Thought Control

Thought control, the second major component of mind control, includes indoctrinating members so thoroughly that they internalize the group doctrine, incorporate a new language system, and use thought-stopping techniques to keep their mind "centered." In order to be a good member, a person must learn to manipulate his own thought processes.

In totalistic cults, the ideology is internalized as "the truth,"the only "map" of reality. The doctrine not only serves to filter incoming information but also regulates how the information can be thought about. Usually, the doctrine is absolutist, dividing everything into "black versus white," "us versus them." All that is good is embodied in the leader and the group. All that is bad is on the outside. The more totalistic groups claim that their doctrine is scientifically proven. The doctrine claims to answer all questions to all problems and situations. A member need not think for himself because the doctrine does the thinking for him.

A destructive cult typically has its own "loaded language" of words and expressions. Since language provides the symbols we use for thinking, controlling certain words helps to control thoughts. Many groups condense complex situations, label them, and thereby reduce them to cult cliches. This label, which is how the loaded language is verbally expressed, governs how one thinks in any situation.

In the Moonies, for example, whenever you have difficulty relating to someone either above or below you in status, it is called a "Cain-Abel problem." It doesn't matter who's involved or what the problem is, it's simply a "Cain-Abel problem." The term itself dictates how the problem must be resolved. Cain must obey Abel and follow him, rather than kill him as was written about in the Old Testament. Case closed. To think otherwise would be to obey Satan's wish that evil Cain should prevail over righteous Abel. A critical thought about a leader's misconduct cannot get past this roadblock in a good member's mind.

The cult's cliches, or loaded language, also put up an invisible wall between believers and outsiders. The language helps to make members feel special and separates them from the general public. It also serves to confuse newcomers, who want to understand what members are talking about, and think they merely have to study hard in order to "understand" the truth. In reality, by incorporating the loaded language they learn how *not* to think. They learn that understanding means believing.

Another key aspect of thought control involves training members to block out any information which is critical of the group. A person's typical defense mechanisms are twisted so they defend the person's new cult identity against his old former identity. The first line of defense includes denial ("What you say isn't happening at all"), rationalization ("This is happening for a good reason"), justification ("This is happening because it ought to"), and wishful thinking ("I'd like it to be true so maybe it really is").

If information transmitted to a cult member is perceived as an attack on either the leader, the doctrine, or the group, a hostile wall goes up. Members are trained to disbelieve any criticism. Critical words have been explained away in advance as "the lies about us that Satan puts in peoples' minds" or "the lies that the World Conspiracy prints in the news media to discredit us, because they know we're onto them." Paradoxically, criticism of the group confirms that the cult's view of the world is correct. The information presented does not register properly.

Perhaps the most widely used and effective way to control cult member's thoughts is *thought-stopping rituals*.[9] Members are taught to use thought-stopping on themselves. They are told it will help them grow or be more effective. Whenever a cult member begins to experience a "bad" thought, he uses thought-stopping to drown out the "negativity" and center himself, thus learning how to shut out anything that threatens his reality.

Different groups use different thought-stopping techniques: concentrated praying, chanting aloud or silently, meditating, "speaking in tongues," singing, or humming. These actions, many of them ordinarily useful and valuable, are perverted in destructive cults. They become quite mechanical because the person is programmed to activate them at the first sign of doubt, anxiety, or uncertainty. In a matter of weeks the technique becomes ingrained. It becomes so automatic, in fact, that the person is usually not even aware that he had just had a "bad" thought. He is only aware that he is chanting or ritualizing all of a sudden. By using thought-stopping, members think they are growing when in reality they are just making themselves into addicts. After leaving a cult that employs extensive thought-stopping techniques, a person goes through a difficult withdrawal process before he can overcome the addiction.

Thought-stopping is the most direct way to short-circuit a person's ability to test reality. Indeed, if someone is able to think *only* positive thoughts about his involvement with the group, he is most certainly stuck. Since the doctrine is perfect and the leader is perfect, any problem that crops up is assumed to be the fault of the individual member. He learns always to blame himself and work harder.

Thought control can effectively block out any feelings that do not correspond with the group doctrine. It can also serve to keep a cult member working as an obedient slave. In any event, when thought is controlled, feelings and behaviors are controlled as well.

Emotional Control

Emotional control, the third part of mind control, attempts to manipulate and narrow the range of a person's feelings. Guilt and fear are necessary tools to keep people under control. Guilt is probably the single most important emotional lever for producing conformity and compliance. Historical guilt (e.g., the fact that the United States dropped the atomic bomb on Hiroshima), identity guilt (e.g., a thought such as "I'm not living up to my potential"), guilt over past actions (e.g., "I cheated on a test"), and social guilt (e.g., "People are dying of starvation") can all be exploited by destructive cult leaders. However, most cult members can't see that guilt and fear are being used to control them. They are so conditioned always to blame themselves that they respond gratefully whenever a leader points out one of their "shortcomings."

Fear is used to bind the group members together in two ways. The first is the creation of an outside enemy who is persecuting you: the FBI who will jail or kill you, Satan who will carry you off to Hell, psychiatrists who will give you electroshock, armed members of rival sects who will shoot or torture you, and, of course, deprogrammers. The second is the terror of discovery and punishment by the leaders. Fear of what can happen to you if you don't do your job well can be quite potent. Some groups claim that nuclear holocaust or other disasters will result if members are lax in their commitment.

In order to control someone through his or her emotions, feelings often have to be redefined. Happiness, for example, is a feeling everyone desires. However, if happiness is defined as being closer to God, and God is unhappy (as He apparently is in many religious cults), then the way to be happy is to be unhappy. Happiness, therefore, consists in suffering so you can grow closer to God. This idea appears in some non-cult theologies too, but in a cult it is a tool for exploitation and control.

In some groups, happiness simply means following the leader's directions, recruiting a lot of new members, or bringing in a lot of money. Happiness is defined as the sense of community provided by the cult, to those who enjoy good status.

Loyalty and devotion are the most highly respected emotions of all. Members are not allowed to feel or express negative emotions, except toward outsiders. Members are taught never to feel for themselves or their own needs but always to think of the group and never to complain. They are never to criticize a leader, but criticize themselves instead.

Many groups exercise complete control over interpersonal relationships. Leaders can and do tell people to avoid certain members or spend time with others. Some even tell members whom they can marry, and control the entire relationship, including their sex lives. Some groups require members to deny or suppress sexual feelings, which become a source of bottled-up frustration that can be channeled into other outlets such as harder work. Other groups *require* sexuality, and a member who hangs back is made to feel selfish. Either way, the group is exercising emotional control.

People are often kept off balance, praised one minute and tongue-lashed the next. This misuse of behavior modification techniques—reward and punishment—fosters a feeling of dependency and helplessness. In some groups, one day you'll be doing public relations before TV cameras in a suit and tie, and the next you'll be in another state doing manual labor as punishment for some imagined sin.

Confession of past sins or wrong attitudes is a powerful device for emotional control, too. Of course, once you have publicly confessed, rarely is your old sin forgiven in the true sense—or forgotten. The minute you get out of line, it will be hauled out and used to manipulate you into obeying. Anyone who finds himself in a cult confession session should remember this warning: Anything you say can *and will* be used against you. This device can even extend to blackmail if you leave the cult.

The most powerful technique for emotional control is phobia indoctrination, mentioned in chapter 3. People are made to have a panic reaction at the thought of leaving: sweating, rapid heartbeat, intense desire to avoid the possibility. They are told that if they leave they will be lost and defenseless in the face of dark horrors: they'll go insane, be killed, become drug addicts, or commit suicide. Actual tales of such cases are constantly told, both in lectures and in hushed tones through informal gossip. It is nearly impossible for an indoctrinated cult member to feel he can have any security outside the group.

When cult leaders tell the public "Members are free to leave any time they want; the door is open," they give the impression that members have free will and are simply choosing to stay. Actually, members may not have a real choice, because they have been indoctrinated to have a phobia of the outside world. Induced phobias eliminate the psychological possibility of a person choosing to leave the group merely because he is unhappy or wants to do something else.

If a person's emotions are successfully brought under the group's control, his thoughts and behavior will follow.

Information Control

Information control is the last component of mind control. Information is the fuel we use to keep our minds working properly. Deny a person the information he requires to make sound judgments, and he will be incapable of doing so. People are trapped in destructive cults because they are not only denied access to critical information but also lack the properly functioning internal mechanisms to process it. Such information control has a dramatic and devastating impact.

In many totalistic cults, people have minimal access to non-cult newspapers, magazines, TV, and radio. This is partly because they are kept so busy they don't have free time. When they do read, it is primarily cult-generated propaganda or material that has been censored to "help" members stay focused.

Information control also extends across all relationships. People are not allowed to talk to each other about anything critical of the leader, doctrine, or organization. Members must spy on each other and report improper activities or comments to leaders. New converts are not permitted to talk to each other without an older member present to chaperone them. Most importantly, people are told to avoid contact with ex-members or critics. Those who could provide the most information are the ones to be especially shunned. Some groups even go so far as to screen members' letters and phone calls.

Information is usually compartmentalized to keep members from knowing the big picture. In larger groups, people are told only as much as they "need to know" in order to perform their jobs. A member in one city will therefore not necessarily know about an important legal decision, media exposé, or internal dispute that is creating turmoil in the group somewhere else. Cult members naturally feel they know more about what's going on in their group than outsiders do, but in counseling ex-members I find that they often know the least.

Destructive organizations also control information by having many levels of "truth." Cult ideologies have "outsider" doctrines and "insider" doctrines. The outsider material is relatively bland stuff for the general public or fresh converts. The inner doctrines are unveiled only gradually as a person gets in deeper.

For example, Moonies always said publicly that they were pro-American, pro-democracy, and pro-family. The Moonies *were* pro-American in that they wanted what they thought was best for America, which was to become a theocracy under Moon's rule. They believed democracy was instituted by God to allow the Unification Church the space to organize a theocratic dictatorship. They were pro-family in believing that every human being's "true" family was Moon, his wife, and his spiritual children. Yet the inner doctrine was—and still is—that America is inferior to Korea and must become subservient to it, that democracy is a foolish system which "God is phasing out,"[10] and that people must be cut off from their "physical" (as opposed to "spiritual") families if they are critical of the cult.

A member can sincerely believe that the outer doctrines are not lies but just a different level of truth. By creating an environment where truth is multi-leveled, cult directors make it nearly impossible for a person to make final, objective assessments. If he has problems, he is told that he's not mature enough to know the whole truth but that all will become clear shortly. If he works hard he'll earn the right to learn the higher levels of truth.

But there are many "inner levels." Often an advanced member who thinks he knows it all is still several layers away from the center. Questioners who insist on knowing too much too fast, of course, are redirected toward an external goal until they get over it.

Behavior control, thought control, emotional control, and information control: each form of control has great power and influence on the human mind. Together, they form a totalistic web, which can manipulate even the strongest-minded people. In fact, it is the strongest-minded individuals who make the most involved and enthusiastic cult members.

No one group does everything described in this section. I have attempted to cover only the broadest and most common practices within each component of mind control. Other practices are surely used by certain cults but are not included here.

Some practices could fall into more than one of these categories. For example, some groups change people's names in order to hasten the formation of the new "cult" identity. This technique could fall under all four categories.

There are many variations between groups. For example, some groups are overt in their phobia indoctrination; others are extremely subtle. What matters most is the overall impact on the individual. Is he or is he not truly in control of his life choices? The only way to tell is to expose him or her to opportunities to reflect, to have free access to all information, to know that there is freedom to leave the environment.

THE THREE STEPS TO GAINING CONTROL OF THE MIND

It is one thing to be able to identify the four components of mind control, but entirely another to know how they are actually used to change the behavior of unsuspecting people. On the surface, the three-step process to gaining control of the mind seems quite simple. I call those three steps *unfreezing, changing,* and *refreezing.*

This three-step model was derived in the late 1940s from the work of Kurt Lewin[11] and was described in Edgar Schein's book *Coercive Persuasion.*[12] Schein, like Lifton, also studied the brainwashing programs in Mao Tse Tung's China in the late 1950s. His book, based on interviews with former American prisoners, is a valuable study of the process. His three conceptual stages apply just as well to non-coercive mind control as they do to brainwashing. As he described them, *unfreezing* consisted of breaking a person down, *changing* constituted the indoctrination process, and *refreezing* was the process of building up and reinforcing the new identity.

Destructive cults today have the added advantage of the thirty years of psychological research and techniques since Mao, making their mind control programs much more effective and dangerous. Hypnotic processes, for example, are much more significant in modern mind control. In addition, modern destructive cults are more flexible in their approach. They are willing and able to change their approach to fit a person's specific psychological make-up, use deception and highly sophisticated loaded language, or employ techniques like thought-stopping and phobia indoctrination.

Let's take a closer look at this three-stage model to see how the step-by-step program creates a well-disciplined member of a destructive cult.

Unfreezing

To ready a person for radical change, his reality must first be shaken up. His indoctrinators must disorient him. His frames of reference for understanding himself and his surroundings must be challenged and broken down. Upsetting his view of reality disarms his natural defenses against concepts that challenge his reality.

Unfreezing can be accomplished by using a variety of approaches. Disorienting a person physiologically can be very effective. Sleep deprivation is one of the most common and powerful techniques for breaking a person down. In addition, new diets and eating schedules also can have a disorienting effect.

Some groups use low-protein, high-sugar diets, or prolonged underfeeding, to undermine a person's stability. Unfreezing is best accomplished in a totally controlled environment, like an isolated country estate, but can be accomplished in more easily accessible places like a hotel ballroom.

Hypnotic processes constitute another powerful tool for unfreezing and side-stepping a person's defense mechanisms. One particularly effective hypnotic technique involves the deliberate use of confusion to induce a trance state. Confusion usually results whenever contradictory information is communicated congruently. For example, if a hypnotist says in an authoritative tone of voice "The more you try to understand what I am saying, the less you will never be able to understand it. Do you understand?" The result is a state of temporary confusion. If you read it over and over again, it may finally make sense. However, if a person is kept in a controlled environment long enough, hearing such disorienting language and confusing information, he will usually suspend his critical judgment and adapt to what he perceives everyone else is doing. In such an environment, the tendency within most people is to doubt themselves and defer to the group.

Sensory overload, like sensory deprivation, also effectively disrupts a person's balance and makes him more open to suggestion. A person can be bombarded by emotionally laden material at a rate faster than he can digest. The result is a feeling of being overwhelmed. The mind snaps into neutral and ceases to evaluate the material pouring in. The newcomer may think this is happening spontaneously within himself, but the group has intentionally structured it that way.

Other hypnotic techniques such as double binds[13] can also be used to help unfreeze a person's sense of reality. A double bind forces a person to do what the controller wants while giving an illusion of choice. For example, a cult leader may say, "For those people who are having doubts about what I am telling you, you should know that *I* am the one putting those doubts inside your mind, so that you will see the truth that I am the true teacher." The person may believe the leader or doubt him, but both bases are covered.

Another example of a double bind is "If you admit there are things in your life that aren't working, then by not taking the seminar, you are giving those things power to control your life." In other words, just being here proves you are incompetent to judge whether to leave.

Exercises such as guided meditations, personal confessions, prayer sessions, vigorous calisthenics, and even group singing can also aid unfreezing. Typically, these activities start out quite innocuously but gradually become more intense and directed as the workshop or seminar progresses. They are almost always conducted with groups. This enforces privacy deprivation and thwarts the person's need to be alone, think, and reflect.

At this stage of unfreezing, as people are weakening, most cults bombard them with the idea that they are badly flawed—incompetent, mentally ill, or spiritually fallen. Any problems that are important to the person, such as doing poorly in school or on the job, being overweight, or having trouble in a relationship, are blown out of proportion to prove how completely messed up the person is. Some groups can be quite vicious in their attacks on individuals, often humiliating them in front of the whole group.

Once a person is broken down, he is ready for the next phase.

Changing

Changing consists of imposing a new personal identity—a new set of behaviors, thoughts, and emotions—to fill the void left by the breakdown of the old one. Indoctrination in this new identity takes place both formally (as in seminars and rituals) and informally (by spending time with members, reading, and listening to tapes and videos). Many of the same techniques used in the unfreezing phase are also carried into this phase as well.

Repetition, monotony, rhythm: these are the lulling, hypnotic cadences in which the formal indoctrination is generally delivered. Material is repeated over and over and over. If the lecturers are sophisticated, they vary their talks somewhat in an attempt to hold interest, but the message is the same every time.

During the "changing" phase, all this repetition focuses on certain central themes. The recruits are told how bad the world is and that the unenlightened have no idea how to fix it. This is because ordinary people lack the new "understanding" that has been brought by the leader. The leader is the only hope of lasting happiness. Recruits are told, "your 'old' self is what's keeping you from fully experiencing the 'new truth.' Your 'old concepts' are what drag you down. Your 'rational' mind is holding you back from fantastic progress. Surrender. Let go. Have faith."

Behaviors are shaped subtly at first, then more forcefully. The material that will make up the new identity is doled out gradually, piece by piece, only as fast as the person is deemed ready to assimilate it. The rule of thumb is "Tell him only what he can accept." When I was a lecturer in the Moonies, I'd often discuss this tactic with other lecturers. To rationalize our manipulations we would use this analogy: "You wouldn't feed a baby thick pieces of steak, would you? You have to feed it something it can digest, like formula. Well, these people (potential converts) are spiritual babies. Don't tell them more than they can handle, or they will die." If a recruit started getting angry because he was learning too much about us, the person working on him would back off and let another member move in to spoonfeed some pablum.

The formal indoctrination sessions can be very droning and rhythmic—a way to induce hypnotic states. It is fairly common for people to fall asleep during these programs. When I was a cult lecturer I chastised people and made them feel guilty if they fell asleep, but in fact they were merely responding well to hypnosis. Later I learned that the hypnotic style is typical of many cults.

Even while lightly dozing, a person is still more or less hearing the material and being affected by it, with his normal intellectual defenses down.

Another potent technique for change is the induced "spiritual experience." This is often contrived in the most artificial manner. Private information about the recruit is collected by his closest buddy in the group and is secretly passed to the leadership. Later, at the right moment, this information can be pulled out suddenly to create an "experience." Perhaps weeks later in another state, a leader suddenly confronts the recruit about his brother's suicide. Knowing that he didn't tell anyone in this new place about it, the recruit thinks the leader has read his thoughts or is being informed directly by the spirit world. He is overcome and begs forgiveness for not being a better brother.

Destructive religious cults are not the only ones to engineer "mystical" experiences. One martial artist and self-professed "mentalist" who was forming his own cult would secretly pay hoodlums to violently "mug" several of his students on the street, in order to heighten their fear of the "outside" world, train harder, and consequently become more dependent on him. A psychotherapist (cult leader) manipulated one of his clients by confronting her inability to stay on her diet. He didn't tell her that he had seen her earlier that day eating an ice cream sundae. She believed that he had unusual powers.

A common technique among religious cults is to instruct people to ask God what He wants them to do. Members are exhorted to study and pray in order to know God's will for them. It is always implied that joining the group is God's will and leaving the group is betraying it. Of course, if a person tells the cult leader that God is warning him to leave, this will not be accepted as valid.

Perhaps the most powerful persuasion is exerted by the other cult members themselves. For the average person, talking with an indoctrinated cultist is quite an experience. You have probably never met anyone else, friend or stranger, who is so absolutely convinced that he knows what is best for you. A dedicated cult member also does not take no for an answer, because he has been indoctrinated to believe that if you don't join, *he* is to blame. This creates a lot of pressure on him to succeed.

When you are completely surrounded by such people, group psychology plays a major role in the "changing" process. People are deliberately organized into specific small groups (or cells). People who ask too many questions are quickly isolated from the main body of other members. In the Moonies, we would set up small group teams at the beginning of a workshop to evaluate the recruits. We would divide them into "sheep" and "goats" and assign them to groups accordingly. The "sheep" were the ones who were "spiritually prepared." "Goats" were stubborn individualists who were not expected to make good members. If they couldn't be "broken," their "negativity" was safely confined to a goat team where sheep couldn't see it, until the goats could be asked to leave. Once again, after I left the group I was amazed to learn that entirely different cults were doing the same thing. We thought we had invented the technique.

But the changing process involves much more than obedience to a cult's authority figures. It includes numerous "sharing" sessions with other ordinary members, where past evils are confessed, present success stories are told, and a sense of community is fostered. These group sessions are very effective in teaching conformity, because the group vigorously reinforces certain behaviors by effusive praise and acknowledgement, while punishing non-group ideas and behaviors with icy silence.

Human beings have an incredible capacity to adapt to new environments. Destructive cults know how to exploit this strength. By controlling a person's environment, using behavior modification to reward some behaviors and suppress others, and inducing hypnotic states, they may indeed reprogram a person's identity. Once the person has "changed," he is ready for the next step.

Refreezing

After someone has been broken down and indoctrinated into the new belief system, he must be built up again as the "new man" (or "new woman," as the case may be). He must be given a new purpose in life and new activities that will solidify his new identity. Again, many of the techniques from the first two stages are carried over into the refreezing phase. Cult leaders must be reasonably sure the new cult identity will be strong when the person leaves the immediate cult environment. So the new values and beliefs must be internalized by the new recruit.

The first and most important task of the "new" person is to denigrate his previous self. The worst thing is for the person to act like himself—unless it is the new cult self, which is fully formed after several months. An individual's memory becomes distorted, minimizing the good things in the past and maximizing the sins, the failings, the hurts, the guilt. Special talents, interests, hobbies, friends, and family must be abandoned—preferably in dramatic public actions—if they compete with commitment to the cause. Confession becomes another way to purge the person's past and embed him in the cult.

During the refreezing phase, the primary method for passing on new information is modeling. New members are paired with older members who are assigned to show them the ropes. The "spiritual child" is instructed to imitate the "spiritual parent" in all ways. This technique, too, serves several purposes. It keeps the "older" member on his best behavior while gratifying his ego, and it whets the new member's appetite to become a respected model so he can train junior members of his own.

The group now forms the member's "true" family; any other is just his outmoded "physical" family. Some cults insist on a very literal transfer of family loyalty. Jim Jones was far from the only cult leader to insist his followers call him "Dad." In my own case, I ceased to be Steve Hassan, son of Milton and Estelle Hassan, and became Steve Hassan, son of Sun Myung Moon and Hak Ja Han, the self-styled "True Parents" of all creation. In every waking moment I was reminded to be a "small Sun Myung Moon." As my cult identity was put into place, I wanted to think like him, feel like him, act like him.

To help refreeze the new identity, some cults give the person a new name. Many change the person's clothing style, haircut, and whatever else would remind him of his past. As mentioned, members often learn to speak a distinctive jargon or loaded language of the group.

Great pressure is usually exerted on the new member to turn over his bank account and other possessions. This serves two purposes besides enriching the cult. Donating one's life savings freezes a person to the new belief system. It would be too painful to admit a mistake, and it also makes financial survival in the outside world appear harder if the person ever does consider leaving.

Sleep deprivation, lack of privacy, and dietary changes are sometimes continued for several months or longer. Relocation of the new member away from familiar surroundings and sources of influence, into a new city where he has never been anything but his new self, fosters a more total dependency on cult authority figures.

The new member is typically assigned to proselytizing duty as soon as possible. Research in social psychology has shown that nothing firms up one's beliefs faster than trying to sell them to others. Making new members do so crystallizes the cult identity quickly.

Some groups finance themselves by difficult and humiliating fundraising methods, such as all-day and all-night begging. These experiences become a form of glorious martyrdom that helps freeze commitment to the group. Running around a supermarket parking lot selling overpriced flowers in the pouring rain is a powerful technique for making you really believe in what you are doing!

After a few weeks of proselytizing and fundraising in the outside world, the member is often sent back for reindoctrination. This cycle can be repeated dozens of times over several years.

After a novice spends enough time with "older" members, the day finally comes when he can be trusted to train other newcomers by himself. Thus, the victim becomes victimizer, to perpetuate the destructive system.

DUAL IDENTITY: THE KEY TO UNDERSTANDING CULT MEMBERS

Given freedom of choice, people will predictably always choose what they believe is best for them. However, the ethical criteria for determining what is "best" should be one's own, not someone else's. In a mind control environment, freedom of choice is the first thing that one loses. The reason for that loss is essentially simple: the cult member is no longer operating as himself. He has a new artificial cult *identity structure* which includes new beliefs and a new language. The cult leaders' doctrine becomes the master "map" for reality of the new cult member.

A member of a mind control cult is at war with himself. Therefore, when dealing with a cult member, it is extremely important to always keep in mind that he has *two* identities.

At first, identifying these dual identities is often confusing for relatives of cult members, especially in the early weeks or months of the involvement when the new identity is most dominant. One moment the person is speaking cultic jargon with a hostile or elitist know-it-all attitude. Then, without warning, he seems to become his old self, with his old attitudes and mannerisms. Just as suddenly, he flips back to being a stranger. This behavior is very familiar to anyone who works with cult members, as I do.

For the sake of convenience, I call these dual identities "John-John" (when "John," to pick a name, is most "himself") and "John-cultist" (when "John" is being a cult "clone"). Ordinarily, only one of these two selves occupies the consciousness at a time. The personality on duty most of the time is the cult identity. Only intermittently does the old identity replace it.

It is essential for family members to sensitize themselves to the differences between the two identity patterns, in terms of both content (what the person talks about) and communication patterns (the ways he speaks and acts). Each one looks and sounds distinctively different.

When John-cultist is talking, his speech is "robot-like" or like a tape recording of a cult lecture—what I call a "tape loop." He will speak with inappropriate intensity and volume. His posture will typically be more rigid, his facial muscles tighter. His eyes will tend to strike family members as glassy, cold, or glazed, and he will often seem to stare through people.

On the other hand, when John-John is talking he will speak with a greater range of emotion. He will be more expressive and will share his feelings more willingly. He will be more spontaneous and may even show a sense of humor. His posture and musculature will appear to be looser and warmer. Eye contact will be more natural.

Such a stark description of a divided personality may seem too simplistic, but it is amazingly accurate. It's an eerie experience to be talking with someone and sense that while you are in mid-sentence, a different personality has taken over his body. Recognizing the change, and acting appropriately, is the key to unlocking the person's real self and freeing it from the cult's bondage, as will be described in upcoming chapters.

As much as cult indoctrination attempts to destroy and suppress the old identity, and empower the new identity, it almost never totally succeeds. Good experiences and positive memories rarely disappear entirely. Of course, the cult identity will try to bury former reference points and submerge the person's past. Yet, over time, the old self exerts itself and seeks out ways to regain its freedom. This process is speeded up by positive exposure to non-members and the accumulation of bad experiences he has while in the group.

It is the "real" identity deep down inside that sees and records contradictions, questions, and disillusioning experiences. It still always amazes me, even though I had this experience myself during my deprogramming, that during the later stages of an intervention, my clients are able to verbalize very specific negative incidents that occurred while they were members. People are able to recall horrible things, like being raped by the cult leader or being forced to lie, cheat, or steal. Even though they knew at the time that they were doing something wrong or were being abused, they couldn't deal with the experience or act on it while the cult identity was in control. It was only when their "real" self was given permission and even encouragement to speak that these things came into consciousness. Indeed, an essential part of exit-counseling involves bringing a person's own experiences into the light, so that he or she can process them.

I have seen time and again in my exit-counseling work that the "real" self holds the keys to what it will take to undo the mind control process. Indeed, this "real" self is responsible for creating the frequent psychosomatic illnesses that cult members experience. I have met people who have developed severe skin problems which excused them from the grueling work schedule and gave them a chance to sleep. I have seen people develop asthma as well as severe allergic reactions in order to seek outside medical attention and help. The "real" self exerts itself in other ways, too. It can exert pressure on the cult self to go home to the family for a visit, using as an excuse the desire to collect clothes or funds or make new recruits. It can also drop hints when speaking to family members or friends that the person wants to be rescued. I have had several families contact me after their cult son or daughter told them *not* to get a professional counselor to get them out. Before the cult member made that remark, the families hadn't even known that there was someone they could contact to help them.

The "real" self has also been responsible for generating thematic dreams. I have met hundreds of former members who reported having nightmares over and over again while a member of a cult. These dreams typically involve themes of being lost, hurt, or trapped. People have told me about having cult dreams of being lost in a dark forest, of being choked or suffocated, of being imprisoned in a concentration camp.

Some people have told me of receiving a "revelation" that they were meant to leave the group. They reported that at the time, they (in their cult identities) didn't want to leave the group, but their "spiritual" experience was so powerful that they followed instructions and eventually were able to get counseling. I believe that God does work through people and is able to signal people to leave destructive cult organizations.

My belief that God works through other people is based, in part, on one of my own experiences. After I had been out of the cult for over four years, I accidentally overheard my mother speaking to another person. She said, "And don't tell Steven, but I was praying for a whole year that God should break his leg! I said, dear God, don't hurt him too much. Just enough so we can find him and rescue him." I was amazed and asked my mother why she hadn't told me this after so many years. She answered, "It's not nice to pray that someone should hurt himself. I didn't want you to be angry with me." I wasn't. I thought back to what the emergency technicians told me as they were prying me out of the wreckage: "It's a miracle you weren't killed!"

In my own life of faith, I believe that God did answer my mother's prayers. My leg was indeed broken. I believe that on some deep unconscious level, the "real" me was influenced from above to fall asleep and wake up at precisely the right moment. Of course, there is no way I can prove this, but I have heard of others being involved in "accidents" which led them eventually to freedom.

No matter how long a person has been involved with a destructive cult, there is still hope that he or she can be helped. This past year I talked with an eighty-five-year-old grandmother who left a destructive cult in New Jersey after fifteen years of membership. Tears came to her eyes when she described how wonderful it was to be free again. I cried as she spoke. I knew exactly what she meant.

Chapter 5

Cult Psychology

Since my departure from the Moon cult, I have counseled or spoken with more than one thousand former members of cults of all kinds. These people have come from every sort of background and ranged in age from twelve to eighty-five. Although some of them clearly had severe emotional problems before becoming involved, the great majority were stable, intelligent, idealistic people who tended to have good educations and come from respectable families.

This fact hardly surprises me, for when I was a leader in the Moonies we selectively recruited "valuable" people—those who were strong, caring, and motivated. People with emotional problems, on the other hand, always had trouble handling the rigorous schedule and enormous psychological pressures we imposed on them. It took lots of time, energy, and money to recruit and indoctrinate a member, so we tried not to waste our resources on someone who seemed liable to break down in less than a year.

Like any other business, all the large cult organizations watch these cost/benefit ratios. They fear that otherwise they may fold within a few years. Those that endure for more than a decade must have competent individuals managing the practical affairs that any organization with long-term objectives must handle.

The big groups can afford to hire outsiders to perform executive and professional tasks, but a hired professional is never trusted as much as someone who is emotionally committed to the group. Moreover, a cult member doesn't have to be paid for his services. Cults try to recruit professionals to run their affairs, to put a respectable face on their organizations, as well as insure success.

Outsiders who deal with the leadership of destructive cults never cease to be amazed that they aren't scatterbrained kooks. A cult will generally target the most educated, active, and capable people it can find. I hear comments such as "I never knew there were so many brilliant people in these types of groups" or "That leader is really a very nice, kind and insightful person—how could he ever join a group like this?"

Occasionally I am asked whether there is some kind of typical "problem family" from which cult members tend to come. The answer to that question is no. Anyone, regardless of family background, can be recruited into a cult. The major variable is not the person's family but the cult recruiter's level of skill.

Participation in destructive cults does provide some people with an outlet for various aspects of themselves that they did not find in their family life or other social activities. Many men and women have a genuine impulse to work together with others as a team for a variety of social or religious causes. Relatively few communities, though, offer such organized activity to idealistic people. Cult life gives them just such an opportunity, along with the apparent benefits of the "togetherness" that comes from an intense group experience. I support anyone's search for more meaningful ways to develop relationships with other people, but I have learned that people who are engaged in that search are often more vulnerable than others to recruitment into destructive cults.

I have also noticed that many idealistic young people recruited into cults are struggling to assert their individuality, and some are going through a period of rebellion. For these people, cult membership can be a way of substituting cult authority figures become a substitute family while they move away from home. I have occasionally come across more serious problems, such as alcoholism or drug addiction within the family, which made the person feel a strong desire to get away from the dysfunctional family as soon as possible. However, there does not appear to be a consistent pattern in the type of family that recruits come from. The majority seem relatively normal.

So what makes a person vulnerable to cults? How does a nice, kind, insightful human being become a member of a destructive cult? If he is like most cult members, he is probably approached during a time of unusual stress, perhaps while undergoing a major life transition.

Intense stress is commonplace in the modern world. Many people experience great pressure at work or school, or tension from family problems, social relationships, health concerns, new jobs, new homes, money crises, or combinations of several of these stresses at once. Usually our defense mechanisms help us cope, but we all have vulnerable moments.

Although we may succumb to mind control in weak moments, it is by no means permanent. Whenever recruits leave the group environment long enough to discover revealing books, articles, or testimonies by former members, they almost always break away. The problem occurs when people rely on the group for all key information. Not knowing any better, they give the cult members or leaders the benefit of the doubt. They may assume that any problem is merely the result of one member's idiosyncratic behavior, not the system itself.

One particular cult member I counseled told me that whenever he had caught his Moonie recruiter in a lie, he disregarded it because he assumed that lying was just a personal problem she had. Such judgment errors are common among people who are ignorant of the nature of cults.

This chapter, then, is designed to help you "put yourself in the shoes" of a cult member—to understand his psychology and something of what his life in a cult is like. The first half of the chapter identifies some of the most basic themes of life in destructive cults, the common denominators they all share in terms of what members do and say. The second half of the chapter focuses on what personal life in a destructive cult is like, through several profiles of people who have been involved in such cults. I have known some of the people mentioned here for a long time. With the exception of Elizabeth Rose, they have all left the cults they were members of, given me permission to use their real names, and checked their stories for accuracy. No matter how strange these stories may sound, they are true.

THE CULT EXPERIENCE

What is it like to be in a destructive cult that uses mind control? How does it feel? How does one think?

Since there are so many different types of mind control cults, it would be impossible to describe the beliefs and practices of each. The best way to learn about a specific group is to locate a former member, or at least a former member's written account. A concerned relative can learn a particular groups special jargon and code words. Ex-members are a great source of information, for no one knows the cult experience better than they do.

Though destructive cults may have individual differences, certain themes of cult membership are more or less universal. By "themes" I refer to aspects of the group's teaching, social life, and beliefs which become powerful factors in—and in fact determine—a member's daily life. Of course, the extent to which these themes influence someone depends on how deeply the person is involved (does he live with the group or have a private home?), how long he has been involved, and what status level he has obtained. But for most cultists, the following themes will very likely ring true to their own experiences.

The Doctrine Is Reality

There is no room in a mind control environment for regarding the group's beliefs as mere theory, or as a way to interpret reality or to seek reality. The doctrine *is* reality. Some groups go so far as to teach that the entire material world is illusion, and therefore all thinking, desires and actions (except those prescribed by the cult) do not really exist.

The most effective cult doctrines are those "which are unverifiable and unevaluable,"[1] in the words of Eric Hoffer. They may be so convoluted that it would take years of effort to untangle them. (Of course, by then people have been directed away from studying the doctrine to more practical pursuits, such as fundraising and recruiting.) The doctrine is to be accepted, not understood. Therefore, the doctrine must be vague and global, yet also symmetrical enough to appear consistent. Its power comes from its assertion that it is the one and only truth: that it encompasses everything.

Since mind control depends on creating a new identity within the individual, cult doctrine always requires that a person distrust his own self. The doctrine becomes the "master program" for all thoughts, feelings, and actions. Since it is the TRUTH, perfect and absolute, any flaw in it is viewed as only a reflection of the believer's own imperfection. He is taught that he must follow the prescribed formula even if he doesn't really understand it. At the same time he is told that he should try to work harder and have more faith so he will come to *understand* the truth more clearly.

Reality Is Black and White, Good Versus Evil

Even the most complex cult doctrines ultimately reduce reality into two basic poles: black versus white; good versus evil; spiritual world versus physical world; us versus them.

There is never room for pluralism. The doctrine allows no outside group to be recognized as valid (good, godly, real) because that would threaten the cult's monopoly on truth. There is also no room for interpretation or deviation. If the doctrine doesn't provide an answer directly, then the member must ask a leader. If the leader doesn't have an answer, he can always brush off the question as unimportant or irrelevant.

Pet devils vary from group to group. They can be political and economic institutions (Communist, socialist, or capitalist), mental-health professionals (psychiatrists, deprogrammers), or metaphysical entities such as Satan, spirits, UFO creatures, or just the cruel laws of nature. Devils are certain to take on the bodies of parents, friends, ex-members, reporters, and anyone else who is critical of the group. The "huge conspiracies" working to thwart the group are, of course, proof of its tremendous importance.

Some groups cultivate a psychic paranoia, telling members that spirit beings are constantly observing them, even taking possession of them whenever they feel or think in non-cult ways. A Moon leader took busloads of members to see the movie *The Exorcist*, which showed horribly graphic scenes of demonic possession. Members were afterward told that they too would become possessed like that if they ever left the group. The movie was a wonderful tool for phobia indoctrination.

Elitist Mentality

Members are made to feel part of an elite corps of mankind. This feeling of being special, of participating in the most important acts in human history with a vanguard of committed believers, is strong emotional glue to keep people sacrificing and working hard.

As a community, they feel they have been chosen (by God, history, or some other supernatural force) to lead mankind out of darkness into a new age of enlightenment. Cult members have a great sense not only of mission but of their special place in history—they will be recognized for their greatness for generations to come. In the Moonies we were told that monuments and historical markers would someday be erected to commemorate us and our sacrifices.

Ironically, members of cults look down on anyone involved in any other cult groups. They are very quick to acknowledge that "Those people are in a cult" or "*They* are the ones who are brainwashed." They are unable to step out of their own situations and look at themselves objectively.

This feeling of elitism and destiny, however, carries a heavy burden of responsibility. Members are told that if they do not fully perform their duties, they are failing all of mankind.

The rank-and-file member is humble before superiors and potential recruits but arrogant to outsiders. Almost all members are told when being recruited that they too will become leaders one day. However, advancement will be achieved only by outstanding performance or by political appointment. In the end, of course, the real power elite stays small. Most members do not become leaders but stay among the rank and file.

Nevertheless, they consider themselves better, more knowledgeable, and more powerful than anyone else in the world. As a result, cult members often feel *more* responsible than they have ever felt in their lives. They walk around feeling as though the world sits on their shoulders. Cult members don't know what outsiders mean when they say you shouldn't try to escape reality and responsibility by joining a cult.

Group Will over Individual Will

In all destructive cults the self must submit to the group. The "whole purpose" must be the focus; the "self purpose" must be subordinated. In any group that qualifies as a destructive cult, thinking *of* oneself or *for* oneself is wrong. The group comes first. Absolute obedience to superiors is one of the most universal themes in cults. Individuality is bad. Conformity is good.

A cultist's entire sense of reality becomes externally referenced: he learns to ignore his inner self and trust the external authority figure. He learns to look to others for direction and meaning. I have observed that rank-and-file cult members universally have trouble making decisions, probably because of the overemphasis on external reference. In this state of extreme dependency, members need someone to tell them what to think, feel, and do.

Leaders of different cults have come up with strikingly similar tactics for fostering dependency. They transfer members frequently to new and strange locations, switch their work duties, promote them and then demote them on whims—all to keep them off balance. Another technique is to assign impossibly high goals, tell members that if they are "pure" they will succeed, and force them to confess impurity when they fail.

Strict Obedience: Modeling the Leader

A new member is often induced to abandon his former behavior patterns and become "dedicated" by being paired with an older cult member who serves as a model for him to imitate. The newcomer is urged to *be* this other person. Mid-level leaders themselves are urged to model their superiors, the cult leader himself being the ultimate model at the top.

One reason why a group of cultists may strike even a naive outsider as spooky or weird is that everyone has similar odd mannerisms, clothing styles, and modes of speech. What the outsider is seeing is the personality of the leader passed down through several layers of modeling.

Happiness through Good Performance

One of the most attractive qualities of cult life is the sense of community that it fosters. The love seems to be unconditional and unlimited at first, and new members are swept away by a honeymoon of praise and attention. But after a few months, as the person becomes more enmeshed, the flattery and attention are turned away toward newer recruits. The cult member learns that love is not unconditional but depends on good performance.

Behaviors are controlled through rewards and punishments. Competitions are used to inspire and shame members into being more productive. If things aren't going well—poor recruitment, media exposés, defections—it is the members' personal fault, and their ration of "happiness" will be withheld until the problem is corrected. In some groups people are required to confess sins to be granted "happiness" and, if they can't think of any, to make some up. Ultimately they come to believe they really committed these made-up sins.

Real friendships are a liability and are covertly discouraged by leaders. A cult member's emotional allegiance should be vertical (up to the leader), not horizontal (toward peers). Friends are dangerous, in part because if one member leaves, he may take others with him. Of course, when anyone does leave the group, the "love" formerly directed to him turns into anger, hatred, and ridicule.

Relationships are usually superficial within these groups because sharing deep personal feelings, especially negative ones, is highly discouraged. This feature of cult life prevails even though a member may feel he is closer to his comrades than he has ever been to anyone before. Indeed, when cult members go through hardship (fundraising in freezing cold or broiling heat) or persecution (being arrested for violations of law or harassed by outsiders), they do feel a depth of camaraderie and shared martyrdom that is exceptional. But because the only real allegiance is to the leader, a closer look shows that such ties are actually shallow and sometimes just private fantasy.

Manipulation through Fear and Guilt

The cult member comes to live within a narrow corridor of fear, guilt, and shame. Problems are always the fault of the member, and are due to *his* weak faith, *his* lack of understanding, "bad ancestors," evil spirits, and so forth. He perpetually feels guilty for not meeting standards. He comes to believe that "evil" is out to get him.

In every destructive cult I have encountered, fear is a major motivator. Each group has its devil lurking around the corner waiting for members to tempt and seduce, to kill or to drive insane. The more vivid and tangible a devil the group can conjure up, the more intense is the cohesiveness it fosters.

Emotional Highs and Lows

Life in a cult is a roller-coaster ride. A member swings between the extreme happiness of experiencing the "truth" with an insider elite, and the crushing weight of guilt, fear, and shame. Problems are always due to *his* inadequacies, not the group's. He perpetually feels guilty for not meeting standards. If he raises objections, he is likely to get the "silent treatment" or be transferred to another part of the group.

These extremes take a heavy toll on a person's ability to function. When members are "high," they can convert their zeal into great productivity and persuasiveness. But when they crash they can become completely dysfunctional.

Most groups don't allow the "lows" to last very long. They typically send the member back through reindoctrination to charge him up again. It is not uncommon for someone to receive a formal reindoctrination several times a year. Some long-term members do burn out without actually quitting. These people can no longer take the burden or pressure of performance. They start to point out inconsistencies in group policy. They may be permanently reassigned to manual labor in out-of-the-way places, where they are expected to remain for the rest of their lives, or if they become a burden, they are asked (or told) to leave. One man I counseled had been sent home to his family after ten years of cult membership because he started to demand more sleep and better treatment.

Changes in Time Orientation

An interesting dynamic of cults is that they tend to change a person's relationship to his past, present, and future. As mentioned before, the member's past is rewritten. He tends to look back at his previous life with a distorted memory that colors everything dark. Even very positive memories are skewed toward the bad.

A cult member's sense of the present is manipulated, too. He feels a great sense of urgency about the tasks at hand. I remember well the constant feeling that a time bomb was ticking beneath my feet and that the world might become a heaven or a hell depending on how well I carried out my current project.

Many groups teach that the apocalypse is just around the corner. Some say they are preventing the apocalypse; others merely believe that they will survive it. When you are kept extremely busy on critical projects all the time—for days, weeks, and months—everything becomes blurred.

To a cult member, the future is a time when you will be rewarded because the great change has finally come—or it is the time when you will be punished. In most groups the leader claims to control, or at least to have unique knowledge of, the future. He knows how to paint visions of future heaven and hell to move members this way or that. Many groups have timetables for the apocalypse, which tends to be two to five years away—far enough not to be discredited any time soon, near enough to carry emotional punch. These predictions have a way of fading into the background as the big date approaches. In other groups, the timetable is believed right until it actually fails to come true.

Usually the leader just issues a new timetable that moves the big event up a few years. After he does this a few times, a few long-term members may become cynical. Of course, by then there is a whole set of new members unaware that the leader has been shifting the timetable. When I was in the Moonies, no one knew about Moon's failed prophecies that the old world would end and the Moon movement would take over in 1960 and then 1967.[2] Moon predicted World War III would occur in 1977. When that didn't happen, all eyes were on 1981. People recruited around 1977 have told me how clearly they remember the magical, whispered excitement of the words "1981!" on their lecturers' lips.[3] When 1981 produced nothing more dramatic for the Unification Church than President Ronald Reagan's inauguration (which Sun Myung Moon himself inexplicably attended), talk had already turned to dates farther ahead.

No Way Out

In a destructive cult, there is never a legitimate reason for leaving. Unlike non-cult organizations that recognize a person's inherent right to choose to move on, mind control groups make it very clear that there is no *legitimate* way to leave. Members are told that the only reasons why people leave are weakness, insanity, temptation, brainwashing (by deprogrammers), pride, sin, and so on.

Members are thoroughly indoctrinated with the belief that if they ever do leave, terrible consequences will befall them, their family, and/or mankind. Although cult members will often say "Show me a way that is better than mine and I will quit," they are not allowed the time or mental tools to prove that statement to themselves. They are locked in a psychological prison.

SOME OF THE PEOPLE WHO'VE BEEN THERE

People who join destructive cults have some experiences that are too painful to remember. Even after counseling, ex-members may not wish to communicate their experiences in a public way. Others have come to believe that people in general should understand the suffering they went through while under mind control, and are not afraid to use their names. While I certainly understand the reticence of people who wish to remain anonymous, I also admire the courage of those who come forward with their stories. Such people are stronger for being able to share their personal stories and also give us an invaluable source of insight into the experience of being recruited, living in a destructive cult, and leaving it.

Carol Giambalvo and est

In the past decade, large numbers of people have experienced the hard-sell recruiting tactics of the large-scale awareness training programs such as est, now renamed the Forum. Werner Erhard estimates that more than 750,000 people have taken the est training/Forum and more than five million people have been enrolled in the Hunger Project. Most people who pay hundreds of dollars to attend Erhard's programs do not go on to become involved in the numerous "graduate" seminars, which are vigorously promoted. Still fewer people become staff members or unpaid volunteers. In the experience of some ex-members I have counseled, the more intensive est programs exhibit certain qualities which I have defined above as characteristic of a cult.[4]

While many est graduates report positive results from the training, others warn of its dangers—among them, psychiatric disturbances.[5] Robert Tucker, executive director of Toronto's Council on Mind Abuse says that the Council has received and continues to receive more complaints about est than about any other single group. "These complaints," he says, "are consistent with our understanding of the effects of cultism. My contention is that Werner Erhard is exploiting people's desire for higher consciousness and marketing a kind of 'instant enlightenment.' I feel that by creating a first-time experience of extended consciousness, he gains control over people who believe that he and his seminars are the source of that experience. In my opinion, this profoundly manipulates and distorts the meaning of enlightenment."[6]

Carol, a lively woman in her mid-forties, met Noel when he was still recovering from his divorce after twenty-five years of marriage. They fell in love, and were married. Noel, a retired elementary school counselor, had taken the est training and recommended it to Carol. Together, they became "workshop junkies," taking seminar after seminar.

During the time of their involvement, Noel's daughter from his previous marriage became associated with the Hare Krishnas. At first, the Giambalvos were very open-minded and supported their daughter's involvement. But then they started noticing drastic personality changes and started to do research on cults and mind control. They tried to have her exit-counseled, but the attempt was unsuccessful and she returned to the group. Later, she had a nervous breakdown and was expelled by the Krishnas. However, because of what they had learned, the Giambalvos became concerned about the cult problem and began to give lectures on the subject. "It is incredible to think," Carol says now, "that we were out there warning the public about the dangers of other groups, and yet were not aware of how deeply entrenched we were in est."

The Giambalvos, like many others, had mistakenly assumed that people must live together in a closed community to be adversely affected by a group involvement. Although their participation in est-related activities was extensive, they lived in a comfortable home on Long Island. Only when they started examining the specific techniques and processes used in est seminars and Hunger Project organizational meetings did they recognize the organization's deceptive and mind-controlling elements.[7] They renounced their affiliation and began the difficult process of analyzing their experiences.

While speaking at a Northeast regional meeting of the Cult Awareness Network, Carol described her moment of "caving in" during her indoctrination.[8] She told the audience, "I remember asking a question of the seminar leader, and his response was something like 'How would you know! You are sitting in the victims row!' When he asked why I was sitting there, I explained it was because I had diabetes. In a matter of moments he accused me of creating my own diabetes in order to get my father's attention when I was a little girl—he embarrassed me in front of two hundred and fifty people. He more or less stated that if I just wanted to 'uncreate' my medical condition, I could do so because I had the power to create reality. It was a good thing I never stopped taking my insulin. I could have died."

Nevertheless, Carol remained in the seminar and took many others. Ultimately she and her husband became one of the first seventy briefing leaders for the Hunger Project, founded by Werner Erhard. They remained active for more than five years, encouraging people to take est and enrolling people in the Hunger Project. At the peak of their involvement, Carol and Noel spent sixty to seventy hours a week working as unpaid volunteers for the Hunger Project— time they now wish they had spent working for an organization that was actually feeding starving people, rather than just raising millions of dollars in order to promote Erhard's idea that if enough people "uncreate hunger," it will disappear.

Carol is currently national coordinator of FOCUS, a national support and information organization for former cult members. With Noel, she spends a good deal of time exit-counseling people from destructive cults.

Elizabeth Rose and the Lyndon LaRouche Organization

Have you ever been at an airport and passed a table filled with literature and signboards that read "Feed Jane Fonda to the Whales," "Quarantine AIDS victims," or "Build particle beam weapons to defend America"? If so, then you have seen members of the LaRouche political organization. Currently under indictment for credit card fraud (taking people's credit card numbers used to purchase the group's periodicals and allegedly charging unauthorized amounts) and obstruction of justice, several members of the LaRouche organization are facing criminal prosecution.[9] LaRouche, who has run for President in the past three elections, asserts that Henry Kissinger acts as a Russian spy, that Queen Elizabeth tolerates drug pushing, and that only he can save America.[10]

LaRouche plays on people's fears and their patriotism in order to get them to support him and his organization.[11] Once a Marxist, he is now virulently right-wing and has even established an "intelligence" network, which over the years has been used by people and governments.[12]

Elizabeth Rose,[13] an eighty-five-year-old woman, was recruited into the LaRouche organization shortly after her husband and sister died, leaving her to live alone for the first time. Members of the LaRouche organization called her on the telephone, found her receptive, and began making frequent late-night visits to her home. Within three weeks, her daughter Nancy Day reports, Elizabeth Rose turned over some $800,000 in family-owned stock to the organization in a loan arrangement, stating that she was going to help "save the world." Elizabeth also told her daughter that through her membership she was going to help "colonize Mars," and perhaps be "the first grandmother on Mars."

In October 1986, the IRS and the state of Virginia raided LaRouche headquarters in Leesburgh and found documents that showed there had been more than 4,500 loan transactions, involving 3,000 individuals in 50 states and 12 countries who had given the organization more than $30 million. It was estimated that at least 70 percent of the victims were elderly, and that they had found no instance of repayment of any loan in strict accordance with the terms of the notes.

Even though Nancy Day was able to go to court and prevent her mother from giving more of her assets to the group, Elizabeth Rose continues to be active with the LaRouche organization. She is very persuasive and is useful in coaxing other elderly persons to turn over their wealth, in exchange for promissory notes with 10 percent interest. In the same way that she was approached by LaRouche members, she appeals to people's sense of patriotism as well as their fear that banks are "unreliable." She travels all over the world defending the LaRouche organization, convinced that it is being persecuted because of left-wing propaganda.

Patrick Ryan and Transcendental Meditation

Patrick Ryan, now a successful entrepreneur, was involved in Transcendental Meditation for ten years. He is a graduate of Maharishi International University (MIU) in Fairfield, Iowa, an accredited institution. Most people think of TM as a harmless way to relax through meditation. But for those who plunge deeply into the TM organization, it takes on cult qualities.

Pat has since founded a support group called TM-Ex for former members, and talks openly about the movement's darker side. "It has all of the characteristics of a destructive cult," he says. "A lot of my friends and I have been greatly damaged by our involvement with it."

Like most destructive cults, TM uses a good deal of deception.[14] Its public spokespeople say that "TM is not a philosophy, a religion, or a lifestyle." Yet, Pat points out, "People become vegetarian, celibate, recite mantras composed of the names of Hindu gods, and worship Maharishi Mahesh Yogi as the 'enlightened master of the universe.' "

In its advertising, TM emphasizes the practical benefits of meditation—particularly the reduction of stress. TM promoters show videos of members from all walks of life testifying to its benefits. TM sales pitches are full of blood pressure charts, heart-rate graphs, and other clinical evidence of TM's effectiveness. Not mentioned is the fact that scientific tests show similar benefits can be obtained by listening to soothing music, or by performing basic relaxation exercises available in books costing a couple of dollars.

After a TM student pays up to $400 and receives his own personal mantra to chant, he is told never to reveal it to another. Why? Because the same "unique" mantra has been given—on the basis of age—to thousands of people.[15]

Most people who learn TM never go beyond the prescribed twenty minutes of meditating twice a day, in the morning and the afternoon. They can hardly be called cult members. But a few continue to visit the TM centers for "checking," and go on to pay for more and more advanced courses. Eventually they may get to the point Pat did. He paid $3,000 to learn how to levitate and fly. In reality, he found himself reciting the more "advanced" mantras while vigorously hopping up and down with his legs crossed in the lotus position for two hours in the morning and two hours in the afternoon.

Not surprisingly, he experienced painful muscle spasms, headaches, and involuntary twitching. He went to his instructors for help. "They told me that I was unstressing," he said. "They told me to go back and meditate and fly harder."

"It wasn't until Bob Kropinsky won the first lawsuit against TM for fraud and negligence that I learned about people who have been hurt by Transcendental Meditation,"[16] Patrick continued. "The top leaders blame the members for everything and haven't done anything to correct their policies." As in other destructive cults, there is never a problem with the leader, the doctrine, or the organization's behavior—it's always the fault of the members.

Pat began to question his involvement with TM only after sitting in on the deprogramming of his sister Michelle from The Way International. As Way ex-members told Michelle the criteria that define a mind control environment, Pat began to hear alarm bells going off in his head. The same methods were used in TM. He realized his problems were a response to practices that were short-circuiting his nervous system.

Pat started digging into every source he could find to understand the history and background of Maharishi and the organization. He discovered from former MIU faculty members that some of the much-touted medical experiments had been conducted without proper scientific procedure.[17] He has now become very critical of the organization in which he was previously involved, and active in warning others of its destructive and deceptive practices.

Gretchen Callahan and the Truth Station

Some destructive cults are so small that they might seem insignificant in comparison with large organizations such as the Unification Church. Yet, small groups can do just as much harm as big ones. Certainly that was true of Gretchen Callahan's involvement in a small fundamentalist Bible cult in southern California called the Truth Station.[18] Its thirty members were led by a man convinced that he was in direct communication with God. They lived in a house together and spent much of their time being indoctrinated. They believed that they were the only people living as "true Christians," and also believed in the practice of faith healing.

Yet Gretchen was to have a first-person encounter in a "faith healing" that failed—with fatal consequences.

Gretchen described the group's long meetings in a crowded living room where the leader would spend hours putting members on the "hot seat"—

verbally ostracizing and humiliating them while everyone watched. "No one was allowed to get up and go to the bathroom during this. They had to stay and be part of the process," Gretchen told me. Members were led to believe that the "sin" in each of them had to be "brought into the light" and destroyed. No one knew whose turn would come next to be on the hot seat, and each would sigh inwardly with relief when another member's name was called.

The group had its own special jargon for dealing with problems. Questioning the leader's authority, for example, was called "giving place" to satanic spirits. Being fully committed to the infallibility of the leadership and the interpretation of the Bible upheld as "The Truth," (i.e., the leader's version of the truth) was seen as the mark of a "true believer." People would go to great lengths to demonstrate that they were, indeed, "true believers."

A young man whom Gretchen refers to simply as David, who was twenty-six years old at the time of her involvement, felt the subtle power of the group pressuring him to become more spiritual. To prove his commitment to the group and be more accepted, he decided to stop taking insulin for his diabetes, believing that God would heal him. The members applauded his faith and encouraged him to throw away his insulin, which he did.

In a matter of days, David's physical health had rapidly deteriorated, and by the end of the week the leader ordered around-the-clock prayer teams. Gretchen's team was on when David took his last breath, yet the group, spurred by the leader's anxious exhortations, was convinced that David would be resurrected. They prayed for fifteen hours over his body. David's father, at that time a group co-leader, beat on his dead son's chest, rebuking Satan and the angel of death, while David's mother had to be removed from the room because her grief and anguish were viewed as "spiritual weakness." Gretchen held David's hand much of the day as his body turned blue and became stiff.

Even after the police arrived and the coroner took away the body, all the members continued to believe that the young man would return. For three months following his death, a place was set for him at the table, and members (including young children) had visions, dreams, and prophecies concerning his resurrection.

A few days later, Gretchen's parents called her from their home in Jamaica because they had heard of David's death. Gretchen succeeded in convincing them that the young man was not actually dead. The leader had told her it would be a great miracle when he awakened, and nonbelievers would flock to the group.

Two years after David's death, Gretchen was kicked out of the group for a "spirit of rebellion." She just couldn't take any more. She gave and gave and it was never enough. "I guess you could say I was burned out," she told former members of other groups during a meeting of FOCUS, the ex-cultist support group. "Something inside me just turned off. Even though I was still frightened of doing the wrong thing or being 'out of the Spirit,' I just couldn't feel repentant any more for the 'sins' they had fabricated about me. I noticed that no one was happy and smiling any more. Everyone was afraid to talk to one another because they might not be speaking 'in the Spirit.' Yet, even after I was thrown out, I still believed they were right and held the exclusive key to salvation. It wasn't until my parents had me deprogrammed that I started to understand that I'd been struggling with the mind-control abuses, not with my relationship with God." A few months after Gretchen left, the group began to use physical beatings, especially on women and small children, to eradicate "satanic spirits."

"It has taken me years to fully understand how deeply they controlled my emotions and thought processes," Gretchen told me. "If I hadn't received good counseling I probably would have kept trying to return to the group." From what I learned of the group, I would venture to say that the leader probably would have allowed her to do so, once he felt she would more fully submit to his will.

Gary Porter and Nichiren Soshu of America

Currently a chiropractor in Philadelphia, Gary Porter met and fell in love with Ann, a woman involved with NSA, or Nichiren Shoshu of America. (Although the organization originated in Japan and claims Buddhist lineage, it has been gaining membership in the United States for over twenty years.) Members of this cult believe that if they chant mystical words repeatedly in front of a rice-paper scroll—the *gohonzon*—they will gain the power to get whatever they wish. Ann had been involved for over two years when she began to chant *"Nam myoho renge kyo"* for hours a day in order to meet and marry a doctor. "People would chant for parking spaces, a new job, good grades in school, whatever," Gary told former members at a FOCUS support-group meeting.

Gary, who had grown up as a Methodist, was at a low point in his life when he met Ann. "I was burned out from four years of chiropractic college, my best friend was killed in a car accident, my siblings were pressuring me to go home and take care of my mother who was ill—I was a sitting duck for anything that promised the keys to solving life's problems."

"I thought the group was weird," he said, "but I agreed to try the chanting. It gave me an incredible high. I bought a *gohonzen* and married Ann and remained in the group for over five years."

NSA made much use of celebrity members such as Tina Turner and Patrick Duffy, both for recruiting and for confirming members' commitment. Its other big selling point was "working for world peace." NSA made members believe that only their chanting would save mankind from destruction. But other than march in NSA-sponsored rallies (shunned by most mainline peace groups), members did little to promote peace. The NSA marches did help dominate the members' time and energies. "We used to have to go to group meetings three or four times a week, not to mention the hours we would spend each day chanting." Relationships between members were manipulated to make sure that doubters were muffled and conformity was rewarded.

Eventually Gary had several confrontations with his leaders in NSA and was threatened with expulsion. Deep down inside, that was exactly what he had hoped for. He was tired of the pressure and manipulation, and his chiropractic work was suffering because of all the time and energy he was putting into NSA.

The two of them were eventually kicked out of the group, but Ann spent the next year on a couch thinking she was dying of terminal cancer. At the time she didn't realize that she was simply acting according to her indoctrination. She, like many other members, had come to fear that if she ever left NSA and stopped chanting, terrible consequences would follow. [19]

Gary and Ann Porter's story is not as dramatic as that of some cult members. Their life in a destructive cult was relatively ordinary to all outward appearances, and certainly they were never asked to stand vigil over a dying member. Fortunately, they were able to leave the cult together. Once Gary and Ann started to study material on mind control and destructive cults, they realized that NSA was using essentially the same techniques of mind control as groups that require members to live together full-time. It took them several years to piece their lives back together.

Wendy Ford and The Way International

Some people have experienced destructive cults which combine the characteristics of small, fundamentalist Bible sects with the sophisticated "training" techniques of groups such as the Forum and the radical politics of purely political cults. Wendy Ford had an experience of this kind during a seven-year involvement with The Way International.

Wendy is a graduate of The Way Corps, a four-year intensive indoctrination course for top leaders in the group. She was originally attracted to The Way by an introductory course called "Power for Abundant Living." At first, she thought she was merely being taught the Bible.

"They referred to themselves as a Biblical research and teaching ministry founded by Dr. Victor Paul Weirwille," she tells audiences today. "I didn't know till my deprogramming that his doctorate was from a mail-order house, [20] and that the so-called 'rightly-divided teachings' were only his twisted interpretations of the scriptures."

Wendy, a businesswoman and talented singer and actress, now works at a major computer company in Massachusetts and is actively involved as a board member of FOCUS. She remembers clearly how The Way taught her to use thought-stopping techniques. "In my group we were taught how to speak in tongues, which was supposed to be a manifestation of the Holy Spirit. We were to do it whenever we started to think for ourselves or question anything."

Like many other Bible-oriented groups, The Way emphasizes the power of the Devil in daily affairs, instilling deep fears in members that they must obey the leadership without question. "Nobody wanted to be possessed by Satan," she says, "so we thought we were remaining centered on God whenever we spoke in tongues. The reality was that we were cutting off our ability to think critically and independently."

As Weirwille became more and more paranoid about Communism, The Way became a survivalist cult, stockpiling food and weapons. Wendy and other members were instructed in how to use a rifle and live off the land in preparation for the impending invasion. "Cars had to have their gas tanks at least half full at all times, and stores of food and weapons were arranged." Fear became an effective tool to bind the group together. "We were afraid of anyone who talked negatively about our organization. We thought we were God's soldiers— the only people who understood the Bible as it was meant to be studied."

The Way continues to operate its college in Emporia, Kansas, and its national headquarters in New Knoxville, Ohio, despite Weirwille's death in 1986. Members number over 100,000, and The Way is still one of the stronger destructive cults in America.[21] However, high-level infighting has caused some leaders to leave. These people have begun to expose The Way's Biblical inaccuracies and corrupt leadership, but very few of them understand the dynamics of mind control.

"I can only hope that more former leaders can get together to share information and resources," said Wendy, "so we can figure out the best way to help others leave this destructive organization."

Linda Blood and the Temple of Set

Satanist rituals involving teenagers have become a favorite subject for journalists throughout the country in the past few years. Yet, not every person who becomes involved in these activities is an adolescent rebelling against authority. Linda Blood's involvement with a Satanist cult, the Temple of Set, demonstrates that such groups often have a powerful appeal to adults.

Linda, a professional knitter and writer, was involved in the Temple of Set for several months. During that time she was under the direct influence of the group's leader, Michael Aquino, a high-ranking officer in the United States Army. She had read a science fiction article by him in a magazine and had written him a letter. After several months of correspondence, she joined the group, met and fell in love with Aquino, and became involved in a complex, emotionally traumatic relationship with him.

"He has since declared that he never really had any romantic or sexual interest in me, so I can only assume that he was lying when he told me he did, and that he seduced me as a way of gaining control over me," she says wryly. "Actually, the sexual involvement was minimal—I think the challenge of seeing how effectively he could manipulate me was what really turned him on."[22]

Linda has no interest in the supernatural and had no interest in the occult until she met Aquino. "I was influenced by him because I believed that he and the other 'Setians' really understood an intense, dramatic, darkly romantic side of my inner self that doesn't find expression in my normal, everyday personality," she told me while we sat and watched Aquino being interviewed on the Oprah Winfrey show.

I was impressed by Aquino's obvious intelligence and his slick presentation, sitting there in his black satanic priest's costume. Even though Linda had been out for several years, it was obvious that he still affected her deeply. It was the first time she had seen him since she left the cult in 1980.

Lt. Col. Aquino is cunning, well educated, and an effective communicator. He has been attached to the Army's psychological warfare division for many years. Despite publicity that has come out about his cult, Army spokesmen defend Aquino's constitutional right to his religious belief.[23]

"I should have gone on the show to oppose him, but I just wasn't sure I was ready to see him close up again," Linda said. "Now, I wish I had. I did and said some stupid things at times when I was emotionally overwrought—both in the cult and after I got out—and he could use that to humiliate me. But it would be worth it for a chance to expose him. Still there is something pathetic in the personality I see on that screen—pompous, distant, cold, aloof, and emotionally deadened. And you can have it."

"I saw the other side of Michael because of our personal relationship. My feeling is that he desperately needs his 'magic' to escape from some inner despair that I perceived in him, and to give him control and power over others. I think it is tragic what he has done to himself."

As Gini Scott points out in her study of the group The Magicians (and as Arthur Lyons has also noted in his book *Satan Wants You*), one of Aquino's aims is to control people without their knowing how they are being controlled.[24] "He controls members by their belief in his alleged magical status and powers, and by their own need to believe that they, too, can gain such powers,"[25] Linda observes. "We were all supposed to be in awe of him and the rest of the high-level members."

Although the Temple of Set is openly Satanist, Linda did not take part in any rituals that included animal or human sacrifices. I asked Linda if she was afraid for her life. "Not from the Temple of Set, because there has never been a murder of an ex-member that I know of," she said. "The Temple of Set operates openly and basically functions like most other 'public' cults, without apparent violence," Linda notes. "But hard-core, violent Satanist cults are much more frightening than the average destructive group."

• • •

In fact, there is no evidence linking the Temple of Set with illegal activity. But the more violent satanist cults operate more secretly, and delight in an evil image. Some use rituals calculated to horrify and impress—often involving ritual sex, bloodletting, and the killing of animals. There have even been cases of ritual murder. Former participants in such activities can't talk about their experiences without setting off intense emotional reactions in their listeners and, possibly, legal action.

These groups are on the rise because young people are being emotionally set up by books, movies, and even heavy metal music to think that Satan worship will give them power. Although that was not her experience, Linda thinks most of these people are recruited by being invited to parties, given hallucinogenic drugs which render them more suggestible and compliant, and subjected to sexual rites of initiation. Step by step, the recruiter gains control over the recruit by winning trust and loyalty. Only when the person is deemed ready is the worship of Satan introduced directly. At that point the new member usually can't get out because of involvement in illegal acts. If people have seen and participated in ritual murder, it is made very clear that they will be killed by the group if they ever leave it.

Chapter 6

Cult Assessment: How to Protect Yourself

Nobody joins a cult. They just postpone the decision to leave.
—Source unknown

I am frequently asked to help people who are involved with a group I have never heard of before. Over the years I have had to develop a way to evaluate a group and assess its negative impact. Many organizations, I have found, which may appear to be unorthodox, or even downright bizarre, are not damaging to their members. I have received occasional calls from concerned relatives and friends about groups that did not, in my opinion, practice mind control.

I have gotten a dozen or so calls from parents who didn't like the man their daughter was marrying and accused him of practicing mind control. In one case the accusation turned out to be true, but in most personal instances, I have simply refused to intervene or become involved in any way. I firmly believe people are entitled to make their own decisions, even bad ones, if they are legally adult. While I am always interested in working to enhance people's opportunities for choice, perspective, and good communication, I will not take every case put before me.

Many groups have certain destructive aspects but are not destructive in and of themselves. These groups fall into what I consider a "gray zone." For some individuals, membership may be regarded as having a destructive effect, while the organization as a whole may not meet the criteria of being a truly destructive cult.

How does one learn how to discern whether or not a group is a destructive cult? What are the crucial elements that separate benign organizations from dangerous ones? In this chapter I attempt to point out in greater detail the general characteristics of destructive cults so that you can protect yourself from their influence. In doing so, I try to answer some of the more frequently asked questions about cults. Last, I include a list of questions which anyone can use to begin evaluating a group.

In examining and evaluating any group I suspect of being a destructive cult, I operate primarily in the realm of psychology and not theology or ideology. My frames of reference for thinking about destructive cults are the influence processes of mind control, hypnosis, and group psychology. I look at *what a group does, not what it believes.* I try to analyze how destructive cults and their members communicate (or fail to communicate), whereas other analysts and critics approach a cult member with the belief that their interpretation of the Bible or political outlook is the *right* one. It seems to me that they want to convert the cult member into *their* own belief system. My orientation, though, is to encourage the individual to sort things out for himself by researching a multitude of perspectives.

A person's right to believe, however, does not grant an automatic license to act indiscriminately on those beliefs. If it did, white supremacy groups would either deport or murder every non-white person in the country, or satanic cults would start *openly* murdering people for their ritual sacrifices.

If a group believes it is good to lie to non-members in order to advance its cause, and that lie infringes on people's constitutionally guaranteed rights, it violates their freedom. Likewise, if a group hiding behind First Amendment privileges, daily violates its members' civil rights as it works to destroy democracy, then freedom is not served. There must be equal protection of liberties under the law. People have a right to be free from undue influence from destructive cults, both socially and as individuals.

Of course, some people may respond by saying something like "Why should I worry about all this? My rights are violated by someone every day, and there's nothing I can do about it!" I'll grant that there are many factors in life which seem beyond our control, but people should have some control when it comes to membership in a group. By preventing others from violating your individual rights, you can keep them from damaging you as a person. After all, what mind control cults destroy are people's lives!

Here's an example. Suppose you meet someone whom you suspect is a recruiter for a destructive cult. Perhaps you might not have even given this person the time of day except for the fact that he or she is particularly attractive. This person keeps trying to get you to come to a certain place for a meeting. You aren't really interested, but are toying with the idea of trying to get to know the person better. In a situation like this, one cardinal rule to follow is this: *Don't give him or her your phone number or address until you know more.* Hold back, even if it's hard to do so, because you might be on the verge of having your right to privacy violated by someone who represents a very organized group that doesn't give up easily.

Many people eventually succumb to constant pressure. With your address or phone number group members can apply that pressure in a very direct way. Once you become a member of a destructive cult, you lose your right to privacy completely, and more serious damage can be done to you later.

I became involved in exposing destructive cults because of my own experience, not because I believe that our government should restrict new, unestablished religions or legislate the beliefs of any type of group whatsoever. What I do believe is that groups can and should be held accountable for their *actions*.

The groups that I label destructive cults have very specific characteristics that undermine individual choice and liberty. In this chapter I will describe my model for evaluating the destructiveness of any group or organization. The three basic areas are *leadership, doctrine,* and *membership*. By examining these three areas, you will quickly be able to determine whether a particular group has the potential to be a destructive cult.

LEADERSHIP

Even though destructive groups try their best to cloak the true nature of their organizations, a good starting point for information gathering and assessment is leadership. Who is the leader of the group in question? What is his or her life history? What kind of education, training or occupation did he have before starting the group? One cult group's leader (Eugene Spriggs) was a carnival barker—the person whose job it is to convince people to go see particular shows.[1] Another cult leader (Werner Erhard of est and The Forum) sold used cars and then encyclopedias.[2] Yet another (Carl Stevens of The Bible Speaks) was a bakery truck driver,[3] while perhaps the most famous of the all (L. Ron Hubbard of Scientology) started as a science fiction writer.[4] One well-known cult leader (Victor Paul Weirwille of The Way International) received his Ph.D. in theology from a mail-order degree mill.[5]

Contrary to public perception, not all cult leaders start a group because they greedily want money or political power. Even the Reverend Jim Jones, who ordered the People's Temple massacre in Jonestown, was a highly respected, ordained church minister who had a long history of helping the poor. His original intentions were in fact quite admirable. However, along the way, he reportedly started to use amphetamines, presumably so he could work longer hours and care for more people. He started to meet others involved in fake faith healings, and began experimenting with these and other techniques to "fire up" his congregation. As his power grew, he became more and more deranged.

Interestingly, many of today's cult leaders were themselves once victims of a mind control cult. Whenever a person is subjected to mind control processes and leaves the group without any counseling, it is easy for him to take what he has learned and practice it on others. Clearly, not every former member starts his own cult, but certain personalities are disposed to do so. It seems obvious to me that some cult leaders have an inferiority complex and a somewhat anti-social personality. Although many cult leaders want and need material opulence, what they require, in my opinion, is attention and power. In fact, power can and does become an extreme addiction. Over time, cult leaders develop a need for more and more power. One thing that makes these people so dangerous is their psychological instability, and the fact that they actually believe their own propaganda. They are not just cunning con artists who want to make money. From my experience, I think that most actually believe they are "God," or the "Messiah," or an enlightened master.

Does the group leader have any known criminal background? If so, what was he charged with? Were there any convictions? For example, Moon was reportedly arrested at least twice while in Korea—with conflicting reports as to the reasons why.[6] In 1985 he served 13 months in a United States federal prison for conspiracy to commit income tax fraud.[7]

Although a leader's background does not necessarily indicate that he is a huckster or charlatan, where there is smoke, there is often fire. It is amazing just how many leaders of destructive cults have questionable backgrounds.

By looking at the leader's background and lifestyle, you can draw some general conclusions about the level of trust you may want to give him. For example, if a person is teaching a course on how to have a successful relationship, the fact that he has been divorced three times is significant. If a leader has a background of drug use and bizarre behavior, like L. Ron Hubbard,[8] I would recommend caution in listening to his claims of being able to solve all of mankind's problems. When Sun Myung Moon says he is working toward world peace, keep in mind that he reportedly owns an M-16 gun factory in Korea.[9]

Another important aspect of leadership involves its organizational flow of power. Does the organization have a structure with a true balance of power? Many destructive groups have boards of directors, but typically they are puppets of the leader. The true structure is that of a pyramid with the cult leader as omnipotent head (apex). Below him (or her) is a core of lieutenants who are totally subservient. Below them are subleaders. The operating structure allows for no checks and balances. The leader has absolute power. Lord Acton said it well when he wrote, "Power tends to corrupt and absolute power corrupts absolutely."

If a leader has a questionable personal background and structures his organization so that power is totally centralized and controlled by him, the group has the beginnings of a destructive cult. If, however, there are checks and balances built into the system and the leader is committed to meeting the member's needs and goals, a much healthier organization will result.

Be warned that a destructive cult will not always have a leader who is glorified (to outsiders) or who enjoys great personal wealth. Since many contemporary destructive cult leaders were themselves once in a cult, they may be acting out of delusion and mind control, not out of a deliberate scheme to make money and use people. I have counseled people out of several groups whose leaders were not "in it for the money" but who were, in my opinion, addicted to personal power. Many destructive Bible cults have leaders who are not conspicuous consumers and who appear to hold God and the Bible above them in authority; yet, their *interpretation* of the Bible and God's will is used to manipulate and control people.

DOCTRINE

Since the Constitution protects people's right to believe whatever they wish to believe, close scrutiny of a group's particular doctrine is unwarranted and unnecessary. However, I believe that *a group's beliefs should be freely disclosed* to any person who wants to join it.

Does the group's doctrine claim publicly to be one thing when it is in fact otherwise? I refer to this structural factor as *insider* doctrine and *outsider* doctrine. For a group to have integrity, it is important that group members truly believe what the group says it believes. However, destructive groups change the "truth" to fit the needs of the situation because they believe that *the ends justify the means.* Helping to "save" someone is a rationalization used to justify deceit or manipulation. Legitimate organizations don't change their doctrine to deceive the public.

MEMBERSHIP

Membership is the last and most important criterion to use in evaluating groups. I subdivide it into three components: *recruitment, group maintenance,* and *freedom to leave.* The impact of group membership on the individual, his identity, his relationships, and the alteration of his goals and interests is primary. This is my main area of concentration when I evaluate a group.

The basic feature of most cult *recruitment* is *deception.* As I have already said, destructive groups have no compunction about using deception in the recruitment of new members. They operate under the assumption that people are too "ignorant" or too "unspiritual" to recognize what is best for them. They therefore take it upon themselves to make decisions for the people they recruit. When an individual's critical faculties are intact and fully functioning, information supplied by the destructive cult is meager. When the individual's critical functions are worn down and less operational, then the cult will supply more information. Deception includes outright lying, leaving out important information, or distorting information.

Most recruiters from destructive cults will deny that they are trying to recruit anyone at all. When questioned as to what they are doing, they normally say that they just want to share something meaningful and want people to make up their own minds about it. What they do not tell the prospective convert is that they may have recruitment quotas to fill.

The practice of deception by destructive cults extends to the use of various "front organizations" to confuse potential recruits and hide the real agenda of the organization. CAUSA, C.A.R.P., Freedom Leadership Foundation, the International Cultural Foundation, and many others are all part of the Moon organization.[10] Dianetics and Narconon are part of the Church of Scientology.[11] The average citizen is not usually aware of the connections among these various organizations.

In a cult recruitment relationship, the recruiter wants to get as much information as possible from the potential convert so as to know the most effective way to bring him into the group. An effective recruiter knows how to hone in on a person's potential weak spots—problems with a boyfriend or girlfriend, parents, family members, job, or school; death of a close friend or relative; a move to a new town, and so on. A good recruiter knows how to make the "target" comfortable, so that very personal and confidential information is disclosed.

Meanwhile, the recruiter reveals as little as possible about himself and especially the group, unless it is absolutely necessary. Most of the information is coming from the recruitee. This kind of imbalanced flow of information is another warning signal that something is wrong.

By far the most common impression received by a potential recruit is that he is making a new friend. However, in the real world, friendships take time to develop. They don't happen overnight. Each person shares more and more personal information in a reciprocal manner, with little or no imbalance, each person giving and taking in a balanced way. There is also no hidden agenda.

Once the potential convert is invited to some cult function or seminar, there is a great deal of pressure, both overt and subtle, to get him to make a commitment as soon as possible. Destructive cults, like good con artists, move in for the kill once they size a person up. It is not in their best interest to encourage thoughtful reflection. In contrast, legitimate groups do not lie to a potential convert or pressure him into making a quick commitment.

A destructive group will recruit new members through the use of mind control techniques, as already discussed. Control of the individual's experience is essential in order to break him down, indoctrinate him, and build him up again in the cult image. During a cult recruitment, the person's identity framework makes a dramatic shift. Sometimes the person doesn't contact family and friends for days or weeks during the indoctrination. When he does see them again, this radical personality change is most evident to them. The individual often changes his style of clothes and speech patterns and behaves in an uncharacteristically distant manner. Often, the person's sense of humor is blunted. Previous interests, hobbies, and goals may be abandoned "because they are no longer important."

This personality change does seem to wear off a bit over time, if the individual doesn't continue to contact the group or participate in its activities. However, when the person maintains contact (over the telephone or by attending group sessions), the new identity can and does grow stronger and stronger.

To family and friends, the person seems not only more distant but deceptive and evasive. Sometimes the person can be coaxed into revealing what he now believes. Frequently, though, the new member asks family members and friends to talk to older members or leaders, "because they can explain it better."

The most tell-tale sign of the work of a destructive cult is this radical personality change of the new member. He may have been politically liberal before but is now a staunch conservative. He may have loved rock music but now thinks it is from the devil. He may have been very loving and close to his family but now doesn't trust them at all. He may have been an atheist; yet now God means everything to him. Granted, people do shift beliefs and values as a natural unfolding of life experience. However, when deception and mind control are involved, the change is dramatic, sudden, and artificially manufactured. Time after time I have heard family members say, "He's a different person now. We don't know him anymore!"

People have been known to change their names, drop out of school or work, donate their bank accounts and property, and move hundreds or thousands of miles away from home once they become involved. However, the absence of these requirements doesn't necessarily mean that the group is not a destructive cult. Increasing numbers of groups have deliberately avoided such practices for some time in order to allay suspicion.

Each situation and each group should be considered individually in terms of its impact on a person's life. Recruitment is done incrementally; in some cases, a person's behavior changes over months, although more typically it takes only days or weeks.

The *maintenance of membership* is achieved by cult activities deliberately designed to undermine the new member's relationships with family and friends. One way this goal is achieved is having the new member recruit everyone he knows. As long as friends and family are "raw meat," as the Church of Scientology likes to call them,[12] recruits have permission to spend time and work on them. As soon as family members and friends express their concerns and announce they will never join the group, cult leaders urge the new member to stop wasting time with non-believers. Ultimately, if the family of a new member is critical enough, he will be instructed to break off all contact.

Destructive cults cannot tolerate opposition of any kind. Either people agree with them (or are seen as potential converts), or they are the enemy.

Once a person becomes a member, his sleep patterns often change significantly. Sleep deprivation is common in many destructive cults. Anyone who has ever experienced several sleepless nights or has had to stay up all night to work or study will remember the difficulty of functioning normally without adequate sleep. Many cult groups make sure that members have only three to five hours of sleep each night. It is not that such groups have a written policy to that effect—most groups don't. They merely make sure that the person is so overworked as to have little time to sleep. They also make sure constantly to praise leaders who are sleeping very little and belittle people who are sleeping too much. In time, members learn to sleep a minimum amount.

Dietary changes also frequently occur with cult recruitment. Some groups practice strict vegetarianism but use excessive amounts of sugar to give members a "high." Some groups encourage long and frequent fasts, with little or no care given to the body before and after. A couple of groups even make members forage in garbage cans for their meals.[13] Drastic weight shifts occur. Although most people lose weight during their membership in destructive cults, some become significantly overweight.

What people eat, their attitude toward food, and how they eat all contribute to a person's sense of self. If a member is made to feel that he has to "die to himself" and his human needs, he may agree to fast a good deal of the time and deny himself any pleasure in eating. If a person is very unhappy and isn't having his emotional needs met, overeating can result. People who are grossly overweight are usually ridiculed by cult members and made to feel guilty and powerless, unless the cult leader happens to be fat or likes fat people. Contrary to public misconceptions, most mind control cults do not systematically deprive members of decent food. If they did so for long, the members' bodies would break down and they would not be able to work.

Destructive cults are characterized, however, by doing little to maintain their members' good health in other ways. Psychosomatic illnesses abound in members, perhaps as a reflection of their unconscious need for help and attention. Medical treatment is minimal, and in some groups it is virtually absent.

In destructive cults, large amounts of time are spent in group activities, with a minimum of time allowed for privacy or for friends and family. Little time is available for reading anything other than cult material or for learning anything other than cult practices. Of course, members go out of their way to convince outsiders that they are living a "normal" life. Yet, if you get cult members into a long discussion of current events, or art, or history, it becomes evident that most are out of touch.

One of the most obvious signs of a person in a mind control group is a lack of independent decision making abilities. Even though cult members try to convince outsiders that they are autonomous, once you probe beyond the surface it becomes obvious that they cannot make important decisions without first asking permission from superiors. This kind of dependency is evident on all levels of cult membership except the top leadership. One mother of a cult member I knew was happy when she thought that her son had decided on his own to come home for Christmas, but crestfallen when she heard her son's explanation of the visit. "No, mom, the yogi told me that my place was to be with you over the holidays," he remarked. I told her that the only reason he was allowed to come home was that she had behaved as though she approved of his involvement, inviting members to dinner often and never openly criticizing the group.

Family members are frequently told by cult members that they "will see" if they can come home for important family events like marriages, deaths, and even birthdays. What this means is that they will ask their leader. Likewise, members have to ask permission to do anything that most people take for granted. It is nearly impossible to imagine a person having to ask permission of a priest to visit a sick relative. However, a member of one of these groups who just goes and does what he feels is necessary is seen as "selfish," "independent," "rebellious," and antagonistic to "positive growth." In fact, the more controlled the group is, the less likely a person is to be able to go and visit a sick relative or attend a wedding, funeral, or any other "outside activity." Some groups go so far as to control all social relationships, telling members not only whom they can or can't date, but also whom they can or can't marry. Some of the more extreme groups actually regulate sexuality, telling members when they can have sex and what positions for lovemaking are acceptable, and even taking children away from their parents in an effort to indoctrinate them more completely.

Life in a destructive cult can vary a great deal. Some people may live with other members in an "ashram," center, or house, while other members may have their own living arrangements. Some members may have quite menial jobs, demanding little or no thinking (as janitors, maintenance men, cooks, cleaners), while others are engaged in quite demanding work (e.g., recruiting, public relations, operating cult businesses). One group, the Children of God, actively encourages its female members to become prostitutes, acting as "Happy Hookers for Jesus,"[14] using sex to make money and gain converts. They operate near many large American military bases overseas, and take advantage of lonely servicemen with their come-ons.

Some people have outside jobs from nine to five, which force them to compartmentalize their cultic thinking process. These people typically continue their jobs once they join, because of the money, the prestige, and the opportunities to recruit and influence. Such people are fortunate to have time away from the group and extensive contact with non-members, and the detrimental effects are minimized.

In the day-to-day lives of members of destructive cults, there is often a wide variation in the degree to which they suffer from thought control, emotional control, behavior control, and information control. Those persons who are forbidden to think "negative thoughts" or have contact with critics or former members, even though they may have outside jobs and live separately, may still be under mind control, though perhaps not as highly controlled as someone who is a full-time, completely devoted member.

The final criterion for judging a group is the members' *freedom to leave.* To put it simply, members of destructive cults are psychological prisoners. As I have explained, destructive cults plant phobias into members' minds so that they fear ever leaving the group. By doing this they shut the door on free choice. People had the freedom to join, but people don't have the freedom to leave a destructive group. In fact, in the eyes of a destructive cult, there is no "legitimate" reason for a person to ever leave the group.

Legitimate groups treat people as adults, capable of determining what is in their best interest. Although every organization wants to retain its membership, legitimate groups never go to the extremes of control through fear and guilt that destructive cults do.

Some of the most destructive cults will actually try to hunt down and silence former members through either overt violence, legal harassment, or emotional intimidation and blackmail. Paul Morantz, a lawyer litigating against Synanon, the drug rehabilitation program, was bitten by a rattlesnake placed in his mailbox by cult members.[15] Stephen Bryant, a former devotee of the Krishnas, was murdered, shot in the head by a member of the group, allegedly at the instruction of one of the Krishna leaders.[16] Bent Corydon, a member of the Church of Scientology for 22 years, has been subjected to extreme forms of legal harassment for writing *L. Ron Hubbard—Messiah or Madman?,* a critical biography of the founder of Scientology.[17] Jeannie Mills, a former member of the People's Temple and outspoken critic of the Reverend Jim Jones, was murdered by persons unknown, along with her husband and children, after the massacre at Jonestown.[18]

Needless to say, people should always retain their right to decide for themselves whether to remain in a group. That freedom of choice should not be taken away from a person who has decided to join any organization.

Questions People Ask About Cults

While one might assume that information about cults might be readily available in bookstores and libraries, there is actually a severe shortage of books, videotapes, films, and other materials containing objective accounts of what cults are and what they do. I have heard more than one report of cult members going into public libraries and bookstores to steal or buy out books on cults, with the intent to keep information detrimental to them out of public circulation.

One question I frequently hear is whether all destructive cults are equally dangerous. The answer is a simple "no," as any common-sense look at cults would prove. Not every group is as destructive, for example, as the People's Temple, or as extreme as the terrorist cults of the Middle East. Nor is every group as deceptive, as demanding, and as dangerous to an individual, his family, or society as is the Moon organization. In talking about destructive cults, we should realize that they fall at the extreme end of the spectrum of influences in our daily lives.

Another question I occasionally encounter is whether destructive cults change over time in significant ways. The answer is yes. Groups that use mind control may start off with extremely good intentions but end up manipulating their members and deceiving the public. That was certainly the case in the People's Temple, which was originally an inner-city ministry oriented toward helping the poor. The tragedy is that the people whom the cult tried to help eventually became the group's own victims and made victims of others. The People's Temple is a group that self-destructed, but others simply fade away or disband. An example of such a "fade-out" is the Democratic Worker's Party of California, which decided to disband after its members became extremely disillusioned with its leader.[19] The Center for Feeling Therapy disbanded when the leaders walked away one day, leaving hundreds of confused and disoriented members.[20]

Another issue is whether a destructive group is uniformly dangerous at every one of its locations throughout the world. Despite the fact that many groups try to present an image of being large, powerful, and monolithic, they are often quite varied in their internal management styles. There can be vast differences in the degree of a cult's destructiveness, depending on the leader's personality, strictness, and style. During my days in the Moonies, there were large differences between the lifestyles of groups on the East Coast and those on the West Coast. For example, in the East (primarily because Moon lived there and oversaw operations personally), militaristic discipline and control were extreme. Men and women were not permitted to hug, kiss, or hold hands unless officially married and given permission. On the West Coast, members were much looser and did all these things, although they were more deceptive in recruitment tactics.

Because many destructive cults offer meditation or therapeutic techniques that are claimed to have universally beneficial results, another legitimate question is whether cults affect some people more adversely than others.

For example, some people simply do not respond well to passive-relaxation techniques. A person recruited into an organization such as Transcendental Meditation (TM), might suffer such negative effects as headaches, insomnia, increased anxiety, and so forth. Since TM members believe that their form of meditation is good for everybody, a person who complains of negative effects may be told that he is simply "unstressing" and should continue meditating. Unfortunately, the results of ignoring such problems may lead to serious health problems, nervous breakdowns, and even, suicidal tendencies.[21]

Large group awareness training programs such as est (now The Forum), Lifespring, and others have been strongly criticized for their lack of professional screening systems to identify people likely to be particularly vulnerable. As a result, many of these organizations have been the subject of a number of serious lawsuits by damaged participants.[22]

Last, there is the consideration of a group's size. Does the degree of a cult's destructiveness stand in some relationship to its size? Not at all. I have seen one-on-one mind control relationships that have been as destructive in their effects as those of big groups. In researching the battered-wife syndrome, I have found many similarities and parallels with members of mind control cults.[23] Some battered women were forced into a nearly totally dependent relationship, often kept away from family and friends critical of the husband's behavior. Some women were not allowed to have access to money, to learn how to drive a car, or to work outside the home. Whenever they tried to communicate their wants or needs, they were beaten. They were made to feel that any problem in their marriage was entirely their fault, and that if they only worked harder to please their husbands, everything would be fine. Such women's self-esteem became so low that they came to believe there was no future for them without their men. Some women had husbands who not only planted phobias in their minds that they could never leave the marriage but told them that they would be hunted down and killed if they ever left on their own.

ASKING QUESTIONS: THE KEY TO PROTECTING YOURSELF FROM DESTRUCTIVE CULTS

Learning to be an educated consumer can help save you time, energy, and money. In the case of destructive cults, being an educated consumer can help save your mind. If you are ever approached by someone who tries to get information from you or invites you to participate in a program, you can ask some very specific questions which will help you avoid over 90 percent of all cult recruiters. *These questions work best if you ask them in a very direct yet friendly manner and demand very specific answers.*

Although most groups use deception, it is important to realize that most cult members don't realize they are lying in the process of recruitment. For that reason, by asking these direct questions one after another, you can usually discover that either you are not being told a straight story, or the cult member doesn't have the straight story to begin with.

Because members have been trained to avoid thinking negatively about the group, you will often receive less than direct responses. Among the more common strategies of cult recruiters are vague generalities, evasive remarks, and attempts to change the subject. Vague generalities such as "We're just trying to help people to overcome their problems" or "We're having a free dinner tonight to discuss some world problems" or "We're just getting together to study the Word of God" should make you suspicious. Evasive remarks such as "I understand you are feeling skeptical; I was too, before I really came to *understand*" or "Is that what you *really* want to know?" should also ring warning bells for you.

Another common technique used by cult recruiters is to change the subject. For example, when you ask a question about whether or not a cult leader has a criminal background, you may hear a long monologue about how all the world's great religious leaders have been persecuted. You may be told about Socrates having been accused of child molestation, or about Jesus having been accused of associating with prostitutes, and so forth. Make sure you don't allow the individual to get you into a debate about Socrates or Jesus—you want a direct answer about the leader of this group. If the recruiter does not answer in a clear, concise, direct way, you may be sure that there is something wrong with his answer. There is always one reply that no recruiter can respond to: you can simply walk away.

As mentioned at the beginning of this chapter, you should never give your address or phone number to someone you suspect might be involved with a cult. Instead, take the individual's name number and address, and initiate contact yourself if you wish. Stay in control! Don't allow yourself to be pressured into revealing personal information. People who have released their addresses and phone numbers have learned the hard way the unbelievable nuisance that can result.

Most of all, though, you will find that the best possible advantage over a cult recruiter is the ability to ask him direct, penetrating questions. The following are some that I have found to be most effective:

- **How long have you (the recruiter) been involved? Are you trying to recruit me into any type of organization?**

I like to find out very quickly who I am dealing with. A person who has been involved in a destructive cult for less than one year is usually very inexperienced. He is less likely to lie, and his lies are not as convincing as those of a more experienced recruiter. If the person has been involved for many years, I expect to get concrete answers to all my questions, and will confront the person with an exclamation such as "You've been a member for X number of years and you don't know the answer!"

When confronted about recruitment, very often the recruiter will answer, "No, I just like you and want to share this with you. What you decide to do with this information will be totally up to you." Fine. Just keep this question in mind, because if the group is a destructive cult, it will become obvious to you at some point that you are indeed being recruited. At that point, you can remember that the recruiter lied to you. Get appropriately angry and walk away.

■ **Can you tell me the names of all other organizations that are affiliated with this group?**

What you are trying to uncover here are the names of front groups. A cult recruiter will usually be taken off guard by this question and ask you what you mean. Ask again if there are any other groups or organizations that the group uses as affiliates, or has ever used in the past. If the recruiter tells you he doesn't know, tell him to find out and write them all down. You will call him tomorrow to find out what the names are.

Even though the person tells you there are no other names, at some point you might discover the person was lying. At that point, get angry, become assertive, and walk out. If you never ask this question, then you will never know specifically that you were lied to.

■ **Who is the top leader? What are his background and qualifications? Does he have any criminal record?**

You may or may not get a straight answer to these questions. The recruiter may or may not tell you the name of the head person of the group. He might use the name of the sub-leader in America, the state, or the city in an effort to cover up. He also might not know anything about the leader's background or criminal record, because he may never have found out himself. You may then ask the person, "How could you have gotten involved with a group without checking these things out first?" Remember, a destructive cult tries to get a person's commitment first, before disclosing important information. A legitimate group will always give information first, and ask for commitment only when the person feels ready.

■ **What does your group believe? Does it believe that the ends justify the means? Is deception allowed in certain circumstances?**

Most cult recruiters will not want to explain what they believe right there on the spot. They are trained to use your curiosity to get you over to hear a lecture, watch a videotape, or attend a program. In this way they know they will have a better chance of influencing you if you are in their environment.

If a person is not willing to summarize the key points of the group's beliefs right there and then, you can be sure that he is hiding something. Of course, he might say that he is just afraid you will get a misconception from a short description. Ask him for it anyway. *Any legitimate group will be able to summarize its central beliefs.* Destructive cults will not want to do so. If you find out later that this description was a gross distortion filled with inaccuracies, you have every right to get angry and leave. The cult members will most assuredly try to convince you that they had to lie to you because you have been brainwashed by the media against them, and you would have never listened if they told you the truth. Don't buy this "ends justify the means" rationalization. No legitimate organization needs to lie to people in order to help them.

- **What are members expected to do once they join? Do I have to quit school or work, donate my money and property, or cut myself off from family members and friends who might oppose my membership?**

If you are being approached by a destructive cult, the person you meet may tell you that you will be expected to do little or nothing once you join. However, this question will make most cult members very uncomfortable and defensive. Watch the recruiter's non-verbal reaction carefully when you ask this question. Ask the person what he did when he first met the group and what he is doing now.

- **Is your group considered to be controversial by anyone? If people are critical of your group, what are their main objections?**

This is a nice open-ended question, something to probe just how much the person knows or is willing to discuss. If you ask this question politely and with a smile, you will be surprised at how many times you will hear "Oh, some people think that we are a cult and that we are all brainwashed! Isn't that silly? Do I look brainwashed?" To that question I will usually respond, "Oh, how are people supposed to look if they are brainwashed?" I generally find that the person I'm speaking to then gets very uncomfortable and, if I continue to probe, finds some excuse to leave.

- **How do you feel about former members of your group? Have you ever sat down to speak with a former member to find out why he left the group? If not, why not? Does your group impose restrictions on communicating with former members?**

This is one of the most revealing sets of questions you can ask any cult member. Any legitimate organization would never discourage contact with former members. Likewise, legitimate groups would support any member's decision to leave, even though they might not like it.

Destructive cults, on the other hand, do not accept any reasons for a person's departure no matter what they are. Likewise, cult groups make sure to instill fear in members, insuring that they stay away from critics and former members. Although you might hear some experienced cult recruiters say "Sure, some of my best friends have left," when you probe further and ask them for specifics, you may find out they have been lying. I always pursue such a response with questions such as "What specific reasons did they give for leaving" and "Do they say that they are happier now that they have left?" Again, the recruiter is usually at a loss for words.

- **What are the three things you like the least about the group and the leader?**

I can't remember how many times I have seen reporters and television hosts ask cult members whether or not they were brainwashed. The cult member usually smiles and says, "Of course not, that's ridiculous." It is absurd, however, to expect an objective answer from someone under mind control. A much better challenge for such people would be "Tell me three things that you don't like about the group or the leader." If you get an opportunity to catch a cult member off guard and ask that question, I suggest you watch his face very carefully. The pupils in his eyes will dilate, and he will act momentarily stunned. When he does answer, he will very likely say that there is nothing he can think of that he doesn't like. Cult members will generally give some variation on that reply because they are simply not permitted to talk critically, particularly on television.

If you get a chance to continue your questioning, ask the person what else he would rather do in his life than be a member of the group. The answer is likely to be "Nothing."

The clincher question is whether or not the person has taken the time to talk with former members and read critical literature in order to make up his own mind. A person under mind control might say that he would be willing to do this. However, I have often seen family members call the member's bluff, and almost always the cult member doesn't follow through. If he does, he is well on his way out of the group.

If you make it through all the above questions and feel reasonably comfortable that the person you spoke with was being straight with you, and you are still interested in learning more about the group, I would strongly suggest that you do several other things. You can ask other members of the group the same questions and see if you get consistent answers. If there are vast differences, you might want to confront them with that fact and see what kind of response you get.

Before you attend any program, be advised that you should still research the group independently. Contact the Cult Awareness Network (CAN) to see if they have any information on this group. It never hurts to be cautious.

If CAN does not have any information on the group, and you still are interested, go to the program with a trusted friend. In this way, you will have someone you can trust to discuss what you see and hear. Destructive cults, as a rule, will always try to find some convenient way to split you up from your friend. "Divide and conquer" is the rule here. Of course, it will seem to be quite spontaneous and benign, but the effect is still the same. Typically, one cult member will start talking to your friend and then another will start to ask you questions. At first you are standing next to each other, within minutes you are several feet away, and if you let it happen, at the end of the evening you are at opposite ends of the room. Some groups are much more obvious and tell participants to pair up with people they don't know. Don't let anyone split you up. Demand to stay with your friend. If you are pressured to conform, or are confronted by group leaders, simply walk out.

If you find yourself in an indoctrination session, stand up and announce that you don't like being manipulated and controlled. The louder you speak, the faster you will be escorted from the room. Who knows? Several other people might jump at the opportunity to leave with you.

Don't let your curiosity get the best of you. Too many people have been recruited into these organizations because they were overconfident that they could "handle" themselves in any situation. Curiosity and overconfidence have been the downfall of many people, including myself. Placing yourself in a potentially dangerous situation just isn't worth it.

Chapter 7

Exit-Counseling: Freedom Without Coercion

W HEN most people begin to search for ways to release friends or relatives from cults, they know little or nothing about mind control, the characteristics of destructive cults, or how to go about rescuing someone in a cult. They may think the only available option is "deprogramming," without knowing that deprogramming involves forcible abduction of the cult member, a fee of from $18,000 to $30,000, and lengthy sessions intended to restore the person to himself.

Non-coercive ways to help now exist. Exit-counselors such as myself are now using therapeutic techniques that are well established in the mental health profession, along with the latest techniques in counseling. In addition, at present almost all exit-counselors are themselves former cult members.

This chapter is intended to serve as a guide to understanding how exit-counseling works, through three case histories of interventions I have conducted. The dialogues in this chapter are reconstructed from memory, but they are a faithful reflection of real events which occurred with real people in my counseling work. I hope to help people understand that there is an effective alternative to deprogramming.

Because I experienced deprogramming I am familiar with its drawbacks. When I was deprogrammed in 1976, very few options were available to my parents and concerned relatives of other cult members. Either they tried to keep in contact with the member and hoped he or she would leave unassisted, or else they hired a deprogrammer. Cult leaders saw deprogramming as a terrible threat because they were losing many long-term, devoted members and leaders—and because these former members were talking to the media and revealing details of the cults' operations. Unlike "walk-away" ex-members, who tended to be ridden with guilt and kept their involvement very quiet, deprogrammees had a support network that understood what they had been through and gave them the strength and encouragement to speak out.

By the late 1970s, the question of cult mind control had become intertwined in the public eye with the issue of forcible deprogramming. This occurrence was partly the result of public relations campaigns financed by certain major cults to discredit critics and divert the debate from the cults themselves.[1]

The propaganda labeled deprogramming as "the greatest threat to religious liberty of all time." Deprogrammers were falsely portrayed as beating and raping people to force them to recant their religious beliefs. Influenced by this campaign, at least one movie portrayed deprogrammers as money-hungry thugs who were just as bad as cult leaders.

For the record, I know of no instance of deprogramming (and I've met hundreds of deprogrammees) that involved any physical abuse such as beating or rape. No family I have ever met would go to the extreme of rescuing a loved one through deprogramming and allow anyone to harm their child in any way.

Nevertheless, the truth is that deprogramming is extremely risky in legal terms, and often emotionally traumatic. In a classic deprogramming, a cult member would be located and physically snatched off a street corner, hurled into a waiting car or van, and driven to some secret location, perhaps a motel room. There the security team would guard him twenty-four hours a day while the deprogrammer, former cult members, and family members presented information, and argued with him. Windows would be nailed shut or barricaded, because members had been known to dive out of a second-story window to avoid the so-called "faith-breaking" process. The member would sometimes be accompanied to the bathroom in an effort to prevent suicide attempts. He would be held for days, perhaps weeks, until he "snapped out of" the cult's mind control or, in some cases, pretended to do so.

In the deprogrammings I participated in during 1976 and 1977, the cult member was usually confronted while visiting home rather than grabbed off a sidewalk. Even so, when the cult member was told he or she couldn't leave, there was almost always a violent reaction. I have been punched, kicked, and spat on; had hot coffee thrown in my face; and had tape recorders hurled at me. Indeed, if I hadn't had a cast on my leg from toes to groin during my own deprogramming, I'm sure I would have done the same. Cult members are indoctrinated to behave that way: to stay "faithful" to the group no matter what. At first the cult member often becomes even more convinced that his family, which has resorted to such extremes, is the very embodiment of evil.

In such situations the cult member's anger and resentment can take years to dissipate, even if the deprogramming is successful. I knew one woman who, several years after she was deprogrammed from a short-term membership in the Moonies, rejoined the group for over a year and then quit on her own—as if, she told me, she had to prove she could do it by herself. Unfortunately, during that time in the group she was paraded around, denouncing deprogramming all over the United States.

There is nothing so terrifying as being held prisoner thinking you are about to be tortured or sexually abused—the experiences that cult leaders drill members to expect in a deprogramming. As you can imagine, good counseling in such a situation is difficult at best. The member immediately clams up, chanting, praying, or meditating to shut out any external influence. It may be hours or days before he sees that the cult leader was wrong—that he isn't going to be tortured, that the deprogrammers are caring, sensitive people, and that there really are legitimate questions to be looked at. Only then does he start to respond.

I decided not to participate in forcible interventions, believing it was imperative to find another approach. Legal and voluntary access to the cult member had to be found; family and friends were the key. But they needed to become knowledgeable about cults and mind control, and they needed to be coached in how to communicate with a cultist effectively.

NON-COERCIVE EXIT COUNSELING: THREE CASE HISTORIES

The non-coercive approach I have developed attempts to accomplish with finesse what deprogramming does with force. Family members and friends have to work together as a team and plan their strategy to influence the cult member. Although the non-coercive approach will not work in every case, it has proved to be the option most families prefer. Forcible intervention can be kept as a last resort if all other attempts fail.

The non-coercive approach requires excellent information in order to succeed. At the first phone call, the information-gathering and information-disseminating begins.

The O'Brien Family [2]

In December 1987, a Mr. O'Brien called me and expressed his concern about his son's involvement with a group known as the Boston Church of Christ (Also known as Multiplying Ministries, the Boston Church of Christ should not be confused with the mainline Church of Christ or with the United Church of Christ, an inheritor of the New England Congregational tradition.[3]). He had gotten my name from Buddy Martin, an evangelist with the Cape Cod Church of Christ (a mainline church) who strongly denounces the authoritarian "shepherding/discipleship" cult tactics used by the group in Boston.[4]

Mr. O'Brien told me he had grown more and more worried about his son's involvement. George had lost a great deal of weight, was always exhausted, had abandoned his plans to graduate from a small liberal arts college in upstate New York, and was becoming more and more incapable of making simple decisions. He always had to get his "discipleship" partner's advice before doing almost anything.

Mr. O'Brien asked about my own background and whether I thought this particular group was a destructive cult. I told him about my background, and that I had successfully counseled some thirty people out of this particular group in the past five years. He was very happy to hear this.

The O'Briens wanted to know what makes a group a destructive cult, and asked several probing questions about my own values and ethics. I told them that, for me, encouraging the person to think for himself was paramount and that I was careful not to impose my own belief system on a client. My role was to present information, to do individual and family counseling as needed, and to facilitate family communication.

We talked for about half an hour, and I agreed to mail information on my approach as well as a background questionnaire and photocopies of articles on the Boston Church of Christ. I also gave them phone numbers of some other families I have worked with. I told them to answer the questions on my form as completely as possible. The more information the family and friends could supply about themselves, the better.

Getting written information from a family is a good place to start. It forces the family to think through a variety of issues about the individual, themselves, the cult involvement, and how they have responded to it so far. It also gives me a good starting point for person-to-person discussions.

It matters to me how much effort a family will make to do a thorough job. The questionnaire elicits different responses from one-line answers to a forty-four-page, single-spaced typewritten response. Normally, six to eight pages are filled out.

Several areas are of special interest. What are the family relationships like between siblings and between them and the parents? What kind of person was the individual now in the cult? Did he have many friends? Use drugs? Have clear-cut life goals? Did he suffer any particular trauma or stress during his life such as the death of a close friend or relative, parental divorce, or a difficult move to a new city? Did he have a well-formed political or social value system? The healthier his family relationships and the healthier his sense of identity before he was in the cult, the easier my job usually is.

In particular, I wanted to know about George. Who was he before he joined, and how had he changed, aside from weight loss and listlessness? I wanted to know who in the family he was closest to. I wanted to know his state of mind just before joining. I also wanted to know about his education, interests and hobbies, work experience, and religious background.

In all my cases, I want to know how long it took the person to be recruited. Did he go straight in when approached one afternoon, or did it take months or years before he became fully involved? What was it that he *thought* he was joining, and does this bear any similarity to what he now thinks he is in? How long has he been in? Where has he been living—with other members, alone, or with non-members? What has he been doing? Has he ever expressed doubts or difficulties about his membership?

Last, I want to know how family members and friends have reacted: what they have said or done about his being in the group. What books or articles have they read; what people (including professionals) have they contacted? I need to know who is willing and who is not willing to help rescue him. Interestingly, a close sibling who starts out unwilling to help often becomes the most important element in a successful case.

Once I get the questionnaire back, the next step is to talk again on the telephone. Now I can ask more specific questions to round out the picture and assess what to do next. In most cases, I ask the family to talk with other people for information and sometimes obtain additional counseling. It is important during this preparation period that the family meet and talk with others who have the same problem, especially others who have successfully rescued someone. It is also good for the family to talk to former members of the group to gain insight into their loved one's mindset.

Next I set up a meeting with as many family members and friends as possible, usually in the family's home. Here I try to observe how the various personalities relate to each other. I spend a lot of time at this meeting teaching about cults and mind control and coaching people on the parts they will need to play. It is crucial that people understand exactly what the problem is and what they can do to help.

I discuss communication strategies: ways to connect with the person and get him to open up. We also may review various plans for an intervention. This meeting is often taped so concerned friends and relatives not able to attend can also benefit from it.

One thing I stress is that every one must pull together and look at the rescue as a team effort. This takes the load off any one person's shoulders and guarantees that the cult member will be influenced by as many people as possible. I urge them to contact other family members and friends and persuade them to help; to study books, articles, and videotapes; and to keep files.

If I am contacted within the first few months of a recruitment, the prognosis for a successful exit within a year is extremely good. On the other hand, if the person has been in the group for ten years when I am contacted, it might be quite some time before an intervention can be successfully attempted (depending on the state of the family's relationship). But long-term members are by no means hopeless. They just require a lot of patience and continued effort. In fact, I have discovered that in many ways it is easier to counsel someone out of a long-term membership. Such a person knows the harsh realities of life in the group—the lies, the manipulations, the broken promises of cult leaders—whereas the new member may still be walking on air during the honeymoon stage.

In this particular case, George had been involved for two and a half years. He was living in an apartment with other "believers." He was still in contact with his mother and father and less so with his sister, Naomi. His parents were not strongly religious and objected to George's rigidity of belief in the group's interpretation of the Bible. George had come to disregard his parents' attitudes as simply "non-Christian." As in so many other families, the cult membership had dredged up some angry and resentful feelings buried on both sides. The family was deadlocked.

By the time George's parents decided on intervention, they had long since realized that the oppositional approach was getting them nowhere. George's father decided to try the opposite tack. He asked George if he could attend a Bible study, and even went to a couple of Sunday services. Of course, George and his discipleship partners interpreted his father's attendance as a sign that "God was moving" in his father's life. Strategically, it was an important step to repairing George's relationship with his family.

Mr. O'Brien explained to him that he wanted to learn more about his son's church because he loved his son. This was true. He could honestly refrain from saying he wanted to join, because he didn't. What he wanted was to do more research and rebuild his relationship with his son. In fact, not only George's father but everyone in the family was deeply involved in trying to learn as much as they could about the group. George never doubted his parents' love for him, nor, deep down, his love for them. He was just taught that people were either part of God (in the church) or on the side of Satan.

After numerous meetings and phone calls, the family and I began to make plans. George had no idea that his family was in touch with me or Buddy Martin. The issue of whether to be deceptive was, as always, important and thorny. The O'Briens had to come to terms with a variety of options. Should they simply tell George what they had learned and ask him to speak with us? Ethically, that was what they wanted to do. And yet they were dealing with a mind control cult. If they told him they wanted him to meet people critical of the group, would he get upset and break off contact?

I encouraged the family to speak with several former members and ask them how a group member would respond to the straightforward approach. Without exception, the ex-members told the family that if they did that, George would immediately consult his discipleship partner for advice. From that moment on, the group would be forewarned and would do everything in its power to convince him to avoid contact with a family obviously controlled by Satan.

My preference is always to have someone ask the cult member if he would be willing to do research on "the other side of the story," and see what reaction this elicits. Such a request should be done by a sibling or a friend rather than a parent. If it is done in that way, it is much less threatening.

If the cult member accepts the opportunity to meet with former members, the place and time should be agreed upon immediately. The person who is to ask for the meeting must also discuss the fact that if other group members find out, they will try to convince him to break the agreement. "Will you fulfill your promise regardless of the group's pressure?" is a question he must be asked. Then a verbal contract is established.

This type of completely "overt" or open intervention works best with people who are not fully indoctrinated or who are having questions or doubts.

I wanted to know whether George had expressed any dissatisfaction or disillusionment with the group. No, the O'Briens said: absolutely none. He was totally committed. He trusted only people within the group. He was pro-grammed to think that all others were "dead," that is, "unspiritual." I advised George's family that the decision was theirs, but that there was only a small chance they would even get access to him if they tried the open approach.

We decided that the best course of action was to arrange for George to be away from the group by inviting him to his grandmother's eighty-sixth birthday party on Cape Cod. After the party on Sunday night, his parents would find some excuse to stay overnight and tell George they would drive back to Boston in the morning. The next morning, the family would tell him at the breakfast table that they were very sorry they had not told him before, but that they had arranged to spend the next three days with a Church of Christ minister, a counselor, and a former member.

I coached the family extensively on what to say and how to say it. I wanted them to make sure he didn't phone the group, and to try their best to talk him out of running away. They needed to reassure him that they were not trying to take him away from God, nor were they trying to hurt him. Indeed, all they wanted was for him to have access to information about the group that he would otherwise have never heard. They were to ask him to pray, and tell him they trusted that his faith in the power of God is stronger than his fear of Satan.

I instructed the family to ask George to agree to a three-day period of research in which he would be free to come and go, to take as many breaks as he wanted, and to decide what areas he wanted to concentrate on.

Monday morning found me in a Cape Cod coffee shop with Buddy Martin and Ellen Queeney, a former member I had counseled out of the Paris branch of the group last summer. We sat around a table and waited for four hours. Meanwhile, the family was trying to persuade George to agree to their terms. They called me half a dozen times for support and advice. The family tried everything I told them to do. George was adamant. He would agree to nothing beyond meeting us for a few hours. We decided to go ahead and do the best we could. Before we left the coffeeshop, a bunch of locals told us that we had just set a record for sitting in one spot. I laughed and thought to myself, "Boy, if they only knew what was going on!"

George was flushed, angry and hostile when we walked in and met him. It was the first time we had ever seen him in person. We introduced ourselves, and he was most surprised to meet Buddy. Here was a Bible-toting fundamentalist minister from a Church of Christ. George asked to speak alone with each of us: first myself, then Ellen, then Buddy. Naturally, he was scared and confused. We tried our best to make him as comfortable as possible and give him as much sense of control as possible. It was imperative that he realize that this situation was an opportunity for him—to learn, to grow, and to prove to his family that he wasn't under mind control and knew what he was doing. That was what I tried to tell him when he wanted to talk to me in private.

George proved to be as indoctrinated as anyone from his cult I have ever worked with. He was extremely resistant to the idea that he might benefit from anything that was being discussed.

Buddy Martin's participation was the key. In his turn alone with George, he began to cite specific Bible verses and asked George what he thought each meant. He began to show George that although the group claimed to be following the Bible, in fact they were taking passages out of context, deliberately ignoring other verses that affected their meaning. Since the group had programmed George to believe in a literal interpretation of the Bible, he could hardly object to examining it. This was the opening by which he began to admit the possibility that the group might be less than perfect.

With that foothold established, George was willing to listen to me give the background of the cult's leader, Kip McKean, and his own recruitment and indoctrination by Chuck Luca into Crossroads, a cult in Gainesville, Florida,[5] back in the 1970s. It was there that McKean may have learned to use the mind control methods he now uses. George had never heard of Crossroads. We showed him a letter written by McKean in March 1986 to Crossroads Church leaders, and printed in their bulletin, saying he "owed his very soul" to them.[6] George was shocked. We produced a letter by the elders of the Memorial Church of Christ in Houston, Texas, written in 1977 to announce why they were firing McKean as one of their ministers because of his un-Biblical teachings.[7]

With that as a starting point we could begin discussing the characteristics of destructive cults and mind control in general. Without this frame of reference it would be impossible to show George what had happened to him. At this point in the discussion I always talk about other groups. In my experience, most modern-day cultists have a negative view of the Moonies (Moonies excepted, of course), so I usually begin with my own story.

This point of departure helps to minimize thought-stopping and defensiveness. I lay out the specific behavioral components of mind control, making sure to point out Lifton's study of Chinese Communist thought reform. Next I describe what it's like inside another, similar group. In this way the parallels between groups become blatantly apparent, and it is more effective because the person makes the connections himself.

The information was very intense for George. He needed to regulate the flow of what he was hearing. Every couple of hours or so, he would stand up and announce that he needed to go for a walk and pray. This happened several times each day for the three days. At night I stayed at a nearby bed-and-breakfast place where I was able to rest and map out strategy. Each time George walked out the door, we were never quite sure whether he would return. It would be easy for him to stick his thumb out as he walked along the road and hitchhike back to Boston or phone the cult for a ride. But to try to stop him would have ensured his lack of trust in us thereafter. We were in this for the long haul. If he walked out now, the family would simply have to continue the information giving process each time they saw or spoke to him. We had to trust that he wanted to do the right thing. Besides, the family knew that I would not participate if they tried any type of forcible intervention.

When George complained about the deception his parents had used to get him to his grandmother's house, they apologized profusely. I asked him to put himself into their shoes and suggest any other course of action they could have taken that would have been effective. He could think of none. He knew that if he had received any advance warning, he would indeed have gone straight to his superiors and they would have dissuaded him.

His parents told him he had turned down a previous offer to meet former members and read critical information. He was astonished; he didn't even remember it. They reminded him he had met his cousin Sally a month earlier. At the parents' request, she had made just such an offer. George had turned her down cold. His parents told him they felt they had no other choice but to proceed with this approach.

During those three days, I was able to do a good deal of counseling with the family on ways to communicate more effectively and work on some of their own issues and concerns quite separate from the cult involvement. In this way George could see that the whole family was learning and growing together and that his involvement could now be a stepping stone to developing closer relationships with everyone.

Even after the three days were over, George was not willing to say he would never return to the group. He did say that he wanted more time to study and think about what he learned. He decided not to return to his apartment but stay with his parents. There he would read books and articles, watch videotapes of shows on cults, and continue to speak with and meet other former members.

Within a month, George declared to his family that he would never return to the Boston Church of Christ. He had attended services and Bible studies at the Burlington Church of Christ, one of the eighteen thousand mainline Churches of Christ, where he met some sixty-five other refugees from the Boston group. He now says he feels far happier than when he was in the cult and has a much better understanding of the Bible. Since leaving, he has spent a good deal of time helping others understand the destructive aspects of this group.

Although George's parents would probably prefer that he attend their Unitarian church with them, they respect his right to choose his own way. His father has been attending a Bible study group with his son on Tuesday nights in order to learn and get closer to him. Indeed, the O'Briens were willing to intervene in his life only to the point where he would be able to recognize and understand the mind control practices of destructive cults. I have never accepted clients who indicate that their reason for making an intervention is at all self-serving. Their commitment must be to help the individual think for himself.

THE BELIEFS UNDERLYING MY APPROACH

Since cults lure people into what amounts to a psychological trap, my job as an exit-counselor is to show a cult member four things.

First, I demonstrate to him that *he is in a trap*—a situation where he is psychologically disabled and can't get out. Second, I show him that *he didn't originally choose to enter a trap.* Third, I point out that *other people in other groups are in similar traps.* Fourth, I tell him that *it is possible to get out of the trap.* While these four points might seem very obvious to people outside a cult, they are not at all immediately apparent to anyone under mind control. It takes someone who understands what it really means to be caught in the trap of a destructive cult to convey this message with the necessary strength and determination. This last reason is why former members, especially former cult leaders, make the best exit-counselors.

My approach rests on several core beliefs about people. One is that *people need and want to grow.* Life is ever-changing, and people inherently move in a direction that will support and encourage growth.

It is important that *people focus on the here-and-now.* What has been done in the past is over. The focus should not be on what they "did wrong" or "didn't do," but on what they can do now. The past is useful only insofar as it provides information that may be valuable to the present.

It is also my observation and belief that *people will always choose what they think is best for them at any given time.* In my experience, people will always do what they believe is *best for them* on the basis of their information and experiences. The member permitted himself to be indoctrinated in the first place only because he believed that the group was wonderful and that he had something to gain from it.

I also believe that *everyone is unique* and *every situation is different.* Each person has a special way of understanding and interacting with reality. Therefore, my approach is totally client-centered. I adjust myself to fit the client's needs. I don't expect him to fit to my needs. In my approach, the counselor's job is to understand the person thoroughly—what he values, what he needs, what he wants, and how he thinks. I have to be able to step inside his head—in a way, to "be him," in order to understand and help him do what *he wants to do*. My approach depends on having faith that deep, deep down, even the most committed member of a mind control group wants out.

Last, *my approach is family-centered*. When someone is recruited into a destructive cult, everyone he knows and loves is affected. Family members and friends are vital in most successful cases. They can be trained to be maximally effective whenever they communicate with the cult member. In this way, emotional and personal leverage can be used to gain his cooperation.

Of course, this way of working demands a lot from the family. They must be willing to learn new ways of communicating, and to deal with troublesome issues that may be lying dormant. If there are any significant family problems, they are best addressed and, it is hoped, resolved before an intervention is attempted.

When the focus is kept on the family, everyone changes. The cult member becomes aware that positive things are occurring outside the group. Family members learn how to build up rapport and trust, and how to plant questions in the cult member's mind.

A family's love is a much stronger force than the conditional love given by cult members and leaders. A family's love supports one's right to grow into an autonomous adult and make one's own life decisions. A cult's love attempts to keep a person forever as a dependent adolescent—threatening to be withdrawn if the person makes his own life decisions that differ from the leader's orders. When family members learn how to interact effectively, they do a great deal to help the individual come away from the group. During the intervention, this factor often becomes crucial.

When I counsel a cultist, I never try to take the group away from him or him away from the group. If I did he would only feel threatened, and rightly so. Instead, I always look for ways for him to grow by offering different perspectives and possibilities. I help people to see choices they didn't know existed, then encourage them to do what they think is best for them. I do whatever I can to let them feel in control.

As I have said before, cult mind control never fully succeeds in erasing a person's core self ("John-John"). It does impose a dominating cult identity ("John-cultist") that continually suppresses the real self. As a Unification Church member I thought that I had successfully "died to myself." I, Steve-Moonie, thought that the old Steve Hassan was dead. Yet the core "me" woke back up during my deprogramming. He had been there all along. I was able to remember all the contradictions, conflicts, and broken promises of Moon that I had experienced—but not acted on—while a member, and that realization enabled me to leave. Somewhere inside I had known it all along.

Successfully connecting with a person's core identity is what enables me to help someone walk away from a cult. If the core identity is happy and content with the cult involvement, there is little I can do. Such a person must not be mind controlled at all. He has chosen to be there. But such people rarely come to my attention. Families call because they observe something terrible happening. And I have discovered that when someone in slavery is given a free choice, he or she does not choose to be enslaved—not when he could be making decisions for his own life, having unrestricted normal relationships with people, and pursuing his own interests and dreams.

Along with these core beliefs, my approach has some very distinctive features. First, I focus on the *process* of change. What this means is that *how* people come to change is more important than *what* or *why* they change. Since I believe that people are interested in growing and learning, my approach is also educational. I do a lot of teaching—about psychology, communication, mind control issues, and other destructive cults, as well as a lot about the particular group's history, leadership, and doctrinal contradictions.

DIFFICULT CASES: THE COVERT INTERVENTION

When a cult member refuses to speak with people who can "offer him the other side of the story," or walks out of an intervention and returns to the cult, all is not lost. Communication about key issues has at least been opened. He might feel badly about how he treated his loved ones and agree to talk at a future date.

The timing of the intervention may have been poor. Perhaps it happened right after the person came from an intensive re-indoctrination experience, or just got married in the group, or received a promotion. Timing can make all the difference. Naturally, the best time is when the member is in a "down" period, and there are cycles of emotional ups and downs in a cult member's life as with anyone else.

After a failed intervention, it might take several weeks or months for a family to re-establish a relationship with the cultist. At that point, they have two choices. They can back off, telling the member that they've done all they can and that when he wants to look at the information or talk to former members, they'll be happy to accommodate him. Or they can choose to attempt a covert intervention.

A covert intervention is the most difficult to accomplish successfully. It is an attempt to counsel the cult member without his knowing that the family is trying to help him re-evaluate his involvement. It is tricky to find a pretext for me to meet the individual and gain enough time to do much good.

Someone observing the preparations for a covert intervention would be reminded of the television program *Mission: Impossible.* A team is assembled. The target's psychological profile is scrutinized for vulnerabilities, interests, and patterns of behavior. A plot is hatched to meet him and get him involved enough to enable the mission to be carried out.

A covert intervention may be necessary if the cult member's relationship with family or friends is severely damaged. Such cases frequently involve long-term members whose families long ago passed their limits of frustration and pain, and said or did things that severed the relationship. Covert interventions involve using deception, something I accuse cults of doing, which makes me uncomfortable. However, I am not trying to make someone into my follower; once my job of presenting information, laying out alternatives, and counseling is accomplished, it is up to the individual to make use of the experience.

Margaret Rogers and the Children of God [8]

Margaret Rogers was a member of Moses David Berg's Children of God cult[9] (now renamed the Family of Love) for some ten years. During most of that time her two sisters and brother had received only half a dozen letters. Margaret, who then went by a name assigned to her by the cult, traveled all over the world with this unusual group. Her family generally had never known how to contact her, except once when they were able to visit her in the Philippines. At that time she was married to another member and had three children.

During that visit, her family pleaded with her to take some time away from the group and talk with former members. She showed a distinct willingness to do so, and in fact badly needed food and rest as well as a thorough medical examination. They didn't mention that they knew the group was making her do "flirty fishing," the Children of God term for a form of prostitution.[10] This is a major way the cult earns money and tries to attract male converts. The Rogers family knew they wouldn't have the stomach to discuss it.

At that meeting, all of them witnessed instants when Margaret momentarily returned to "herself"—her face and demeanor relaxing and becoming like the person they once knew—particularly when her brother and sisters talked about memories of childhood, or people and events back in their hometown. It was also clear that her husband was a hard-core cult member who showed no such flashes of his former identity. Furthermore, he always made the decisions for her. Margaret's family returned to the United States glad to have seen her and their grandchildren—and committed to trying to rescue her.

Her parents attended one of my communications workshops for family members and asked me to help. They told me they wished they had had the workshop's guidance before their trip to the Philippines, or even that they had taken me along. I told them to keep learning all they could about the group: its buzz words, lifestyle, and beliefs. To this end I put them in touch with several former members. I also encouraged them to continue practicing the communications techniques I taught them. Within a year, Margaret contacted them from Mexico and asked if they could again come to visit.

We sat down and discussed the options. How could we get me to her, keep the husband away as long as possible, and evoke a minimum of suspicion all at the same time? We concluded that the parents would not make the trip at all. They represented the clearest threat to Margaret's cult involvement, having been bitterly critical from the very start. Her two sisters and brother would go for a week. I would go too, posing as her sister Lisa's boyfriend.

We manufactured a story that Mr. Rogers was under doctor's orders not to take such a trip—he had a problem with his heart. Mrs. Rogers was unable to get time off from work and felt obliged to stay close to home to help her husband if necessary. Bob, Margaret's brother, called up his company's branch office in Mexico City and talked them into giving a job interview to Margaret's husband, who we knew was looking for a way to earn some legitimate and steady money. The cult's colony in Mexico was scattered, and member families had been told to work on their own.

Bob next convinced the husband to follow up the offer of a job interview. Bob would accompany him to Mexico City for a few days to give us time alone with Margaret.

The plan was to assess Margaret's state of mind and try to convince her to come back to the United States with her children. We hoped that after the previous visit she might be more homesick, and that if she didn't really love her husband, as we suspected, we had a good chance of succeeding.

Everything started out smoothly. When we arrived, Margaret and her husband showed little or no sign of anxiety. We all spent the first day together, and our group painted a rosy picture of ourselves. In no way did we indicate that we were bothered by their lifestyle. We went out to eat lots of good food, went shopping and bought the whole family new clothes, and had a good time. We were interested to notice that Margaret and her husband did not try to sell the group to us in any way.

Bob left with the husband the next day, and we invited Margaret to our hotel and took a room for her and the kids. We volunteered to take the kids out and recommended that she lie down and catch up on some sleep in the meanwhile.

When we returned five hours later, she was still asleep. She was obviously exhausted. When she got up, her face had a lot more color. We ordered up room service. It was clear that she was not used to eating so well or to being served in such a nice hotel. And she was thoroughly enjoying it!

After dinner we started up a conversation. It began with talk of pleasant childhood memories. Then her sisters started talking more and more about how they missed her, and how they felt robbed of a sister they loved so much. Tears started to flow and long hugs were shared. Then the discussion turned to the children, and their future. Was this the way she always envisioned raising a family? Was Tom her vision of an ideal husband?

The time seemed ripe. "Hey, listen, Margaret," said one of her sisters. "How would you like to come back with us to Connecticut?"

"Oh my gosh, I'd love that!" Margaret answered excitedly. But then just as quickly she sank back into the couch and said. "Oh, I can't do that."

"Why not?" Lisa asked.

"Because I just can't."

I stepped in. "Is it because you believe God wouldn't like it if you did?"

"Yes," she said. "Besides, Tom would never do it unless he was told to by Elias." Elias was the closest leader. It was the first time Margaret had mentioned this aspect of the group to her sisters.

"What would *you* like to do?" I asked again.

"I don't know, I don't think I can," she said with a tone of disgust.

"What would happen if God came and told you to go back to Connecticut?" I asked.

"He would never do that," she answered.

"But what if he did?" I pressed. "What if he told you in a loud clear voice that his will was to take the children and go to Connecticut for a few months? Would you be obedient?" I said, my voice rising. "Where is your commitment, to God or to the group?"

She thought about it for a while and answered "If God told me to go to Connecticut, then I would go."

"Even if your husband or another member told you to stay?" I asked, insistently. I was pushing it, but I wanted to see how far I could get.

"If God told me to go, I would go, even if others told me to stay," she declared.

Very good, I thought. Now for the next step. I asked her "How would you *know* if God wanted you to go, if you don't pray and ask him what his will is? Have you ever asked him a question like this one?"

"No, but I will tonight. But I don't think he wants me to go to Connecticut."

"Oh, so you're going to tell God what to answer," I said. "Why don't you reach down to the bottom of your soul and pray without any foregone conclusions about what God wants for you and your children in this life?" My voice was intense. "Pray fervently and clearly, putting your total faith that what he wants will be what is right for you."

Margaret asked me if I really believed in God that strongly and I told her I did. Then she asked me about my spiritual life. That gave me all the opening I needed to launch into my experience in the Moonies—how I came to believe that God was speaking through my leaders and that I couldn't doubt, ask critical questions, or even leave the group. I explained phobia indoctrination, and showed her how I was finally able to imagine a future for myself outside of the group because I had met so many former Moonies who still were very spiritual, good people after they left.

She was listening attentively. I explained that I had come to distrust my own inner voice while I was in the Moonies, and to believe that it was evil, when in fact, I came to learn, it was a direct link to God. I described how I had been controlled by fear and guilt, and how in both the Moonies and the Children of God there was complete control over the information we received. Both leaders saw themselves as God's chosen one on Earth, both had absolute authority, and both were extremely wealthy.

"Do you believe that God gave man free will just so he could take it away through deception and mind control?" I asked her. "Think about it: do you believe in a God that wants his children to be robots or at the very best slaves? If he wanted that," I pointed out, "he never would have given Adam and Eve free will! Isn't it a big contradiction?"

Margaret's mouth hung open and her eyes were wide as saucers. I gave her a hug and excused myself. I announced that I needed to be by myself and was going for a walk. She needed time to absorb what I had said. I was confident that her sisters would help her start working it through and deal with her feelings as they came up.

Later that night I talked with her for a few more hours, mostly trying to empower her. She had a good mind, I told her, she should use it. She had always been an ethical person—did she really believe that the ends justify the means? Was it Christian to use sex to recruit people? She loved her family. Would she let her fears be stronger than her love? I also appealed to her maternal instinct and asked how she felt letting her children grow up in virtual poverty, with no formal education, and with little or no medical attention. I knew that she knew other members' children had died because they didn't get to see doctors.

Before she went to bed I reminded her to pray, and pray hard. "Pray like you never prayed before. Beseech God to show you the way. Ask him what *he* wants you to do!"

That night we let the children sleep with us so she could get an undisturbed night's rest. The next morning Margaret told us of incredible dreams filled with symbols of great struggle and turmoil. In one dream she was lost at night in a forest, not knowing how to get out. In another she was being bombarded by stormy ocean waves alone in a small boat. The third dream she had was of wandering in a field of wildflowers in the middle of a warm, sunny, spring day.

Over breakfast I asked her if she was aware of God's answer to her question. She flashed a smile, which then turned into a frown. She got up from the table and walked to the window. Then after staring outside for a while, she turned and said, "In my heart I think I should go back to the States, but I don't think I can."

I felt as though a hundred-pound weight had just been lifted from my chest, but I tried to show little excitement. Her sisters started to cry.

"What is stopping you?" I queried.

She sighed and thought for a long time. Then she said, "I am afraid."

Her sisters and I went over and the four of us stood there in one massive hug. "Don't worry," I reassured her. "We'll help you in every way we can. Trust God."

We acted as if that settled the matter. Now was the time to get moving. Within two hours we were on our way to the airport. We phoned ahead to her parents and told them the good news. Margaret left a long letter to Tom saying that we were on our way to the States, that she wanted to be alone with the kids and her family for a few weeks, and that she would contact him and let him know when he could come visit, if he wanted to. She assured him that she had decided on this voluntarily—that she had been very unhappy for a long time, and felt that God wanted her to do it.

There were no hitches at the airport. In a situation like this I'm always apprehensive that some crazy thing will go wrong, such as all the planes being full or members of the cult showing up in the waiting area. We talked on the plane ride home, and I told her that I had a few friends who were former members of the Children of God. But I decided that I wasn't going to explain my role until a couple of weeks had passed so she would have time to stabilize. There are a couple of other clients who do not know to this day that I was brought in to counsel them at their family's request.

When she walked into her house for the first time in ten years, she saw balloons and a huge WELCOME HOME! sign hanging from the ceiling. The house was filled with relatives and friends. Tears came streaming down her face. She had forgotten how wonderful life had been for her there. She told me later that she felt like a prisoner of war who had just been released from ten years of captivity. So many people had grown up and changed. The neighborhood had changed a lot. And she was totally unaware of the national and world events of the last decade. She had plenty of catching up to do.

Within a couple of days I arranged for her to sit down with some former members. I was lucky enough to locate someone she had known while in the group. Margaret improved dramatically day by day. She put on weight, started to make jokes, and had color and expression in her face. Her children adapted quickly and joyfully to their new life. Arrangements were made later to help her husband with the support of his family.

No one can come out of a long-term experience like that without emotional problems, and she was no exception. Not all cases, though, are successful. Especially in the early years of my counseling work, I took on several cases in which I was not able to help the person to come out of the cult. In retrospect, some cases had just too many factors going against success, but I tried anyway. Some cases involved the psychopathology of the individual in the group, or in family members themselves. Other cases involved families who neglected to tell me everything about their family history, while in others, there was intentional sabotage by one of the family members.

Alan Brown and the Foundation for Human Understanding[11]

Herbert and Julia Brown's son Alan had been involved in Roy Masters' group, the Foundation for Human Understanding, for over two years. Masters is a professional hypnotist who has a national radio show called *How Your Mind Can Keep You Well* in which he attracts new followers. Alan got involved by listening one night, and sent in his money to order Masters audiotapes on "meditation." Having listened to the tapes myself, I was able to understand that Masters was doing a powerful hypnotic induction—not meditation—as it was claimed. Later, as I studied Roy Masters, I learned that he had gotten into the "exorcism" business: discovering people in his audience who he claimed were possessed and then liberating them—for pay. His place of work was normally a hotel ballroom packed with people.[12]

Unlike most of my clients, the Browns had serious psychological problems. Unfortunately, I didn't realize that until I came to Michigan to do an intervention with their son before he went away for a one-month residential course at Masters' ranch in Oregon.

I knew something was seriously wrong when I walked in the door. The family dog was virtually uncontrollable: jumping, barking, running all over the furniture. The Browns apologized to me, but it was evident that they were at their wits' end. They were constantly undermining each other's authority with the dog: one would tell him to go lie down, and then the other would encourage the dog to sit on his lap. The dog was past being spoiled—the dog was ruined.

Later, when I met Alan, I observed an only child who was obviously spoiled and overprotected. He was also slowly being driven crazy because he was constantly receiving conflicting messages from his two parents, messages they were unaware they were sending. One minute his mother would praise him for mowing the lawn, and the next his father was criticizing him for taking two weeks to actually do it. The father would tell Alan he should get a job, but the mother would tell him he should wait a few more weeks.

It was obvious to me that Alan was desperately trying to get away from his parents' influence. He wanted to be independent, but he didn't know how to begin to do so. He wanted to prove to his parents that he was capable, but his self-esteem was so low that he seemed to be always on the verge of depression. Alan had difficulty socially and had no friends outside of the group when I met him.

In this case, Alan-Alan was not happy or successful. He was truly miserable. From an exit-counseling point of view, there was little from the past that could be used for him to connect with.

Despite disturbing traits of his cult group,[13] as long as his parents continued their dysfunctional style of relating and communicating with him, it seemed that staying in the group at that time was the better choice for him. At least the group offered him an opportunity to socialize with other people, as well as the hope that he would get better by following his savior, Masters.

Clearly, understanding mind control and destructive cults was not enough for Alan. He needed a safe, supportive environment and a good deal of personal and family counseling. Unfortunately, although his parents loved him, they were unwilling to get the help they needed. They wanted me to "get Alan out of the cult," and that was all. On top of that, the Browns also didn't want to invest the money required in a good rehabilitation program for Alan. He absolutely needed to have the experience of being somewhere healthy—not at home or in the cult.

Despite all my efforts, the intervention was doomed from the start. The parents did not understand cults and mind control thoroughly, nor were they willing to examine their own behavior and take the necessary steps to change. At that time, Alan was getting too much from the cult (hope, attention, connection with people) to even consider giving it up. However, rarely do people like him "make it" within a cult. More often than not, they get pushed to their limit, burn out, and either walk out or get kicked out. Perhaps when that day came he would remember some of the things I told him.

When I left that case in 1980, I learned several valuable lessons. First, I learned that meeting with, screening, and preparing the family is vital. If the family is not willing to invest the time, energy, and money necessary for a successful intervention, I should not take the case. Second, if the family isn't willing to address its own problems and make an effort to change and grow, it will undermine the cult member's progress.

Over the years, I have certainly had my share of unsuccessful cases. Recently, however, I have come to understand the critical variables for success and will only attempt an intervention if I am sure it will be a positive step for the individual and his family. In addition, three full days of exit-counseling seems to insure success. In the past three years or so, the only people I have been unsuccessful with went back to the group without giving their families three days' time.

These are just three examples of the many hundreds of people I have worked with since my exit from the Moonies. From my own experience I learned the incredible lengths to which people will go for a cause they believe is great and just. I have also learned that no one wants to sacrifice his time, energy, and dreams for a cause that is harmful and untrue. Once the phobia against leaving is addressed and I can make contact with a person's true self and let that person know what has been done to him, he almost always chooses to be free, because people will choose what they believe is best for them.

Finally, it is important that former cult members and their families not view everything that happened in the cult as negative. I always encourage people to *remember the good and take it with them* when they decide to leave. Still, there is no question that belonging to a destructive cult changes you forever. You realize how many things you've taken for granted: family, friends, education, your ability to make decisions, your individuality, your whole belief system. Cult withdrawal affords a unique opportunity to sit "naked" with yourself and analyze everything you ever knew or believed in. Such a process can be liberating and also quite terrifying. It is a chance to start your life all over again.

Chapter 8

How to Help

IF someone you know and love becomes a member of a destructive cult, you will probably find yourself facing one of the toughest situations of your life. In helping a person you love return to being himself, it's easy to fall into mistakes that could make your job even harder. Yet, if you respond to the challenge in a planned, emotionally balanced way, the chances are good that your effort will be successful, and it will be a very rewarding and ultimately joyful experience. That, at least, is what I have seen time and time again in the families I've worked with as an exit-counselor.

This chapter is intended to give you some basic, practical ideas of what people should and should not do when trying to help a cult member leave, what to do for yourself and the other members of your family, while involved in this effort. Taking a few basic precautions can save you a lot of frustration.

The best place to start is with examples of the contrasting responses of two families to the problem of losing a child to a destructive cult. The following are composite stories based on real people whom I have counseled. Their names, and the names of the cults with which they were involved, have been changed.

The Johnson Family and the World Brethren

When Bill and Lorna Johnson first noticed that their daughter Nancy was acting strangely, they simply wrote it off as the growing pains of a nineteen-year-old girl away from home for the summer. Her older brother Neil had gone through his own share of episodes of strange and atypical behavior when he was about the same age. Nancy was then in the Midwest, selling books door to door to earn extra money for college, but she was experiencing a slump in sales. Yet, when she phoned her parents to tell them about her difficulties with her job, she surprised them by sounding emotionally cool, as though she didn't have a care in the world. Knowing Nancy to be a go-getter, Bill and Lorna would have expected their daughter to sound frustrated and anxious. Something wasn't right, but they couldn't put their finger on it.

Several weeks later they received a telephone call from Leslie, one of Nancy's close friends. Leslie told Bill and Lorna that she had just received a disturbing letter from Nancy. Leslie had hesitated before calling her friend's parents—she didn't want to betray her confidence. But the content of the letter was so unlike Nancy that she felt she had to risk alienating her friend.

The letter read, in part: "I have truly found my place in the world, Leslie. God has summoned me to be part of the Brethren who are the only true Christians on Earth. I have thrown away my blue jeans, for I realize that they were part of my Satanic past. . . .A woman's place is beneath a man . . . the Word of God says so, and I am learning to destroy this vain ego of mine that longs to be part of this wicked world."

Nancy's favorite clothes had always been her blue jeans. Normally a very happy-go-lucky person, Nancy was always easy to get along with because she was so nonjudgmental. Also, she had been something of a feminist. Such subservient sentiments were very uncharacteristic of her. All these things had bothered Leslie. Nancy's parents were even more disturbed, though, because Nancy had apparently been hiding her involvement from them. Why hadn't Nancy even mentioned this group to them? She had always been so open and honest with them. It was unlike her to lie deliberately to them about her involvement with a religious group. When they asked her what was new, she answered, "Not much." From her letter, a lot seemed to be new.

The Johnsons immediately got on the phone to ask their minister's advice. He came right over. He agreed that Nancy was indeed acting strangely, and said that maybe she had gotten involved in a religious cult. At the mention of the word "cult" the Johnsons began to panic. Mr. Johnson came close to making a typical mistake. His first impulse was to call Nancy and confront her about the name of the group, her letter to Leslie, and her lies to them. Fortunately, he didn't.

Mrs. Johnson started to sob uncontrollably. She felt she had failed as a parent. Something must have been lacking in Nancy's life that would allow her to get into one of these groups. She began to review in her mind every detail of every significant incident in Nancy's life that had made her so susceptible. She decided to ask Neil to drop whatever he was doing and come over.

When Neil walked into the living room, his father was pacing back and forth, his mother was still in tears, Leslie was sitting near her on the sofa with her hands clasped on her lap, and the minister had a bewildered expression on his face. "What's going on here?" Neil asked as he sat down and put his arm around his mother. Mr. Johnson said, "We think that Nancy has gotten into some type of religious cult." "Nancy? Never; no way," Neil declared. "She would never fall for something like that." Then they told him everything they knew. He was astonished.

Fortunately, the minister was able to persuade the Johnsons to do nothing for the moment. He assured them that he would do his best to try to find more information about the group called the Brethren and get some advice on what they should do to help. That was the first of many sleepless nights that lay ahead for the Johnsons in the next few weeks. Through the minister's knowledge of the Cult Awareness Network, he was able to get my name and telephone number and give it to the family.

As soon as we were able to get enough concrete information to go on, the Johnsons asked their friends and relatives to come over the next Saturday to be part of a one-day counseling and training program. I advised them to try to get as much help and support as they could find. I was able to arrange for a former member of the group in another city to make a videotape describing as much as he could remember about the group, its leaders, its beliefs, and its practices. With this as the foundation, we were able quickly to arrange an intervention.

Since Nancy and the group were unaware that her family knew about her involvement, it was relatively easy to plan a surprise intervention. The family agreed that we should all fly out the following week. We staked out the cult house the morning after we arrived and waited for Nancy to leave. We figured that it would be much easier to talk with her if she was off the group's property and away from other members.

Within a couple of hours, she and another woman got into a station wagon and drove off. We followed them to a supermarket in a nearby shopping mall where they were apparently buying groceries. I coached the Johnsons extensively on what to say and do. The plan was to try to wait until Nancy was by herself if possible. At that point, they were to walk right up to her and give her a big hug. Naturally, we counted on Nancy's being totally surprised and shocked. Since she hadn't told her family about the group, it would be more difficult for her to resist their insistent invitation to go out to eat. Mr. and Mrs. Johnson would tell her that they needed to discuss very urgent family business, and nothing more. They would be affectionate and friendly, but firm. Neil would make sure that the other woman would not interfere with their leaving.

I watched through the outside window. Nancy put up no resistance at all. She seemed really happy to see her family and yet very shocked and confused. When Nancy said "Let me go tell Claire," Neil volunteered to do that and walked off. "I think she is in the produce department," Nancy called out to him. "Don't worry," Neil said as he looked back. His parents were already walking towards the door. Neil waited around the corner for a minute and then came running out. "She said fine," Neil told her as he got into the car—a fabrication. I would take a cab back to the hotel and wait in the second room we had taken next door until the family was ready for me. I reported what had transpired to the former member of the group I had brought along for this intervention.

We didn't have to wait long. As instructed, the Johnsons waited until they were settled in their room before telling Nancy that they had flown out because they were concerned about the group she was involved with. At first Nancy denied any involvement. Then Mr. Johnson produced her letter to Leslie. They told me that her face turned beet red and then she started to cry. "Why did you lie to us?" Mr. Johnson asked sternly. "That's not like you, honey," Mrs. Johnson added. More tears from Nancy.

"We're here because we love you and we are worried about you," Neil said, wiping the tears from his face. "Why don't you tell us all about it?" Mr. Johnson asked. "Why don't you start from the beginning," he suggested.

As Nancy recounted what had happened, she reached a point where she became very cultish and started quoting from the Bible and from her leader. This scared the Johnsons, they told me later. Her faced changed and she became like a different person. They asked Nancy if deep down in her heart she loved them and trusted them. She thought for a moment and said, "Yes."

"Will you stay with us for the next three days and not talk to or see people from the group?" Mrs. Johnson asked.

"Why?" Nancy wanted to know.

"Because there is important information we think you will want to hear, and we've arranged for some people to come to share what they know with you," Mrs. Johnson continued.

Nancy thought about it for what must have seemed like an eternity. She wanted to know who these people were and why it had to be for three days. Mr. Johnson said, "Honey, you can find out for yourself. They're waiting next door. All that we ask is that you trust us and that you give them a chance to tell you facts the group might not want you to hear."

The intervention took only two days. Nancy listened eagerly to us once she saw we were sincere and didn't have horns on the tops of our heads. She was immensely grateful for all the concern and love shown to her. She had had her doubts about the group but, like most new cult members, thought that she just wasn't spiritual enough to criticize what the older members were telling her.

WHY THE JOHNSONS SUCCEEDED

Even though their daughter had been recruited into a destructive cult, the Johnsons were very fortunate. First, since they talked with Nancy weekly, they were able to notice some of the changes in her voice and in her personality very early on. They instinctively knew that they should stay in close touch, because Nancy was young, half way across the country, and experiencing a great deal of stress in her sales work. While the Johnsons could have made sure that Nancy knew about destructive cults before she left, they didn't realize that the problem could affect anyone, even a member of their family. Once they understood the techniques and effects of mind control, they were able to move toward constructive solutions rather than allow the guilt of having "failed" as parents to cripple their decision-making abilities.

Leslie turned out to be a hero. She was able to overcome her fear of angering Nancy and acted like a true friend by contacting her parents. Because she had done so, the Johnsons were able to identify and resolve the problem quickly. As soon as Nancy was out of the group, she thanked Leslie profusely.

The Johnsons were also quite fortunate in getting good advice from their minister, who quickly came to their aid. Not only did he help them to put a finger on the problem, but also he was able to keep them from making the classic mistakes that make the exiting process much more difficult and complicated. Unlike most clergymen, their minister had attended a workshop earlier that year on destructive cults and was able to be of great help. He realized that the family should not do anything rash. Knowing that too many people try to exit-counsel a friend or relative on their own, he was aware that they needed to slow down and map out a plan with experts. Since his workshop had been sponsored by an affiliate of the Cult Awareness Network, he knew where to turn for information and help.

The Marlowes and The Word

Roger and Kitty Marlowe were not as fortunate as the Johnsons. Their son was recruited into The Word while he was away at college. They too noticed some very drastic changes in his personality and his disposition, but for the most part they thought those changes had been quite positive. Henry had stopped using swear words, and he told them that he had given up smoking and drinking. When they came to visit him on parents' day, they were delighted to see his dormitory room so neat, and his once favorite magazine, *Playboy,* noticeably absent.

Henry introduced his parents to several of his friends from the group. They thought it was odd he had become so religious. He had never before expressed an interest in Christianity. On the whole, they were impressed by many of the people in the fellowship. They seemed to be groomed nicely, were obviously very intelligent, came from apparently good homes, and were extremely friendly. The Marlowes didn't even think to check up on The Word. On the surface, it seemed fine with them.

They did become concerned when they saw his grades at the end of that semester. Henry's A minus average had plummeted to a C plus. When they confronted him about his grades, Henry was very defensive. He told them that he was doing the best he could, but he felt he had gotten really bad teachers that term. Besides, he was thinking of changing his major. Marketing no longer interested him. He wanted to become a religious studies major.

Henry had always been a headstrong, independent kid. His parents reasoned that he knew what he was doing. Of course, they wanted him to be able to support himself. Yet, if he was feeling a spiritual calling, who were they to question it? He was almost twenty years old. Another semester came and went, and still the Marlowes didn't understand what was going on. Henry managed to pull his grades up to a B, still well below his average.

That summer he told them that he was planning to go to Kansas for a "once-a-year gathering of believers." However, once he was there, he phoned to say that he had felt "called by the Lord" to take a leave from college. He was going to make a one-year commitment to go wherever they sent him, take a part-time job to cover expenses, and evangelize at least twenty hours a week.

His father was infuriated. "Why don't you finish your senior year and then evangelize?" he said with considerable irritation.

Henry got angry at his father's tone of voice. "Because, Dad, I feel like this is the right thing for me to do!" he said, imploring his father to support him.

At that point, Henry's mother intervened. "Why don't you come home and we will discuss this," said Mrs. Marlowe. She had been listening on the extension phone.

"Mom, trust me. I know what I'm doing," Henry said.

Roger and Kitty could now hear mumbling on the line. It sounded as though someone was standing next to Henry, telling him how to handle them.

"Is there someone telling you what to say?" his father demanded.

"What?" Henry asked.

"Is there someone there telling you what to say to us?" his father repeated.

"Uh, er no," Henry stammered.

"Son, have you gotten sucked into one of those religious cults?" his father demanded.

"We're a Bible research and teaching fellowship," Henry said in a defensive tone, repeating the words as though he had just read them from a brochure.

"I want you to come home right now, young man!" his father ordered, getting angrier every moment. "If you don't, I'll never respect you again," he threatened.

"Now calm down, Roger. Henry, your father is very upset. Henry, you're not in a cult, are you?" his mother asked naively.

"No mom, of course not," Henry answered.

"You see, Roger, Henry's not in a cult," she repeated, as if repetition of these words would magically make them true.

Henry did not return home to discuss anything with his parents. Instead, he went to St. Louis to work for the group, recruiting other members for The Word. He asked his parents to put some of his belongings in boxes, and they shipped them off to him as he requested. They even sent him $500 in cash to help him get started.

Henry's father was disgusted. He went to the library, started making copies of articles which described The Word as a cult, and mailed them to Henry. He thought these articles would prove to Henry that what he had objected to was documented proof. It backfired. All it proved to Henry was that his parents were possessed by the Devil and weren't to be trusted.

His mother believed that her son was too intelligent to stay in such a group for very long. She convinced herself that he would see his mistake and walk out. When months passed and he seemed to become more and more distant, she grew hysterical, loading herself and her husband with guilt. Henry's sister Amy, seventeen, and brother Bernie, fourteen, were caught in the emotional upheaval left by Henry. Day after day, they had to endure their parents' obsession with Henry's cult involvement and began to get angry at Henry for putting the family through this ordeal.

Time after time, his parents took turns confronting Henry with new pieces of information they had found about The Word. They told him that the founder and leader of the group was a plagiarist who drank and swore excessively, but this information did not deter Henry.

Throughout this time, the Marlowes remained silent with their friends and relatives about Henry's cult involvement. Roger was a state politician and was concerned about his career. Kitty felt that people would think she was a bad parent for her son to be so disturbed. Whenever friends or relatives asked about him, they merely told them that he was fine, had taken a leave of absence from college, and had decided to work for a while. They were deathly afraid of what everyone would think if they told them the truth.

With each passing year, Henry became more and more estranged from his family. They spoke very infrequently on the phone and wrote only sporadically. Henry felt there was no reason to see his family. As far as he was concerned, they were under Satan's power.

LESSONS TO BE LEARNED

Here are two different families, the Johnsons and the Marlowes, whose responses to a cult problem were very different. The Johnsons were able to find out very quickly that something was wrong and were able to get good advice. The Marlowes didn't pick up the signs, and when they realized their son had a cult problem, didn't seek out help. Mr. Marlowe lost valuable leverage by confronting his son and issuing what amounted to an ultimatum to him. Some people actually disown children who have fallen victim to destructive cults. Unfortunately, the mistakes the Marlowes made are very common and happen with the majority of families. In the case of destructive cults, parents' instinctive reactions frequently do more damage than good.

There are several lessons to be learned here. Any sudden, uncharacteristic change in a friend or a loved one should be investigated thoroughly. If the person is suddenly spending a good deal of time away, find out why. Ask a lot of questions in a non-threatening tone. Avoid wishful thinking. Remember: when people join cults, they often become deceptive or evasive when questioned about life changes.

If you are concerned, consult with as many of the person's friends and relatives as possible. Don't do what the Marlowes did, and try to keep the problem hidden from friends and relatives. By doing so, they cut themselves off from very valuable emotional support as well as possible help. Perhaps someone they knew could have located for them the name of a former member or an exit-counselor who could advise them. Perhaps one of the friends or relatives could have been used to meet with Henry and work with him.

Usually, the person going into the cult has tried to confide in someone, possibly in an effort at recruitment. When people delay talking with others about the possible problem in the hope that the person will snap out of it himself, the consequences can be disastrous. If you see a friend getting into trouble, make sure to contact his family. They will almost always be grateful for your concern.

CLASSIC INEFFECTIVE RESPONSES

Since most people do not understand mind control and the practices of destructive cults, it is easy for them to fall into behavior patterns that are not effective.

The most common problem is that family members typically feel an *excessive amount of guilt and shame.* People seem consistently to blame themselves because of their loved one's cult involvement. Guilt for things done or not done in the past is one of the greatest hindrances to positive and effective action. People need to know that they are not at fault. Cults exist. Mind control exists. As with most modern problems, people just don't realize how pernicious cults are until they absorb someone they know.

Another common emotional problem is that *people neglect their own needs.* The best way to help someone else is to make sure that you take care of your own needs. The cult involvement has to be placed in a manageable perspective. People can do only what is within their capacity to do. Life has to go on. People wind up hurting themselves and their loved ones when they aren't able to rest, relax, and do other things they need in order to cope. Burn-out occurs when an obsession sets in, and often alienates other family members who want to help.

For example, the Marlowes inadvertently punished their other children because they devoted too much ineffective energy to Henry. They wound up exhausted and hopeless. No matter how long a person has been involved with a destructive cult, there is never cause to give up hope. I have met people who have been in a group for thirty years but have come out and resumed a happy and successful life. Learning how to cope with your needs and those of your family will enable you to be more helpful to the person in the group.

Another mistake is that people *emotionally overreact to the cult involvement*. This can be even more dangerous than doing nothing. A person can get driven further into a cult by hysterical tirades and inappropriate uses of words like "cult" and "brainwashing." Getting emotionally aggressive with a cult member almost always backfires.

A common mistake is that *relatives try to argue the person out of an involvement by using a condescending, confrontational approach*. Unless you are extremely knowledgeable, a gifted communicator, and very lucky, trying to argue a person out of a group with a direct approach is doomed to failure. Rational discussions are simply not effective with someone who has been indoctrinated with mind control.

Someone who is recruited into a destructive cult should not be blamed. Family members and friends should regard what happened as an example of destructive mind control. I have been told time and again that a person who comes out of a destructive cult feels psychologically raped. Get angry with the cult. Get angry at all mind control cults. But *don't get angry at the person who has been victimized*. It isn't his fault!

If you want to get even with the group, get the person out first. Then do as much as you can to expose the group to the public. Take it to court, if possible. In the past, destructive cults have appeared to dominate the legal system because of their financial clout. It's time to use the law to ensure justice.

Focus on helping the person who was recruited. To this end, information and strategy are your two most important tools. The overall objective should be this: ***Do everything within your power to create the necessary conditions to help the cult member* change *and* grow.**

Family members and friends should keep this objective in mind at all times when deciding what to do or say. Notice that I have omitted saying that the objective should be "getting the person out of the group." I make that omission deliberately, because I have found that people get out of destructive cults as a natural consequence of *changing* and *growing*. If people are focused on positive growth, there will be less resistance and everyone will be happier and more effective.

It is essential to adopt the positive attitude that *the individual is going to leave the group*. The only question is whether it will be sooner or later and whether the transition will be easy and smooth or difficult and painful. People can do only that which is within their control to do. People can help to create the positive conditions necessary to help a person trapped in a cult to grow beyond the shackles of mind control.

The best way for you to help the cult member leave his group is for you to be adequately prepared to undertake the job. Here are some ways to make sure that you're able to handle the stress you'll inevitably encounter.

PREPARING FOR A SUCCESSFUL INTERVENTION

Take Care of Your Emotional Needs

Learning not to expect instant results and pacing oneself for the long haul will help you keep a balanced perspective. Particularly if the cult member has been involved for many years, efforts to help him should not be done at the expense of another's health or well-being. One of my clients, from Germany, flew to the United States against his doctor's advice to try to see his son in the Moonies, and had a heart attack and died. Imagine the guilt the son will have to live with after he leaves the group.

Remember that you are in a kind of war with the cult. As part of the preparation process, identify and address everyone's concerns and emotional needs whenever possible. Good individual and family counseling can be enormously helpful.

Parents and other family members should try to keep the cult problem in a balanced perspective. Life for them and their family has to go on, particularly if the person has been a member for a long time.

Consolidate Your Resources

Following the example of the Johnsons, involve as many family members and friends in the intervention as you feel comfortable with, and help educate them. Try to invite them to participate in a preparatory workshop. Contact knowledgeable clergy, mental health professionals, former cult members, families who have had a cult problem, and anyone who might be able to offer any assistance. If there isn't anyone locally, then find someone wherever you can. Also, find local people who are willing to learn. Coordination, teamwork, and good communication all combine for success.

If a key member of your family is very close to the individual in a cult, do everything within your power to get that person involved. Countless times, I have found a situation in which a brother or sister who had a lot of clout with the cult member did not want to help effect a rescue because they didn't understand cult mind control and felt a loyalty to the sibling. If necessary, plan a mini-intervention with that person first. Then, with that person on your side, it will be much easier to get the person out of the group.

Get Organized and Make a Plan

Start learning as much as you can. Good preparation is the key to success. Study the "enemy" (the specific cult group) as well as similar destructive cults. Learn how they think and how they operate. Become knowledgeable about mind control. The more clearly you understand it, the more easily you will be able to explain it to others—and particularly to the person in the cult when the time comes.

Keep organized files, making copies of important articles to share with everyone concerned. Make copies of every letter written to the member and every letter received by him. This may be quite important during or after the intervention. I have frequently shown the cult member letters he had written in which he made promises that he later broke, or even instances in which he blatantly lied to his family.

Update everyone concerned regularly. Consistent communication with the cult member is always better than sporadic contact. Send a little card or note once a week, every week. This is far better than writing a fourteen-page letter one week and then missing the next month. Ask the cult member to call collect whenever and wherever he is if he needs to talk.

Selecting the right exit-counselor is a key step in organizing and making a plan. He or she can help you step by step through your own particular situation. Most of these people are first-rate and have demonstrated their expertise by helping a tremendous number of people out of cult groups.

While the Cult Awareness Network will try to assist people with names of exit-counselors whenever they can, at this time there is no centralized list of exit-counselors. Be aware that different state affiliates may recommend only local people, or people they have worked with before. Also, contrary to cult propaganda, CAN does not support or promote forcible deprogramming, so you will not be able to find deprogrammers, should you want one, through any of their offices. Involuntary deprogramming is against the law and, as stated before, involves great risk. The only way to locate one is to track down someone who at one time hired a deprogrammer.

Above all, be a good consumer. After the Jonestown tragedy, a dozen or so con artists calling themselves deprogrammers appeared out of the woodwork, took advantage of numerous families, and stole their money. Some of these people were cult members themselves, attempting to give deprogramming a bad name. Be careful. A person's claims to be an exit-counselor don't make him one.

Check the person's credentials from as many sources as possible. In my opinion, the best exit-counselors are people who were actually once cult members themselves. They know what it feels like to be under mind control. Also, the best exit-counselors have had a lot of experience. Check with several families the exit-counselor has worked with over the years. Consult with other exit-counselors too. Find out whether they have had any counseling training; my own training has helped me enormously. However, training in counseling isn't enough. A tremendous number of mental health professionals know nothing about counseling someone out of a cult.

Remember at all times that you are the employer. You have the right to decide what is or is not done when it comes to your loved one's well being. In addition to checking an exit-counselor's credentials, trust your instincts when you select him. You have to feel that the *cult member* will be able to trust and relate to him as a person. Exit-counseling is very serious and is no place for amateurs.

Exit-counselors charge fees that range from $250 to $1,000 a day. Former members who assist the exit-counselor receive between $100 and $300 a day on the average. Usually all expenses, such as travel and accommodations, are extra. Although each case is quite different, most interventions are accomplished within three days time. The average cost of an intervention lies between $2,000 and $5,000; most exit-counselors will try to accommodate hardship cases whenever possible. After the intervention some follow-up is required, either at a formal rehabilitation center or by introducing the person to as many former members as possible.

Once you've accomplished all the preliminary preparations, it is important to make up a one-month, three-month, six-month and one-year plan. Although interventions should be done as soon as possible, they should not be rushed. Most interventions are conducted within one year, preferably as soon as preparation is completed and as soon as there is a good opportunity. Keep in mind that arrangements to reserve an exit-counseling team are usually made several months in advance.

HOW TO HELP A CULT MEMBER CHANGE AND GROW AS A PERSON

It may seem that getting a cult member to go through a personal change is the long way toward getting him out of a cult. After all, isn't it most important to get him physically away from the people who practice mind control on him? While a certain degree of impatience is understandable, it is vital to recognize that the only permanent way of getting people out of destructive cults is to help them get back in touch with their real selves, and help them start growing towards meeting a new personal goal that means something to them.

Keeping the long-term objective in mind, then, everyone concerned with helping a cult member should focus attention on three main short-term objectives. The first is *building rapport and trust*. Without trust, nothing you do will be effective. The second objective is *gathering information,* specifically information about how the cult member thinks, feels, and views reality. The third objective is using specific techniques and skills to *plant seeds of doubt about the cult* and *promote a new perspective.*

Build Rapport and Trust

When you first become aware of a problem with a cult member, try to act as though you do not know he is in a cult. Don't tip your hand. Don't tell the member that you are in contact with anti-cult information or people. If you do, the result will be breakdown of trust.

A *curious yet concerned posture* is the most effective stance anyone can take in relating to the cult member. It is relatively easy to elicit rapport and trust when you are acting curious because all you are doing is asking questions in a non-judgmental way. You care about the person, therefore you want to know everything that is important to him.

Show approval and respect of the individual and his ideals and talents. However, be careful to show only conditional approval of his participation in the group. Let him know that you are withholding final judgment on the group until all of the facts are in. In some cases, it might be appropriate for you to tell him you have a feeling in the pit of your stomach that something is not right about the group, but you are not sure. If the cult member tries to give credit to the group for good aspects of his life, like not using pot or alcohol anymore, tell him you think that is great, but remind him that *he* deserves the credit for the good things, not the group.

Evaluate your present relationship with the person in a cult. Do the two of you have a great deal of rapport and trust? If not, start thinking about ways you can rebuild the relationship. Remember, the more people he feels connected to who are outside of the cult, the better off he will be. He will always be closer to some people than others, but everyone should be making a natural effort to get closer to the person. Coordinate the flow of communication to him. It wouldn't seem natural if ten people wrote him at one time. You don't want him to get suspicious.

Avoid sending money, particularly cash, because it will most likely be turned over to the group. It is far better to send clothes, pictures, books, and other objects with a more personal and long-lasting meaning. Grandma's home-made cookies go a long way towards establishing rapport and are much better than a card and a check.

Ask the member what you can do to get closer to him. Try to get him to be specific. Try your best to accommodate his needs, but act sensibly. If he asks you to read one of the group's books, tell him that you would be willing to do a swap and ask him to read a book you recommend. If he tells you he wants you to stop criticizing the group, ask him how you can communicate your questions and concerns without his getting defensive.

People have done many creative things to help build trust and rapport.

They have written poems and short stories, put together elaborate photo albums, and painted pictures and portraits. They have sent shoes, winter jackets, and tickets to performances that they know the person will love. Some people have even invited the cult member to go with them for a trip overseas, and in some cases were able to induce the person to be away from the group long enough to be counseled.

Collect Valuable Information

Once rapport is established, information gathering will become much easier. The more information you collect, the better will be your ability to know what is going on inside the mind of the member. Communicate as regularly as possible. If you can see each other, try to do it one-on-one. It is nearly impossible to get anywhere while talking to two or more cult members at a time.

Expect at some point that you will be invited to talk with older members or leaders. Stall for as long as you can. Tell the person that you care about him and trust him. You are not interested in talking with strangers. You want *him* to explain everything to you. If he says that he doesn't know the answers to your questions, you can gently point out that you are concerned that if he doesn't know the answers, he may have made a commitment to the group before he was ready to do so. Suggest that he take a step back, and spend a few weeks researching the group objectively. If the group is legitimate, what does he have to lose?

Information can also help one understand just how fully indoctrinated a person is. When I was speaking with Bruce, I was able to ascertain his stage of involvement, so I knew that to tell him about the Moonie pledge service would be very disillusioning to him. If a family can determine what a member knows and doesn't know, then that makes the exit-counselor's job much easier and raises the chances of success.

Develop Specific Skills to Promote a New Perspective

When you are able to establish good rapport and accumulate a good deal of information, the last step is actually developing the skills and strategies to undermine or side step the mind control used by the group. Too many people try to jump to this step before they have accomplished the first two. This is a big mistake. Only when you have laid the groundwork can you really be effective.

Remember that you want to connect and empower the person's real self and not his cult self. Reminding him of earlier positive life experiences is the most effective way to do this. For example, a friend calls up the member and says "Hi! It's been a long time. You know I was down visiting the old school today, and I remembered when you and I used to go early, so we could play handball on the school wall. Do you remember the time when the gym teacher chased us across the field demanding the ball because we accidentally cracked his window?"

A father could try an approach such as this: "You know, son, I was flipping through the channels on TV the other day and I saw a show on bass fishing. We haven't done that in years. I sure would love to go back up to the lake with you sometime this summer. It would be so good to spend some time with you, just you and me and the fish." Evoking these kinds of feelings and memories can be a powerful way to undermine the cult programming. However, be cautious about overusing this technique and arousing suspicion.

By being in close contact with the member and pooling information gathered by family members and friends, you can give strategic messages. For example, if the member tells one of his old friends that he really misses skiing, and that friend tells the family, then they can plan a family ski trip and invite the friend along. The cult member may think it is coincidental or perhaps even spiritually destined. Even if he isn't allowed to go, it will help to stir a strong desire within him.

Whenever you communicate, make sure to concentrate on just one or two points each time. It is better to make one point thoroughly than to try a "shotgun" approach. Again, the follow-up is critical. For example, if you write the member that you saw one of the leaders of the group on television saying that members could come home to visit whenever they wanted to do so, you might mention that you remember a conversation with him just a few months earlier when he told you that he "had to ask permission to visit." If he neglects to answer that point in the next letter or phone call, ask him again about it. Ask him gently, but firmly, why there seems to be a contradiction: "Was the leader lying? Were you the one who was lying? Help me to understand because I am confused." Too many people make really good points but don't follow up with them. Perhaps they find it difficult to ask the follow-up question in a non-threatening tone—one that forces the cult member to have to think about the contradiction.

Don't send unsolicited critical articles, as Mr. Marlowe did. Such information actually does more harm than good. If you feel your rapport is very good with the member, try to have a personal discussion. If it will be some time before you can see the person, talk with him on the telephone, first about the article and what it says. If he expresses an interest in seeing it, tell him you will send it, if he promises to go over it point by point with you. Too many people don't get the person's permission first, and then if they do, they don't follow up on it.

Remember to stay in your normal character. The member will be suspicious if you are very different from your usual self. Also, don't worry about making mistakes. If you feel you must weigh every word and action, you will incapacitate yourself. Keep learning from your mistakes, and over time you will become effective.

• • •

Since every situation is different, no one book can possibly cover every-one's particular needs. Under ideal circumstances, someone who recognizes that a friend or loved one is becoming a member of a destructive cult will immediately seek out professional assistance. The important point is this: *don't delay.*

If you know of someone who has been in a cult for many years, start to work now. What would you do if you received a call tonight from the cult member and he told you he wanted to come home for a long visit tomorrow? As surprising as it is, this kind of sudden event (perhaps an appeal for help) happens time and time again.

Usually, at that point it is too late to do all of the necessary groundwork to insure a successful intervention. The best thing is simply to start preparing for such a possibility. Talk with other families who have been through the cult problem. Meet and talk with former members. Talk with exit-counselors and other professionals. If you do your homework and get involved in this process, it will be one of the most challenging and rewarding things you will ever do in your life.

Chapter 9

Unlocking Cult Mind Control

Wherever I go—to the supermarket, to the YMCA, or on an airplane trip—I meet people who are involved with destructive cults. My heart goes out to them, because I was once in a similar trap. With all the cult members I meet, I try to remember that they are *enslaved*. They are also somebody's son or daughter, sister or brother. Whenever I meet people like these, I feel extremely grateful that I am free. I was one of the lucky ones who had the opportunity to be counseled out. Since people helped me, I try to share my good fortune.

In these fleeting personal encounters, I know that I will have only a few minutes, but I try to say or do something to help. Although usually I never hear from someone like this again, occasionally I do find out that the meeting had some long-term impact.

Back in 1980, I started to deliberately go out of my way to conduct impromptu mini-interventions. At that time I was eager to research and practice the non-coercive approach to exit-counseling. I looked at every cult member I met as an opportunity to hone my skills.

These mini-interventions, taught me more effective ways of communicating with cult members—methods that serve as "keys" to unlock cult mind control. This chapter is a summary of those keys, with some examples of how I use them during an intervention.

Briefly, these are the three most basic keys to helping a cult member:

Key No. 1: build rapport and trust.

Key No. 2: use goal-oriented communications.

Key No. 3: develop models of identity.

After presenting two examples of sample interventions I have conducted (and a mini-intervention that was conducted on me when I was still a cult member), I will discuss at greater length the keys that enable an intervention to be carried through to a successful conclusion:

Key No. 4: access the pre-cult identity.

Key No. 5: get the cult member to look at reality from many different perspectives.

Key No. 6: side-step the thought-stopping process by giving information in an indirect way.

Key No. 7: visualize a happy future to undo phobia indoctrination.

Key No. 8: offer the cult member concrete definitions of mind control and characteristics of a destructive cult.

KEY NO. 1: BUILD RAPPORT AND TRUST

I have already emphasized the importance of building rapport; several techniques for building non-verbal rapport can help. The first is to simply mirror the body language of the person with whom I am speaking. I also use a non-threatening tone of voice and line of questioning and try to avoid judgmental statements. Like riding a bicycle or learning a foreign language, rapport-building is a skill that anyone can learn and develop.

KEY NO. 2: USE GOAL-ORIENTED COMMUNICATIONS

Practiced mainly in the business world, goal-oriented communication represents the best way to influence people in a deliberate way. This style is drastically different from the ones people traditionally use when interacting with family members or friends. When we are intimate with people we usually say whatever we think or feel, because we are being "ourselves." We don't have an agenda to influence others.

In the business world, most people have to think through their goals and objectives and how best to accomplish them. Top business executives understand that they often have to establish a step-by-step plan to make their dreams a reality.

Let us assume, then, that I've already outlined a goal (helping someone leave a cult) and have outlined a step-by-step plan of action. The next thing is to find out just *who* it is that I'm trying to influence. Understanding a person "from the inside out" is an invaluable asset. Whenever a great actor prepares for a role, he must first research the character thoroughly and go to as many sources as possible to find out how the person "ticks." The actor creates a model of this character in his mind and then steps inside it, letting go of his own identity, beliefs, and values. He can then test a communication and see whether it elicits the desired response. The rule of thumb is to *do what works*. If what you are doing doesn't work, try a different approach. Keep focusing on the goal.

KEY NO. 3: DEVELOP MODELS OF IDENTITY

By gathering information, family members and friends can thoroughly research the cult member they hope to influence. In order to be most effective, three models of who that persons is (also called "mindsets") need to be constructed.

The first model is *who the person was before he joined*—how he thought about himself, the world, his relationships, his strengths, and his weaknesses. This is the way *he* viewed all these things. This information is best gathered from what he has written or has said to friends and relatives.

The second model is that of *a typical cult member of that group*. Any former member can provide a generic model of how the typical Moonie or any other cult member views "reality." Ideally, people can role-play what it feels like to be a cult member. Just as the actor rehearses his lines in character, what is important here is the characterization, even though the lines are impromptu. Former members can serve as coaches, teaching you how to think like a cult member. Different family members can take turns interacting with the "cult member" as well as "being" the cult member. The more they are able to role-play and practice, the better they will understand how the cult member thinks.

The third model is that of *the person actually in the cult*. At each level of membership this model will change somewhat. By contrasting it with the model of the generic cult member and the real person, you can get a good idea when the person is being very "cultish," or when he is being more himself. Remember, every person is different, and every cult member is at war between his cult identity and his real identity. At any time, you can actually see the person visibly switching back and forth.

Many people desperately try to fight off the cult identity whenever they can. For example, there are groups whose members are supposed to be vegetarian and not use drugs or alcohol. Yet, I have met several people in one such group who told me they used to sneak off the communal property and drive thirty-five miles so they could have a hamburger and a beer. A sibling or close friend who has good rapport could discover and make constructive use of such information. At any moment the member could shift into his "real" self or into the "cult" self.

These three models are what I use in effective exit-counseling. Before meeting the person, I want to have as complete a sense of all three as possible. Then when I am with the person, I am able to continue refining the models by asking specific kinds of questions. Within three days, I am able to develop a sophisticated set of maps.

Like an actor, I am able to step into a role and imagine myself as the person I am counseling. I am able to immerse myself in his "reality." Throughout the process, I continually keep switching back and forth.

I use the model of who the person is now (the person still in the cult) and test out the model by anticipating how he will respond by having an imaginary conversation with him. Then I ask him the same question and note how accurately I was able to predict his response. As the exit-counseling goes on, I am able to refine this model more and more.

The more rapport I am able to establish, the more easily I will get the needed information. The faster I am able to create an accurate model of the cult member, the faster I can "become" him. Once I become him, I can then figure out what needs to be said or done to help him regain control over his life.

Indeed, it is the real identity who shows me how to unlock the doors. He tells me what keys are necessary to use, where, and in what order. This process of discovery can be demonstrated in the following interaction with a young member of a cult that stresses meditation under the leadership of a man named Guru Maharaj Ji.

A Sample Intervention: Gary and the Divine Light Mission

"I'm curious: how long have you been involved with Divine Light Mission?" I asked, gazing at the brochures the young man was carrying. We were both waiting for the bus to come.

"For about seven years," he answered. His eyes moved up slowly until they focused on mine.

"That's a long time," I said. "How old were you when you first got involved?" I tried to sound innocent, as though I were an old friend of his.

"I was twenty," the young man responded.

"I'm Steve," I said holding out my hand to shake his. "I'm sorry if I'm bothering you. What's your name?" I asked.

"My name is Gary," he said, somewhat bewildered. He looked as though he didn't know what to make of me.

I continued, "Gary, I'm just curious: what were you doing at that time in your life?"

"Why do you want to know?" he asked with a look of puzzlement.

"I love to talk to people who have made unorthodox choices in their life. I like trying to figure out why people do what they do," I offered as an explanation, and shrugged my shoulders a bit.

"Oh. Well, back then I was working for a construction company putting up buildings," he said, warming up.

"Anything else?" I asked.

"Yeh, well I liked to hang out with my friends and I was also into animals. I had two dogs, a cat, some tropical fish, and a rabbit," Gary told me. A warm smile lit up his face as he recalled his friends and his pets.

"You certainly were into pets. Was any one your favorite?" I asked.

"Well, my dog, Inferno, was pretty special. He and I used to be best buddies," Gary said.

"What made him so special?" I asked.

"He was an independent spirit. He loved adventure. He loved to go with me into the woods," Gary stated. It was obvious to me that he missed his dog a great deal.

"So, you love an independent spirit. Do you admire anyone who stands up and does what he feels is right no matter what others say?" I was trying my best to empower Gary by reminding him of the qualities he used to admire.

"That's right. Inferno did what he wanted to do. And I loved him for that, too," Gary said in a somewhat defensive, self-righteous tone.

"So Gary, tell me, what was it that made you decide that the Divine Light Mission was the group that you wanted to spend your life in?" I asked.

"I never thought of it that way," he said, his face growing sullen.

"Well then, what was it that got you involved?" I asked in an upbeat voice.

"At the time, my girlfriend Carol started going to *satsang,* you know— group meetings—and I went along. We listened to the people all talk so glowingly about their experience of knowledge, and how high it made them feel," Gary explained.

"Did you decide to get initiated first or did Carol?" I continued to probe.

"She did. At first, I thought the whole thing was a bit strange. But after she started meditating, I got curious and decided to do it too," he said, sounding as though he had been very skeptical.

"What year was this?" I asked for clarification.

"In 1973," he answered.

"And at the time, what did you think of Guru Maharaj Ji?" I inquired.

"I thought he was this young dude from India who was going to usher in an age of world peace," he said, with a touch of sarcasm.

"Were you at that big meeting at the Houston Astrodome?" I asked.

"Yes," he answered.

"And what ever became of Carol?" I asked.

"I don't know. We sort of broke up a few months after we got involved," Gary said, his face darkening again.

"When was the last time you spoke to her?" I asked.

"About four years ago she wrote me that she had decided to go back to school and wasn't going to practice the knowledge anymore," he told me.

"Why did she say that she wasn't going to be part of the group anymore?" I asked, increduous.

"I don't remember," he said, staring at the pavement.

"So the person who got you involved left the group four years ago?" I repeated.

"Uh huh."

"And you have never really sat down with her to find out why she left after belonging to the group for three years?" I asked one more time for emphasis.

"Why are you looking at me like that?" Gary said, looking up at me.

I smiled, then looked down, and then looked him right in the eye. "Well, I don't understand, Gary. If my ex-girlfriend left the group that she introduced me to, I would certainly want to sit down with her and find out everything I could from her. She must have had some really good reasons why she left after three years. And she obviously cared enough about you to contact you and let you know her decision."

I paused for a couple of minutes as Gary stood there, silent. Then I continued, "I suppose there is no way for you to get in touch with her anymore."

"Actually, her parents probably live at the same address. I could look it up in the directory."

"Might be a good idea. Well, I wish you good luck, Gary. It was really good talking to you. Thanks." I said as my bus arrived.

He waved to me as my bus pulled away.

The preceding conversation demonstrates how much can be done to help someone in a mind control cult in just a few minutes. During that time I was able to quickly establish rapport, collect very valuable information about Gary, and use what I learned to help him take a very important step away from his cult group.

As stated before, rapport building is essential for gaining influence. If I had used a threatening or even condescending tone of voice, I would never have gotten to first base. Because I used a curious, interested tone, Gary was happy to kill some time and chat with a friendly stranger.

Once I found out how long Gary had been involved, I was able to quickly ascertain that he wasn't gung-ho for a seven-year member. It was relatively easy for me to get Gary to reminisce about his pre-cult life. When he remembered what he had done before, he was able to reaccess his real identity and get in touch with how he thought, felt, and acted before being indoctrinated into the cult. He not only remembered his favorite dog but talked about how he used to value an independent and adventurous spirit—a valuable resource needed to help him walk away from a seven-year commitment to Guru Maharaj Ji.

Gary also remembered what he had first thought of the group before becoming involved. He stepped back into time and looked at the group with his pre-cult eyes, thinking that it was a bit weird. Back then he certainly never intended to join the group for life. An important strategy for reality testing is to go backward in time from the present viewpoint and ask, "if you had known then what you know now, would you have made the same decision?" For Gary, apparently the answer would have been no.

Then, as I was fishing for more information, Gary stunned me by telling me that Carol, his ex-girlfriend who initially recruited him, had left the group. Since everyone under mind control has been made to be phobic about leaving the group, it didn't surprise me that Gary didn't know why she had left. Four years before, he was probably not able to consider talking with her, even if she had been a close friend. However, it was clear to me that Gary was still curious about why Carol left the group. He was now at a point in his life where he was more open to this possibility. I gave him a nudge to go and talk to Carol.

An Early Experience of a Mini-Intervention

When I first got out of the Moonies and searched my memory for times I had questions or doubts, I remembered several occasions when I was momentarily thinking outside the Moonie framework. Even though these experiences weren't enough to get me to leave, they proved significant when I was deprogrammed. One of these involved a caring person I accidentally met one day. During my first year as a member, I was fundraising on a steamy summer day in Manhattan. I approached a man who must have been in his sixties, and asked him if he wanted to buy some flowers.

"What are you selling flowers for, young man?" he asked with a warm smile.

"For Christian youth programs," I answered, hoping I could sell him a dozen carnations.

"My, my, you look very hot," he commented.

"Yes sir. But this cause is very important, so I don't mind," I answered.

"How would you feel if I took you inside this coffeeshop and bought you something cold to drink?" he asked.

I thought to myself, "This guy is nice, but he has got to buy some flowers, otherwise he will not have a connection to 'Father.' " Then I remembered Jesus saying that anyone who gives water to a thirsty person is doing the will of God.

"Just for five minutes. It will refresh you so you will be able to sell even more flowers," he said, with a twinkle in his eye.

"Okay. Thank you very much," I answered as we walked into the air-conditioned shop. It felt so good to be out of the sun.

When we sat down at a table, he said, "So tell me a little about yourself."

"Well, I grew up in a Jewish family in Queens," I started.

"Oh, so you're Jewish. Me too," he said with a warm smile.

I thought to myself that perhaps God had sent this person to me to "witness to" (the term we used in the group to recruit). We had been instructed that while fundraising, we should never spend more than a couple of minutes with any person. But since my main job was recruiting, and I had been sent out on Saturday to fundraise, I thought maybe it was okay to spend a few extra minutes with him.

I must have spent at least half an hour with him. He got me to do most of the talking. During that time I became incredibly homesick, not only for my family and friends, but for playing basketball, writing poetry, and reading books. Before I left, he insisted that I call home and walked me to the phone and put in the dime himself. I remember feeling that this man reminded me of my grandfather, someone I loved dearly. I didn't have the will power to refuse. Besides, it would look bad for the group if I refused to talk to my parents. I spoke with my mom for a few minutes.

After that I felt that I had to pry myself away from this man. My cult identity was starting to exert itself strongly. I started to feel guilty that I hadn't been out raising money and allowing people to "pay indemnity" and connect themselves to the Messiah.

I was spaced out and couldn't sell for the rest of the day. Eventually, a Moonie leader told me that I had created a bad condition by going inside for a cold drink, that Satan had tempted me, and I had failed. He told me that at that moment I had crucified Jesus on the cross one more time. That evening I prayed and repented and tried to quash any memory of what had happened. I never thought of that experience again until after I was deprogrammed.

Another Intervention: Phil and the Hare Krishna Sect

The following is a description of part of an intervention I made with Phil, a member of the Hare Krishna sect for over three years. Phil had gotten involved with the group about six months after his twin brother was killed in an automobile accident. The death hit his family hard and sent Phil into a severe depression, in which he contemplated suicide. Despite medication and therapy, nothing seemed to help Phil. Then one day, while walking downtown, he was approached by a person from the Krishnas.

I met Phil during one of his infrequent visits home and was introduced as a family counselor who had been working with his parents and his two sisters for many months. I told him that I felt I needed to speak with him alone before I would do any family sessions. I told him that in my view he was a very significant member of the family and that his participation was appreciated and badly needed.

After introducing myself to him, I suggested we go outside for a walk so that we could get acquainted. He was dressed in full Krishna clothes and wore sandals. I spent the first few minutes explaining my background as a counselor who specialized in communication strategies and family dynamics and was committed to helping everyone grow and enjoy better relationships with their loved ones. He used the name Gorivinda.

"So Gorivinda—Phil—would you mind telling me about how you feel toward your family now?" I asked, my hands in my pockets and my eyes directed toward the pavement.

"I don't know," he responded, shrugging his shoulders slightly.

"Well," I continued. "Are you happy with your present relationship with your mother? your father? your siblings?"

He answered, "Things have gotten a lot better since they stopped criticizing my religious commitment."

"How do you feel when you come home for a visit?" I asked, trying to be as gentle as possible.

"To be honest, it's a bit strange," he said.

I was glad at his response. "What do you mean?" I probed for more information.

"Well, its like coming to another world. It's so different from devotional life at the temple," he responded.

"Are there any good feelings that you are aware of when you come home?" I continued.

"Yes," he said warmly. "I love my parents and my sisters and brother very much." Then he caught himself and added, "But they are living in the material world."

"I see," I said, a bit disheartened that he had caught himself and injected the cult perspective. "Would you mind telling me about your twin brother and what his death meant to you?" I asked, hoping to steer him back into his pre-cult identity.

"Why?" he asked suspiciously.

"Because as a mental health professional, I believe that your whole family is still suffering from that tragedy," I stated, hoping he would buy it.

When I said that, Phil started to cry and choke up. I was struck by the power of his feelings. Then he put his hands together and started rocking back and forth. I thought to myself, "He's chanting to shut himself down." After a few minutes he was recomposed.

"Tom and I were very close," he said, beginning to lose control of himself again.

"Tell me about him when he was alive," I asked. "What was he like? What did he like to do?"

Phil's face started to shine as he reminisced about his brother. "Tom was bright, energetic, had a great sense of humor. He was the more aggressive of the two of us. He helped motivate me to do things all of the time."

"Tell me, Phil, what do you think he would be doing today if he hadn't had the car accident?" I was hoping to get Phil to think again about the kind of life Tom would have had.

"That's a hard one," Phil answered.

"Do you think *he* would have joined the Krishnas?" I asked with a smile.

"No, never," Phil said definitively. "Tom was never into religion much at all, although he was very spiritual."

"So what do you think he would have been doing?" I repeated.

"He always said that he wanted to go into the media—to work in television," Phil explained. "He wanted to be an anchorman for the six o'clock news."

"So he liked news. Did he like investigative journalism?" I asked. I knew that if he said yes, I would have another angle to work on later with Phil.

"That was his favorite!" he said.

This had hit home. I decided to explore another angle first, though. I asked, "Back then, what did you see yourself doing?"

"Back then? I wanted to become a musician," he said with enthusiasm.

"That's right," I said. "Your sister mentioned to me that you used to play electric guitar—used to write songs, too." I felt that Phil was making some of the important connections I was hoping he would make.

"Yeah."

"So did you want to have your own band and make records—the whole bit?" I asked, wanting to get Phil to remember as much detail as he could.

"Sure. I loved music so much. I remember singing my songs with Tom. He would help me with the lyrics sometimes, too," he said with considerable pride.

"So you could imagine being a successful musician, living a happy and spiritually fulfilled life?" I asked, nodding my head. I wanted him to make as powerful a mental image as he could. I wanted to anchor it.

"You bet!" Phil said, his eyes defocused. He was obviously enjoying what he was experiencing.

"Can you imagine how good it feels to be up on stage, singing your songs, touching people with your creativity, making them happy?" I asked. I wanted Phil to get in touch with how good he would feel as a musician.

"Yes! It's a wonderful feeling," he said.

"Great. Just imagine enjoying your music, and perhaps see your friends there, too. They must admire and respect your talent a great deal. Perhaps you are even happily married, maybe have kids," I continued. I knew that I was taking a risk, but he seemed to enjoy adding the wife and kids to his fantasy. I waited a few minutes in silence and waited for Phil to return from his pleasant voyage.

"Now I have another question." I paused for a deep breath. "What do you think Tom would say now if he saw you in the Hare Krishnas?"

Phil looked stunned. Then he said, "He'd laugh at me and tell me to rejoin the real world. He wouldn't understand at all!"

That response was just what I was hoping for. I decided to press the point.

"If Tom were sitting right here, right now, how would you explain to him why you went into the Krishnas?" I asked.

I have to admit I was caught off guard when Phil burst into intense sobbing, which continued for a full five minutes. By this time we were sitting together in a quiet park. Phil clutched his chest and rocked back and forth. The loud crying seemed to echo from deep within. I debated with myself whether or not to put my arm around Phil and console him; I decided not to interrupt. Eventually, he stopped and collected himself once more. I looked compassionately at Phil and decided to try the question again.

"Really, what would you tell Tom?" I asked.

Phil wiped his eyes and stated quite categorically, "I don't want to talk about it anymore, okay?"

I nodded and remained silent for a while. I decided to let him think about the question some more, hoping he would answer it within himself. I suggested we get up and walk some more. I wanted him to shift his frame of mind.

"There are a few more things I would like to discuss with you before we go back to the house," I started up again. "If you could put yourself in your parent's shoes, how would you feel to lose a son?"

"What?" he asked looking up at me.

"Imagine being your mother," I said. "She carried Tom and you, gave birth to both of you, nursed, diapered, washed both of you. Cared for you when you were sick. Played with you, taught you, watched you grow to adulthood. Can you feel what it must have been like for her to lose Tom?"

"Yes. It was horrible," he said. He was indeed talking as though he was his mother.

"And your father. Can you stop and think about what it was like for him?" I added.

Phil said, "Dad was always the closest to Tom. It hit him real hard."

"Yes," I said. "Now can you imagine what it felt like to watch your other son become suicidally depressed and then a few months later, change his name, shave his head, and move away to a group which is considered to be very controversial?"

"It would be horrible," he repeated. "I would feel angry. I would feel like I lost two sons."

"That's exactly how they told me they felt," I said. "Can you see that now? That is why they were so critical of the group when you got involved."

I paused and let him think for a few more moments before I went on.

"I'm curious to know what was going on in your mind when you first met the member of the group. What was it that caught your attention and attracted you to learn more?" I asked.

Phil looked up at the sky for a moment, looked down at the ground, took a deep sigh, and said, "Well, when he asked me why I looked so depressed, I told him about Tom's death. I told him that I just couldn't understand why it would happen to such a wonderful person like him. It just didn't seem right. He began to explain the laws of karma to me, and how this material world is just illusion anyway, and how I should be happy that Tom left his material consciousness so that he could come back as a more highly evolved being in his next life."

"I see—so the devotee helped you understand what had happened to Tom in a way that took away your fear and confusion," I said.

"And guilt," he added.

"And guilt?" I asked.

"Yes, you see, I had asked Tom to go to the store that day to buy me another guitar string. He was on his way there when he was killed," Phil said.

"So you blamed yourself for his death because you figured that if you hadn't asked him to go to the store he never would have been in the accident?" I asked.

"I guess so," Phil said, sadly.

It occurred to me that I had better try to offer Phil some other perspectives on the incident. I began by saying, "If Tom had been killed in a swimming accident at the far end of the lake, would you have blamed yourself for not staying closer to him?"

He thought for a moment. "Maybe."

"Can you imagine any way Tom could have died that wouldn't have been your fault?" I asked.

He paused again before answering. "I guess not. But the fact remains that he was going to the store for me."

"Is it possible that he also had some other things to buy, or some other errands to run? Is it possible that he decided to take a different route to the store than he ordinarily took, and that was where the accident occurred?" I asked.

Phil seemed nonplused.

"How would Tom feel now, if it had been you who had gone to the store one day and were killed in a car accident?" I asked. "Would he get depressed, think about committing suicide, and then join the Hare Krishnas?"

Phil laughed.

I knew this was a bullseye. Within a few minutes it was Phil who started asking me questions.

"How do you feel about the Krishnas, Steve?" Phil asked.

I thought he was genuinely trying to test his "reality," not just trying to find fault with me and write me off.

"Boy. That's a tough one," I said, scratching my head.

He then said, "I want to know."

"My role as a professional, Phil, is to do counseling and not to make value judgments on what people do with their lives. I do have personal feelings though," I said.

"I want to know what you think personally," said Phil, quietly.

"Well, to be honest, I am very concerned. You see, fourteen years ago I myself joined a religious group which my family disapproved of. I too had been depressed before I met the members and wasn't sure what I wanted to do with my life. Back then, I thought that they were trying to interfere with my rights as an adult to choose what I wanted to do."

"What group?" Phil asked, with curiosity.

I decided to give the long answer first. "The Holy Spirit Association for the Unification of World Christianity. It is also known as the Unification Church," I said. "Anyway, I was a devoted member of the group for more than two years. I slept three hours a night, and even did several seven-day fasts drinking just water."

"That's a long fast," Phil said admiringly. I could tell that he was listening to every word I said.

"Yeah. I lost an average of fifteen pounds at the end of the week. Anyway, in my group we revered the leader as one of the greatest spiritual masters who has ever lived. In fact, we believed that he had met with Jesus, Buddha, Muhammed, Krishna, and every other great spiritual leader."[1]

"You believed *that?*" He was amazed.

"Yes. We believed in a spirit world. In fact, we believed that whenever someone died, like Tom, it was to pay indemnity for some past sin in the person's lineage. In this way, another member of the family could join the group, serve the man we revered as the living Messiah, and then later intervene to save the person who had passed on to the spirit world. In this way, God could not only restore the whole world back to its original state of goodness, but restore all of the spiritual beings in the spirit world who were unable to advance without earthly 'vitality elements' provided by those on earth."

Phil's jaw hung open a bit. He asked, "You really believed that?"

"At the time, absolutely," I said. "You see, in the church, members were not allowed to ask critical questions of anything the leader said or did. We were taught to believe that anything that challenged the leader or the group's beliefs was 'negative' and was caused by evil spirits. We were taught to do thought-stopping to shut down our minds. In my group we did this by praying intensely as well as chanting whenever we started to doubt, or whenever we felt homesick."[2]

"What was the name of the group again?" he asked.

"The Unification Church," I said. "You probably know it as the Moonies."

"You were in the Moonies? No—I don't believe it!" Phil exclaimed.

"It's true. In fact, I was a devoted follower of Sun Myung Moon. I would have gladly died on command if he had told me to," I replied.

"That's incredible!" Phil said.

"Not only that, but we were literally made to feel that if we ever left the group our lives would fall to pieces," I continued. "We were told that we would be betraying God, the Messiah, ten generations of our ancestors—the whole world, in fact—if we ever left. We were told that all of our relatives now in the spirit world would accuse us throughout eternity for betraying God.[3] It was quite a heavy trip. We were told to avoid all former members because they were controlled by evil. If someone we were close to left the group we were made to feel that he or she was now a Benedict Arnold and was possessed by demonic spirits.[4] Can you put yourself in my shoes and imagine what I felt when I was in there?"

"Yes," Phil said. "Amazing. How did you get out?"

"Well, I was in an automobile accident in which I was almost killed," I said. "After two weeks in the hospital and an operation on my leg, I was able to get permission to go visit my sister. She had given birth to my nephew over a year earlier, but I had never seen him. I had never been able to get permission from my central figure. Anyway, my parents hired some former Moonies to come talk with me."

"Didn't you try to resist?" asked Phil.

"Of course. I had been taught in the group about deprogramming," I said. "I was told that they would torture me and try to break my faith in God. Of course I tried to get away, but with a broken leg and no crutches I couldn't get very far."

"So then what made you decide to leave?" said Phil. I could see he really wanted to know.

I explained to him all the things I had learned during my intervention. I told him I had realized the former members still loved God and were genuinely good people. I described them as people who had decided to leave the group because they no longer wanted to follow a demagogue who was interested in creating a world in which everyone was identical in thought, feeling, and action. The ex-members told me of their belief that God gave them free will so that they could choose to do the right thing, and not be forced by mind control to do what the leader thought was the right thing. I told him that any group that told its members not to think, but rather to obey their leaders blindly, was dangerous. I told him that any organization that told members not to talk to former members or read critical information was exercising information control—an essential component of mind control.

I told him that during my counseling I began to remember specific questions I had had, and specific contradictions that I had observed but had never had time to ponder while I was surrounded by members because as a "good" member I had to use thought-stopping nearly all the time. Once encouraged to get in touch with who I really was and rethink my entire experience objectively, I was able to see that I had really been very unhappy in the group: I had given up my individuality, my creativity, my autonomy.

"I was also involved in bringing others in the group and forcing them to be the same way. I had a lot of guilt over things that I had done while a member, Phil."

We talked for a long time before we went back to the house. I told the family that maybe we should take a few hours out before we started family counseling. Not surprisingly, Phil wanted to be by himself for a while and do some thinking.

The family counseling that took place later built on the work I had done with Phil. By the time we stopped for the evening, the family had communicated their intense desire to Phil that he give himself a chance to really listen to the "whole story." Phil agreed to spend several days listening and talking to former members and re-evaluating his involvement in the Hare Krishna group. Several people were brought in to assist him in this process. I was able to help the family resolve some of their pain and conflict, and Phil eventually made the decision to leave the cult.

Phil is presently pursuing a music career.

For Every Lock There Is a Key

In my intervention with Phil, I not only built rapport, used goal-oriented techniques of communication, and developed a model of his identity, but deliberately began to try to get Phil to look at his situation from another perspective. I then intentionally applied the keys to the remaining locks of mind control, and he responded positively. These keys reach into the deepest levels of a person, and the changes that they bring on can be very profound, as in the case of Phil's sudden collapse into cathartic sobbing.

KEY NO. 4: GET THE PERSON IN TOUCH WITH HIS PRE-CULT IDENTITY

When a person begins to remember who he was before becoming a cult member, I am able to reanchor his personal reference point on reality to a time when there was no cult identity and consequently no mind control. I enable the person to review what he was thinking and feeling at each stage of the recruitment process. Almost always, the person had significant doubts or questions at that time which have long since been suppressed. As I have said earlier, it is quite common that through the pressure of indoctrination, people silence their inner voice, which is trying to warn them away.

It is within this pre-cult personality that I can learn exactly what a person needs to see, hear, or feel in order to walk out of the group. For some people, the criteria can be to show them how their leader misinterprets the Bible. For others, it is to learn about the leader's criminal background and dealings. Others need to be shown specific contradictions within the doctrine. The question "How will you know when it's time for you to leave the group?" can reveal that individual's bottom-line criterion. Will he leave if God tells him to? Will he leave if he discovers he's been lied to? As soon as a member can tell me explicitly what he would need to decide to leave the group, then I can try my best to get him the proof he requires.

In the case of Phil, prior to joining he was a depressed, suicidal person wracked with guilt because he felt responsible for his brother's death. If I hadn't been able to help him face his feelings and "reframe" the accident, he never would have been able to leave the group. One could speculate that on some unconscious level, he was punishing himself for his "crime" by being involved in the group. Until he could rethink the circumstances of his brother's death and verbalize what he felt, he would never be able to take a fresh step forward.

In this and other cases like it, if the individual was not happy or healthy just before joining the group, it is imperative to find some positive reference point for the person to use as an identity anchor. If there are no strong positive experiences to use for this purpose, then one has to be made up or cultivated. Imagination can be used to create some positive experiences. For example, one might ask questions such as "If you had had a warm, loving family, what would it feel like?" or "If your father had been everything you wanted when you were growing up, what qualities would he have had and what kinds of things would you want to do together?"

In order for Phil to even consider leaving the Krishnas, he needed to remember his previous self and recall how good it felt to play guitar, write songs, and enjoy his friends and family. His unresolved grief and irrational feeling of guilt had to be brought up and worked out. He needed to remember Tom as a person full of life, not just as a victim. Phil was able to resurrect Tom in his inner life—his desire to be an investigative journalist, his dislike of organized religion, his aggressive stance to life. Since twins are almost always extremely close, it was imperative that he reestablish his positive emotional link with Tom.

KEY NO. 5: GET THE CULT MEMBER TO LOOK AT REALITY FROM MANY DIFFERENT PERSPECTIVES

During my intervention with Phil, I asked him to look at himself from a variety of different viewpoints. When I asked Phil to switch perspectives and think like Tom, everything seemed to make a dramatic shift for him. I asked him, "What would Tom do if you were the one who had died? Would he have joined the Krishnas?" Phil had become so frozen in his grief that he had never been able to get a perspective on it. When I asked him "What would Tom say if he knew you were in the Krishnas?" the answer came back "He'd laugh at me and tell me to rejoin the real world."

Another important perspective that I wanted Phil to have was that of his parents. He needed to connect with their grief and sense of loss. Phil had been so wrapped up in his own pain that he hadn't realized how deeply everyone else had been affected. Indeed, his parents had felt that they had to hold themselves together in order to help the children. They had never been able to go fully through the stages of mourning.

Helping Phil to remember and process his experience of being recruited into the cult was another important perspective for him. By asking him to verbalize what he was thinking and feeling when he first met the member, Phil's long-suppressed guilt feelings about asking Tom to buy him the guitar string on that fateful day came to the surface for the first time in years. Not only that, but by remembering his recruitment, Phil was able to remember some of the questions and doubts he must have had then. He remembered how important the devotee's explanation of karma was to him. It helped him to put an ideological box around his brother's death and say to himself that Tom was one step closer to enlightenment. He remembered that when he first started chanting, it made the pain go away. He remembered thinking to himself at the time, "This is a whole lot better than feeling suicidal."

In other interventions, it is important to introduce different perspectives. Each time a cult member takes a different perspective, the cult hold is weakened somewhat. In addition to asking a person to remember who he was before the group, it can also be quite valuable to ask him to imagine the future. What will he be like in a year, two years, five years, or even ten years? What does he realistically see himself doing then—selling flowers on street corners? If not, how would he feel if he still is unable to do anything else but sell flowers on the street, ten years down the line?

Another valuable perspective can also be that of the cult leader. I asked one woman, "If you were the Messiah, would you live the way Rev. Moon is living—in a palatial mansion, with two $250,000 personal yachts, limousines, etc.?" She answered, "Definitely not. I would give all my money to help the poor. I would live very simply." At this, I was able to ask her why she thinks *he* does it. She told me, "It troubles me. It has always troubled me!"

When I told Phil what it felt like to be in the Moonies, I especially tried to convey what it felt like to be around Mr. Moon—the excitement, the honor, the awe. I could have asked him to imagine what it feels like to be a Moonie who believes that Moon is ten times greater than Jesus Christ, to feel the incredible honor of living on earth and seeing the Messiah in person. When Phil stepped into the shoes of a Moonie, his experience as a Krishna devotee was altered forever.

Each time the member is able to step out of his shoes and into the shoes of another—whether a member of a different group, or even his parents or his leader—he is weakening his psychological rigidity. Indeed, encouraging a cult member psychologically to take another perspective enables him to test his reality. In this process, the information he was programmed with takes on a new light.

The way to undo blind faith is to introduce new perspectives.

KEY NO. 6: SIDE-STEP THE THOUGHT-STOPPING PROCESS BY GIVING INFORMATION IN AN INDIRECT WAY

Every person in a cult has been programmed to stop all "negative" thoughts about the leader, the doctrine, or the organization, and has also been indoctrinated to believe that this group is superior to all other groups and different from all other groups.

This thought-stopping process is triggered whenever there is a "frontal attack," or, in other words, whenever the person perceives that someone is attacking the validity of the group. In this way, thought-stopping acts as a shield to be held up against any perceived enemy.

However, a cult member does not use thought-stopping when there is no perception of "danger." Since a cult member believes that he is not in a cult, but that there are other groups which are cults, it is relatively easy to have long detailed conversations with the cult member without his ever feeling that you are attacking his leader or his group. Therefore, the way to communicate with a cult member is through an indirect approach.

If he is a member of The Way International, he will not be threatened in the least if you tell him about the Moonies. If you are talking with a member of the Moonies, he will not be threatened if you tell him about The Way. He thinks his group is so different, so superior to these other groups. In this way one can outline the specific mind control processes and techniques used by this other group in a soft, subtle manner. You will be providing the person's unconscious (his "John-John" identity) with the essential frames of reference to begin to analyze what has happened to him.

Notice that in Phil's case I was careful not to attack the Krishnas. If I had done so, he probably would have become defensive and started chanting, and if I had kept it up, he would have walked away. All the information was based on the Moonies and other groups. This indirect method of conveying information bypasses the thought-stopping mechanism.

KEY NO. 7: VISUALIZE A HAPPY FUTURE OUTSIDE THE CULT TO UNDO PHOBIA INDOCTRINATION

Phobia indoctrination—fear of ever leaving the group—is usually accomplished on an unconscious level. The cult identity never thinks of leaving the group. Indeed, he is perpetually happy, enthusiastic, and incredibly obedient to his superiors. It is "John-John" who has been enslaved.

I helped Phil to begin to unlock the phobia indoctrination by asking him to *visualize a picture of the future that he would really enjoy*—playing music, friends, a wife, kids, being close to his family. Then I asked him to "step into the picture" and enjoy the experience. By doing this, I was helping Phil open a door out of the Krishnas. This one visualization technique began to dismantle the phobia indoctrination. It became a bridge to another possible life.

In other cases, I often ask the member, "If you had never met this group, and you were doing exactly what you wanted to be doing, what would that be?" After some moments of confusion and resistance, I usually have to repeat the question several times. "Really, just imagine, if you were doing exactly what you wanted to be doing, so that you were totally happy, spiritually and personally fulfilled, and you never knew the group even existed, what would you be doing?"

The answers vary. "I'd be a doctor and work in a clinic serving poor people." "I'd be a tennis pro." "I'd be sailing around the world." Once the person verbalizes the fantasy, I try to get him to step inside his visualization of this new life and encourage him to emotionally involve himself in it.

By taking this step, I am able to begin neutralizing the cult member's programmed negative feelings about doing anything other than being a member. Once a positive personal reference point is established, the cult-generated picture of a dark, disaster-filled life outside the group begins to be altered. When a positive picture is in place, a bridge to other possibilities opens. People outside the group can be seen as warm and loving. There are a lot of interesting things to learn outside the group. There are lots of enjoyments to be had. Religious and spiritual fulfillment can be accomplished. Once the outside world becomes filled with positive experiences, the group loses full control over the cult member's sense of reality. A cult member can then be in a better position to decide whether he wants to stay where he is or cross the bridge and do something personally more valuable and fulfilling.

KEY NO. 8: OFFER THE CULT MEMBER CONCRETE DEFINITIONS OF MIND CONTROL AND CHARACTERISTICS OF A DESTRUCTIVE CULT

My intervention with Phil shows the importance of giving a cult member specific information about cults. Because I was able to establish good rapport with Phil, I was able to get a lot of information from him and help him. In the process, Phil became curious about me and wanted to know what I thought.

At that point, I was able to begin conveying specific information about cults and mind control through my own story of being in the Moonies. I was able to explain what happened during my deprogramming and show how it enabled me to understand that I had been subjected to mind control and that, in fact, I was in a destructive cult. In my own case, until my counselors taught me what the Chinese Communists of the 1950s were doing, I did not truly understand the process of "brainwashing." Until they were able to show me how other destructive cults, like the Krishnas,[5] were structured in the same authoritarian manner as is the Unification Church, I had believed that the Moonies were different from all other groups.

I was also able to explain some of the Moonies' beliefs to Phil to show him that, as strange as they sounded, some of them did seem to make sense, if you believed in the whole doctrine. I made sure to include the Moonies' view on why "accidental deaths" happen, so that he could see that there were alternative belief systems that offered another explanation. It was also important for him to see that there are other groups who are led by people claiming to be spiritually superior. When I eventually told him that there were some three thousand cult groups, and that if one of them was in fact led by the one legitimate great leader (which I seriously doubted), then the odds that he would have found the right one on the first pick were three thousand to one. Not very good odds.

I also showed him that I was a dedicated member, and that I chose to leave the group for the "right" reasons. I wanted to challenge his indoctrination that people who leave the group do so for the wrong reasons—because they are weak or undisciplined or want to indulge in materialism. I wanted him to know that I left the group out of strength and integrity.

I left the group because I came to see objectively what I had been doing. I had devoted myself to a "fantasy" created in the Moonie indoctrination workshops. I thought I was following the Messiah, the person who would be able to end war, poverty, disease, and corruption, and establish a Kingdom of Heaven on Earth. I didn't mind sacrificing myself for these noble causes. I thought that as a member, I was teaching people the ultimate standard of love and truth, and living an exemplary life.

Instead, I realized to my horror that I had learned to compromise my integrity in the name of God. I realized that the higher I rose in the organization, and the closer I got to Moon, the more obsessed I had become. Power became almost an addiction, and I began making choices based on what would protect and enhance my power, not on what was morally right.

I left when I realized that deception and mind control can never be part of any legitimate spiritual movement: that through their use, the group had created a virtual "Hell on Earth," a kingdom of slaves. Once I was able to realize that even though I *wanted* to believe it was true (Moon as Messiah, Divine Principle as Truth) *my belief didn't make it true,* I saw that even if I remained in the group for another fifty years, the fantasy I was sacrificing myself for would never come true.

By being given some clear definitions of mind control, I was able to see clearly how I had been victimized and how I had learned to victimize others. I personally had to come to terms with my own values, beliefs, and ideals. Once I did that, even though I had invested so much of myself in the group, become a leader, and developed close bonds with many members, I had to walk away. I could never go back to becoming a "true believer" again.

Chapter 10

Strategies for Recovery

PEOPLE leave a group in three basic ways: they walk out, they get kicked out (often in a very "burned-out" condition, both psychologically and physically), or they get counseled out. Although they are fortunate to leave the destructive cult, the adjustments to life in the "real world" can be extremely difficult. If they don't get good information and counseling after they leave, the cult-induced phobias they carry with them will make them into walking "time bombs." Also, many cult members have lived for so long without any kind of normal work or social life that the process of readjustment to adult life is an uphill climb. Some people leave cults only to voluntarily return to the cult. While in my experience such people are generally the exception to the rule, they point out the vulnerability of people who have just left a mind control environment.

WALK-OUTS

Undoubtedly the largest number of former members fall into the first category, the walk-outs. These are the people who have managed to physically remove themselves from the cult but have received no exit-counseling at all. I occasionally meet them socially and find that some of them, even years after the cult involvement, are still dealing with the problems of mind control indoctrination.

For example, I once met a woman at a dinner party who had "walked out" of the Moonies. During our conversation she remarked that even though she had been happily married for more than six years, she was deeply afraid of having children. She told me that she couldn't figure it out at all, because she had wanted to have children ever since she was a little girl. Now she was in her early thirties and realized that she was in a race against time to have children, but she still couldn't get over her fear.

As we talked, I learned that she had been recruited into the Moonies in 1969—more than twelve years prior to our conversation—but had stayed in the group for only three months.

"When they started making too many demands on me, I left," she told me. It was clear that she had brushed off her encounter as simply a close call.

"Did it ever occur to you that your fear of having children might be related to your experience in the Moonies?" I asked.

She looked puzzled. "What do you mean?" she said.

"Do you remember ever being told anything about having children, when you were in the Moonies?" I asked.

She rolled her head up slightly, as if her eyes were scanning the ceiling. After a few moments, her face became flushed and she shrieked.

"Yes! I do remember something!" she said. To my surprise, she took hold of me by the shoulders and shook me back and forth.

"I remember being told that if anyone ever betrayed the Messiah and left the movement, their children would be stillborn!"[1] she exclaimed.

Her excitement at remembering the source of her fear of having children was tremendous, and I couldn't help but share it. It seemed as though we could hear the psychological chains that had been locking her mind fall to the floor with a thud.

At that point, I realized I had to explain phobia indoctrination to her. I told her that even though she had been involved with the Moonies for only a few months, her recruiters and trainers had successfully implanted a phobia of giving birth to a dead child in her unconscious mind.

"Even though I didn't believe in Moon anymore?" she asked.

"The mind is capable of learning new information and retaining it forever," I said. "This goes for harmful things as well as helpful things. You may have thought that you were finished with the Moonies when you walked out the door, but it has taken you twelve years to locate and eliminate that time bomb they put inside your mind."

Of course, it is somewhat rare to have a conversation with a former cult member whom I meet socially which leads to a sudden breakthrough about phobia indoctrination. Yet, a great number of people, just like this woman, are somehow coping with the damaging aftereffects of cult participation. Their problems are often made worse by the fact that many mental health professionals are not knowledgeable about mind control and do not know how to effectively help people suffering from its lingering aftereffects.

Many people *are* able to walk out, particularly during the early phase of indoctrination. This woman was able to rebel and assert herself in 1969, when the Moonies were much less effective in their indoctrination. People may be able to escape the cult if they are exposed to too much of the inner doctrine before they are ready to swallow it. For example, one woman I was recruiting found out that Moon was going to assign her a husband in the first few weeks of her indoctrination, and it so infuriated her that she simply stormed out of the group. A man I was recruiting discovered that we believed Moon was the Messiah[2] before we had had enough time to prepare him for that conclusion.

Other people walk out when they become victims of internal politics or personality conflicts. For example, many people have gotten fed up and walked out because they couldn't relate to or follow their immediate superior. Other long-time members have walked out when they felt that group policy was not being fairly and uniformly applied and there was a struggle for power.

Over the years I have met dozens of people who have walked out of their group because they couldn't stand it anymore, but they still believe in the top leader. There are thousands of ex-Moonies who still believe that Moon is the Messiah, but just can't tolerate the way the Moonies are run. In their minds they are waiting for the day that the group reforms its policies so they can return. They do not understand that the group is structured and run the way it is *because* of Moon.

KICK-OUTS

I've encountered quite a few people who were kicked out of their group, ostensibly because they were bucking authority and asking too many questions. Others were abused to such an extent that they were burned out and no longer "productive." Still others had developed serious physical or psychological problems that required too much money for treatment, and had become a liability to the group.

The people who have been kicked out of a destructive cult are always in the worst shape of all former cult members. They feel rejection not only from the group members but, in the case of religious cults, from God Himself. Most of them devoted their entire lives to the group, turning over bank accounts and property when they joined. They were told that the group was now their "family," which would take care of them for the rest of their lives. Then, years later, they were told that they were not living up to the group's standards and would have to leave. These people, phobic toward the world outside their cults, have been cast into what they view as utter darkness.

For many "kick-outs," suicide seems a real alternative to their suffering.[3] No one knows how many people have killed themselves because of involvement in a destructive cult. I knew personally of three people who killed themselves because of their cult involvement.

Of those who unsuccessfully attempt suicide, many are incorrectly diagnosed as schizophrenic when they are brought in for psychiatric evaluation.

Uninformed doctors can hardly be blamed. How else could they treat a person screaming for Satan to come out of them? How could they know that the person had been doing high-speed silent chanting for hours and that it was causing him to be so spaced out that he appeared catatonic?

One man I worked with was kicked out of his guru-oriented cult after his father threatened the group leader with lawsuits and other forms of harassment. The young man had been programmed for six years with the idea that leaving the guru meant instant insanity. After he left (surprise!) he went crazy. His parents took him to a mental hospital, and the doctors confirmed that in their opinion, the boy was crazy—in fact schizophrenic. The young man interpreted this diagnosis as proof that his leader was right: that anyone who leaves the guru goes crazy.

Once in a psychiatric hospital, he started to pound his head vigorously against the wall. He was put in a straight jacket and put under constant surveillance. No one stopped to ask him why he was doing it. I found out that while he was a member during a visit to India, he had been shown the actual rock the Guru had banged his head against until, in his words, "he managed to reach gross consciousness." In his effort to replicate his guru's spiritual path, the young man nearly killed himself. To top it all off, it only "proved" to the doctors that he was schizophrenic.

Only when I began to exit-counsel him did he begin to see how he had been programmed by the cult, and how he inadvertently reinforced that programming whenever he remembered cult jargon and his indoctrination as a devoted follower. By internally repeating his cult leader's teaching, he continued to keep himself indoctrinated and impair his progress for many years.

He was also struggling with the years of negative "help" he had received from mental health professionals while in "treatment." He said that some of his doctors had actually told him that his involvement with the group was one of the healthier things he had done in his life. One case worker even encouraged him to read cult literature. All the time, he was being reminded daily that he was schizophrenic.

One ex-member I worked with from an occult group was absolutely convinced that her spiritual body was disintegrating and that she was in the process of dying. She would suffer tremendous anxiety attacks, particularly in the middle of the night, and felt pains in her chest. She had been tested by doctors for every conceivable problem, and it was determined that the problem was all "in her mind." She had been programmed to self-destruct by the group if she ever left it, and once she was out, that was exactly what started to happen—until her exit-counseling.

When people who have walked out or have been kicked out are not able to receive cult exit-counseling, their suffering is usually prolonged. Still, many manage, with the help of family and friends, to pick up the pieces and move forward in their lives. However, if these people never come to understand mind control and how it was used to recruit and indoctrinate them, they will never be able to live as full a life as they could if they did. These people may have temporarily managed to put their cult experience on a shelf and forget about it. At some point, though, it could burst back into their lives.

Rick was one of these people. He had walked out of the Children of God with his wife and three kids after a six-year membership. Five years later, a piece of cult literature turned up in his mailbox. All his cult indoctrination was triggered by this one letter from the leader, and his mind started racing out of control. At one point, he said he started hearing a voice in his head that told him to go upstairs and choke his children. Fortunately, he didn't listen. Rick was able to receive exit-counseling and is today a successful computer consultant.

COUNSELED-OUTS

For those people who were counseled out of a group, most were fortunate that they were able to get the help and information they needed. However, many people, particularly some who were deprogrammed in the 1970s and even 1980s, are still carrying around cult-related psychological baggage. Just because a person has been out of the group for years, does not mean that all of the issues are resolved. Nothing could be further from the truth.

Much more is now known about mind control and exit-counseling than even a few years ago, and there are many more counselors to help. The FOCUS support organization for former cult members has groups in several major cities. Meeting and talking with former members of one's particular group and other groups is most effective in helping one to identify and resolve these problems.

PSYCHOLOGICAL PROBLEMS OF EX-CULT MEMBERS

Former members report a variety of psychological difficulties after they leave a cult. Probably the most common is the *depression* they feel during the first few months after leaving. It is difficult to describe the pain of realizing that you have been lied to and enslaved in a mind control cult—when you discover your "dream" is really a nightmare.

Many of the people I have met described the experience as having fallen deeply in love, giving every ounce of love, trust, and commitment to someone, and then finding out that person was a false lover and was just using them. The pain and sense of betrayal is enormous.

Others describe the realization in more graphic terms: feeling as though they had been spiritually and psychologically raped. The sense of personal violation is indescribable. I myself came to realize that all of the love and devotion I felt towards Sun Myung Moon and Hak Ja Han as my "True Parents" was totally one-sided. I realized after I left that they didn't care about me personally at all. If they had, they would have tried to contact me to try to find out why I had left. Instead, I was automatically labeled "Satanic" and a traitor.[4]

When people are depressed, they tend to only see the bad side of things. Their pain can be so great that it blots out the hope of a positive future. It is essential that former members acknowledge and work through their pain, and go through the necessary grieving period. What seems to help the most is to enable people to realize that positive things did come out of their involvement, and to show them how they can now be much stronger because of the experience. Also helpful is encouraging them to put their experience in a manageable and hopeful perspective. There are always examples of people whose experience was much worse than their own, and who were able to not only survive but thrive after coming out.

Another common problem is an overwhelming tendency toward *continued dependence* on others for direction and authority. In groups where members lived communally, most life decisions were made by leaders. Members were encouraged to be selfless and obedient. This form of dependency creates low self-esteem and retards the desire and ability for individual development.

One specific form taken by this dependency is *difficulty in decision making*. I have worked with people who didn't know what they wanted to eat at restaurants, what clothes to wear, what book to read, what movie to go to, or what they should do next with regard to education or employment. For those who always had to ask their superiors for permission to do ordinary things, being thrust back into the world of personal responsibility can be quite overwhelming.

When I first left the Moonies, I didn't seem to have that difficulty. My deprogrammers told my parents that I would have trouble making decisions. My parents were quite confused when we went out to eat, because I easily knew what I wanted. They told me later that they thought, in some twisted way, that this meant that I hadn't been deprogrammed. What they hadn't taken into account was that I had not been a rank-and-file member. I had been a leader and was used to making certain kinds of decisions for myself as well as for others. Day-to-day decisions were easy for me; bigger decisions, like where to go back to college, were more difficult.

Like most skills, decision making becomes easier with practice. In time, people learn how to resume control over their lives. This process can be speeded up by the gentle but firm insistence by family members and friends that ex-members make up their own mind about what they want to eat or do. By bolstering the ex-member's self esteem and confidence, the dependency problem is usually overcome.

"FLOATING": DEALING WITH THE CULT IDENTITY AFTER LEAVING

A more difficult problem that former members experience is a phenomenon known as "floating."[5] It may be described as an experience in which the former member suddenly starts to "float" back in time to the days of his group involvement, and starts to think from within his former identity. Here is an example.

Margot Sutherland, a 19-year-old college student, was recruited into Lifespring during a summer job in 1987. Although she had completed the basic course and was one weekend away from completing her leadership training course, she didn't like the pressure being put on her to recruit new members. Fortunately, she lived in Maine and was not in the immediate vicinity of the central group in New England, based in Boston. This provided her a great deal more space, even though they called nearly every day to check in. Margot's mother, an ordained Methodist minister, saw the personality changes in her daughter and was concerned enough to borrow money to do an intervention.

As part of an investigation of Lifespring, ABC's "20/20" interviewed psychiatrist and cult expert Dr. John Clark of Harvard Medical School. Although Lifespring takes a different view, Dr. Clark stated during the interview tha Lifespring does, in his opinion, practice mind control and brainwashing.[6] For Margot, one of the biggest problems after the intervention was hearing music come on the radio, like Steve Winwood's "Higher Love," and getting flashbacks of the training. Groups like Lifespring like to use popular music as part of their indoctrination for that very reason. It creates a strong association in the individual's unconscious, which without proper counseling can take months, sometimes years, to overcome. Music is used by many cults for indoctrination because it forms a strong anchor for memory.

This stimulus-response mechanism that caused the flashback, or "floating," can be a significant problem for former members. This experience is triggered when a former member sees, hears, or feels some external or internal stimulus which was part of the conditioning process. This can briefly jolt them back into the cult mindset.

For the first year after I left the Moonies, every time I heard the word "moon" I would think "Father" and remember sitting at Moon's feet. Another example of this phenomenon occurred a month or so after I left the group. I was driving to a friend's house and had the thought "This would be an excellent fundraising area!" I had to catch myself and tell myself that I was no longer in the Moonies. This thought was triggered because for the last five months of my membership, I spent fifteen to twenty hours a day driving around looking for places to drop off members to solicit money.

For those people involved for a long time in groups that required excessive meditation, chanting, "decreeing,"[7] speaking in tongues and so forth, one may expect to see involuntary episodes occur for at least one year after they have left the cult. Many of my clients have complained to me that suddenly in the middle of a sentence while holding a normal conversation, they find themselves doing the mind-numbing technique they had practiced for years. This can be especially dangerous when someone is driving a car.

"It is very frustrating to realize over and over again that your mind is out of your control. Particularly when I'm in a stressful situation, I will suddenly discover I'm babbling nonsense words and syllables (speaking in tongues) inside my head, and I've become disoriented from whatever I was doing," one former member of a Bible cult told me.

Floating, if not understood and responded to appropriately, can cause a former member who is depressed, lonely, and confused to go back to the cult. For those fortunate enough to receive exit-counseling, floating is rarely a major problem. However, for people who don't understand mind control, it can be a terrifying experience. Suddenly, you can pop back into the cult mindset, and be hit with a tremendous rush of fear and guilt that you have betrayed the group and its leader. You can lose rational control and begin to think magically. By this I mean that one can interpret recent world and personal events from the cult perspective. For example, you didn't get that job "because God wants you to go back to the group," or the Korean Air Lines Flight 007 was shot down by the Russians "because you left the Moonies."

If an ex-member starts to float, what he should do is simply but firmly remind himself that the experience was just triggered by some stimulus, that it will pass, and find someone who understands cult mind control with whom he can talk it out rationally. Remember, floating is a natural by-product of being subjected to mind control. It will decrease over time, and there are techniques you can use to exercise control over it.

The most powerful and effective technique is to identify the trigger. For example, it could be hearing a song, seeing someone who looks like a member of the group, or behaving in a manner associated with being a member. Once you know what triggered you, you can deliberately call forth the stimulus, and this time make a new association for yourself. Do this over and over again until it becomes a *new learned response.*

In my case, for example, I would hear the word "moon" and make a picture in my mind of a beautiful full moon. I would say to myself "The earth only has one natural satellite, the moon." For about a week I systematically said to myself "moon," and repeated the pattern over and over again. I referred to the leader of the group as Mr. Moon, not wishing to call him "Reverend," since that was a self-appointed title anyway.

One ex-member of est told me that even though she loves the beach, she avoided it because the sounds of ocean waves always reminded her of the group indoctrination. Even though she had been out of the group for five years, that association was still inhibiting her ability to enjoy something she had always loved. I told her to change the association! She could hear the sound of waves, and deliberately program in a new and personally gratifying association. I told her to repeat the new association until it automatically overrode the cult programming. Within a few days she was able to visit the beach again.

OVERCOMING "LOADED LANGUAGE"

Substituting real language for the cult's "loaded language" can speed up a person's full recovery. By eradicating the cult jargon put inside my head, I was able to begin looking at the world again without wearing cult "glasses." The cult's "loaded language" had created little cubbyholes in my mind, and when I was a member, all reality was filtered through them. The faster an ex-member reclaims words and their real meaning, the faster his recovery.

When I was in the Moonies, all relationships between people were described as either a "Cain-Abel" or a "chapter 2" problem. The term "Cain-Abel," as explained earlier, was used to categorize everyone as either someone's superior or his subordinate. "Chapter 2 problems" were anything that had to do with sexuality, and any attraction members felt towards others. Therefore, all personal relationships fell into either of these two categories.

The most common mistake made by ex-members is to tell themselves that they should not think of the cult word. The mind doesn't know how *not* to think of something. Language is structured so that we have to think in positive associations. So, if you are an ex-member, make a new association, just as I described for the problem of "floating." If you are an ex-Moonie and have trouble getting along with a person, think of it as a personality conflict or a communication problem.

LOSS OF PSYCHOLOGICAL POWER

Another common problem is the loss of concentration and memory. Before I got involved in the Moonies, I used to read a book at one sitting, averaging three books a week. However, in the two and a half years I spent in the group, virtually all I read was Moonie propaganda. When I first left the group, I remember how frustrated I felt whenever I tried to read non-cult literature. At first, getting through one entire paragraph was nearly impossible. I would continually "space out," or have to stop to look up words which I once knew but now couldn't remember. I had to read and reread sections before I was able to force the creaky gears of my mind into operation. I also needed to look at old photographs and be reminded of people I knew and things I had done prior to being in the group.

Fortunately, the mind is like a muscle. Although it tends to atrophy from disuse, with effort it can be built up again. It took me nearly a full year to get back to my pre-cult level of functioning.

NIGHTMARES, GUILT, AND OTHER EMOTIONAL PROBLEMS

Nightmares are a good indicator that the former member needs to receive additional counseling in order to work through his cult experience. These unpleasant dreams come from an unconscious mind which is still wrestling with the issues of cult involvement. Some common nightmares include being trapped somewhere, feeling that people are out to get you, and being in the midst of a storm or a war. Former members also frequently report having unpleasant dreams in which they are talking with friends still in the group and trying to get them to leave, while their friends are pressuring them to rejoin.

Another key issue for some former members is *bad feelings about things they did in the group*. Some people were involved in illegal acts, such as fraud, arson, prostitution, and the use and sale of drugs. I have met people who went AWOL from the armed services because they were recruited by a destructive cult group, and had great trouble when they tried to clear themselves later.

Fortunately, the vast majority of former members I have met have not been involved in such things. However, most have to cope with how they treated their family and friends during the time of their cult membership. For example, some people, when their father or mother became ill, followed cult leaders' orders and refused to visit them in the hospital. In some cases the parent died and the member was not allowed to go to the funeral, even though it might have taken place only twenty miles away. It can be extremely painful for a person to walk out of a destructive cult and have to deal with the havoc and emotional damage that his membership caused.

When I first left the Moonies, I felt an incredible sense of guilt about my role as a leader. I blamed myself for lying and manipulating hundreds of people. I felt I had allowed myself to be used as an American "front" man, a stooge for the Koreans and Japanese, who really held the reins of power in the group.

Another issue involves the feelings towards friends still in the group. When I left, I desperately wanted to rescue those people I had personally recruited. Unfortunately, the Moonie leadership cleverly shipped the people who were closest to me away from the New York area. They were told that I was "away on a secret mission." The people I had recruited, my "spiritual children," didn't find out that I had left the group for more than three months. I believe they were told then only because at that point I started appearing on television to speak against the group.

About six months after I left, I went back to Queens College, where I had started a chapter of C.A.R.P., and gave a public lecture on cults and mind control for the psychology department. In the audience were my top three disciples,[8] Brian, Willie, and Luis. They sat and listened to me lecture for over an hour about mind control. I gave specific examples of how I had lied and tricked each one of them into membership. After the lecture was over, I walked over to them, and anxiously asked them what they thought. Willie smiled and said to me, "Steve, you shouldn't forget the heart of the Divine Principle or the heart of Father." I was crushed. They didn't appear to have heard a single thing I said. I remembered how, when I was a member, I had been instructed by Mr. Kamiyama to "raise my spiritual children to be faithful, even if I left the group." I didn't realize at the time why he had me do that, because I never imagined leaving. Now I understood. To my knowledge, Brian has since left the group, and I have no information about Willie or Luis.

Many people involved in faith-healing cults have to deal with the death of a child or loved one who was blocked from medical treatment. The remorse they feel when they leave such a group should not be turned on themselves in the form of blame or guilt. *They must realize that they were victims too and did what they believed to be right at the time.*

Others have to deal with the anger and resentment of their children, who in some cases were beaten, neglected, or sexually abused, as well as deprived of an education and a normal childhood. The horror some of these children have gone through is almost unimaginable. Some groups, like the Krishnas, systematically separate children from their parents and allow them to visit only infrequently.[9] Yogi Bhajan's 3HO group sometimes sends members' children to their school in India, in this way separating the children from their parents so that their allegiance is solely to the group.[10]

For others involved in less destructive cults, the emotional toll on children can ultimately yield positive results. I saw that in the life of Barbara, who called me last year for help. She explained how for most of her life she had thought she was crazy, and how she had just realized from talking with a friend that the group her parents had been involved with for the previous ten years was considered a destructive cult. Now twenty-two, she had spent a good deal of her childhood growing up with her family on the group's commune. She and her brother had been taught since early childhood that all negative emotions were harmful. Sadness, anger, jealousy, embarrassment, guilt, and fear were all to be avoided and not "indulged in." Barbara and her brother, Carl, were very relieved to know that their lifelong problems were not signs of mental illness and that there was help for them.

Since they had been ten and twelve years old, Barbara and Carl had tried to do what they were told by attending cult indoctrination programs but had never felt right about it. Nevertheless, they loved their parents and tried to do what would please them. Now that they were old enough and in college, as soon as they discovered that the group was a cult, they arranged for me and a former member to come and counsel them all.

Both parents were bright, successful people, now in their fifties. He is a practicing attorney, and she an elementary school teacher. He had been recruited into the group by an old friend from college. As a lawyer, he was quite skeptical at first, but was eventually drawn further and further into the group. He and his wife eventually ran the group's meetings in their city.

The intervention was a complete success, and the entire family is now closer than ever before. Now both parents are helping others in the group to re-evaluate their commitment. Several have already left the group.

HARASSMENT AND THREATS

Another issue for some former members involves harassment, threats, break-ins, lawsuits, blackmail, and even murder, particularly if the person goes public. Since groups believe that anyone who leaves is an enemy, there is always some risk that something bad will be done to a defector.

I have been threatened by cult members more than once, usually by mail or the telephone, but also in person, particularly when I am picketing, demonstrating, or otherwise exposing a particular group's activities. Only once was I physically assaulted, when a Moonie punched me in the face and tried to get me into a fist fight. I looked him in the eye and asked him, "Is this what the Kingdom of Heaven is going to be like—silencing the opposition?" I took him to court and he pleaded no contest. The judge ordered him to pay for a new pair of glasses and gave him a stern warning to stay away from me. Years later, he left the group and contacted me. He apologized for the incident, and told me he was only doing what he had been instructed to do: "Take care of Steve Hassan."

While violence towards former members is relatively rare, the fear factor has kept many people from going public and telling their story. What they don't realize is that once their story is told, along with many others, it would be stupid for a group to retaliate because it would only incriminate them more. When I started Ex-Moon Inc. in 1979, it was partly because I realized there would be much more strength and safety in numbers. The strategy was successful.

Some of the larger, more aggressive groups, like the Church of Scientology, have characteristically believed in attacking critics rather than defending themselves.[11] They have initiated hundreds of law suits against former members and critics, including Paulette Cooper, author of *The Scandal of Scientology*, and Gabe Cazares, former mayor of Clearwater, Florida. As far as I know, most of these suits were filed purely to harass and financially drain their opponents. To a certain extent, their strategy has been successful: most former members of Scientology are afraid to take any public action against the organization.[12] However, when the FBI raided Scientology headquarters, documents were obtained that proved the illegality of many activities conducted by the organization. In fact, Hubbard's wife and other top leaders were sent to jail.

PROBLEMS WITH INTIMATE RELATIONSHIPS

Former cult members who begin to live in the "real world" sooner or later have to deal with the fact that, for years, their emotional need for a satisfying intimate relationship with another individual was never met. Yet, the experience of having been taken advantage of while in a group makes it genuinely hard for people to take the emotional risk of forming a close relationship with others. Some people have denied their own sexuality for so long that they may have difficulty, even out of the group, in overcoming their inhibitions towards expressing their sexuality.

Someone who didn't live in a group environment surrounded by members but was involved in cults which permitted people to live in normal society may also find a new perspective on personal relationships after leaving the group. Perhaps he or she got into a sexual relationship with a "trainer" or leader who manipulated the member with little regard for feelings. Leaving such relationships behind is difficult for anyone, but the grief of separation and disillusionment can be overcome. In both cases, it's best to seek therapy with someone who understands cult mind control.

WAYS TO HEAL YOURSELF

The most effective emotional and informational support is provided by former members. In 1986, I served for a year as the national coordinator of FOCUS, a loosely knit group of former members who want to help themselves and others. It is quite a feat to coordinate a group of people who have all been burned by a group. It took a full year after my experience with the Moonies before I gingerly allowed myself to get involved again with a group, in this case with a peer counseling organization when I returned to college in 1977.

FOCUS, a non-profit organization affiliated with the Cult Awareness Network, gets funded to the tune of $500 a year, which means that the coordinator gets some of the telephone and mailing expenses paid, and that's all. It is up to specific former members in different cities to have meetings whenever they can. Here in Boston, thanks to Dean Thornburg, we meet in the basement of Marsh Chapel on the campus of Boston University. Between ten and twenty people show up each month and spend the two hours talking about our respective experiences, problems we are addressing, and ways to heal our wounds.

One woman who attends the FOCUS group in Boston contacted me after she heard me on a local radio show. Deborah had been involved with a politically oriented group. As far as I could tell, it was a social action group run like an authoritarian cult. She had been involved for some ten years. One day she broke one of the group's rules. She had lunch alone with a non-member, and rather than face being "grilled" by the cult leader in front of the entire membership, she called up her parents and asked them for a plane ticket. She later decided that she was afraid to go home and wound up living on the streets of Boulder for several months until she was able to slowly work her way back into society. When I met her last year, she was a successful businesswoman.

Even though she had been out of the group for eight years, she had never talked about her group experience until she started attending FOCUS meetings. "I feel like the whole thing is one big black box, and I'm afraid to open it up," she explained to the fifteen people present one Wednesday night. "Yet, I know that I am being hampered in my ability to trust my boyfriend and make a commitment to him. I think it is connected to what I went through."

We were all amazed at how successfully Deborah was able to compartmentalize her mind control experience for such a long time. When she did start talking about it, huge chunks of time were unaccounted for. The more she talked, the more we asked her questions and prodded her memory. Month by month, she got more and more in touch with what had happened to her. She had been subjected to an unusually intense degree of emotional and personal abuse while in the group.

"I am really glad that I was able to meet and talk with other former members," she told us one night. "It's nice to see other bright, talented people who went through something like what I went through. I just could never talk about the group to anyone without them thinking that I was crazy or sick!"

Indeed, being part of a support group can show people how mind control operates within very different organizations. It also enables those who are still grappling with these issues to hope that they will be able to go on with their lives and be happy, productive people. For most people who leave a destructive cult, the first step should be getting a handle on their group experience. Then, if there are other issues or problems that existed before their membership, they can begin to resolve them also.

When looking for a support group in your area, it might be best to contact the FOCUS coordinator to find out about resources in your area. (See appendix for more information about FOCUS.) If there is no FOCUS group in your city, start one! In addition, you may find a group therapy center in your area and find a group you would like to participate in. If that is the case, I would simply recommend applying to this group the same questions that I have suggested you apply to any other group, as I have outlined in chapter 6. Be a good consumer, especially in evaluating the group leader.

It becomes apparent to former cult members in the first year after leaving that any pre-cult problems they may have had were never resolved while they were members of a destructive cult. This can be very disappointing to the ex-member, because the illusion of becoming healthier was one of the factors that reinforced continuing membership, sometimes for many years.

This realization is often more difficult for long-term members. Imagine going into a group at eighteen and coming out at age thirty. The individual has been deprived of a huge amount of life experience. His twenties, typically reserved for self-exploration and experimentation as well as education, job skill development, and relationship building, have been lost.

Some long-term former members liken the experience to that of POWs coming home after the Vietnam War. In fact, post-traumatic stress syndrome seems to apply perfectly to some cult member veterans. When they come home, they have to catch up on everything. One person I worked with had never heard of the Watergate scandal, didn't know who James Taylor was, and wasn't aware that we had landed and walked on the surface of the moon.

Chronologically, the person is thirty. Psychologically, he probably feels eighteen. His friends from high school have good positions; many are married; some have children; some have houses and one or two cars. At thirty, he is inexperienced at dating and has been out of touch with current events and world affairs for more than a decade. At a party, he has little to talk about, unless he wants to talk about his cult experience, which can exacerbate the feeling of being in a goldfish bowl.

Such a person often feels *an acute sense of having to make up for lost time.* This pressure can become stressful. The reality is that the person has been out of the mainstream of society for twelve years. He has to learn that he must have time to heal, grow, and develop. He has to recognize that he has his own path, his own time clock, and should be concerned about his needs and not compare himself with other people.

One sensitive parent of a former member expressed the situation of a former cult member when he said, "If someone gets hit by a Mack truck, naturally you expect that it will take time to recover. You wouldn't expect someone to get up out of bed, and go and get a job the next week, would you?"

Every person who has been in a cult is different and has different needs. Some people are able to adjust more quickly. Others who have been more severely traumatized need more time. In the case of this parent, his daughter lived at home for the first year and a half. He didn't pressure her to move out or seek employment during that time. He recognized that she was doing the very best she could.

Former members need to *learn how to trust themselves again.* They have to become their own best friend, as well as their own best therapist. They have to realize that they didn't choose to be lied to or abused. They are not at fault. Eventually, as they learn to trust themselves and their own inherent wisdom and instincts, they learn that it's okay to begin trusting others. They have to realize that all groups are not evil. In fact, the good part of being involved with a healthy group, be it a religious, social, or political group, is that you *can* exercise control over your participation. You do not have to stay one minute longer than you want to. Nor do you have to sit silently and blame yourself when you don't understand what is being said or done. You can question and you can question some more. Not only is that all right—it is your constitutional right!

Learning how to get in touch with emotions and channel them effectively is another significant process for any ex-member. Often when a person first comes out, many of his emotions remain suppressed. But as the person adjusts, he begins to feel shame and embarrassment, then often anger and indignation. The person moves from "What is wrong with me?" to "How dare they do that to me!"

At some point, the person may begin a voracious research project to find out everything he can about his group and answer every one of his questions to his satisfaction. This is a very positive therapeutic step. Often, the number one priority of someone who has just left a cult is to help rescue the friends who were left behind. For cult members, their major regret in leaving is usually losing contact with people they came to know and care for in the group. It becomes particularly difficult when a former member realizes that the friendships he thought were so good were conditional on continued membership. A former member can quickly see the strength of mind control bonds when his closest friend in the group refuses to meet him unless he brings another member along.

Eventually, when all the questions are answered, and all the cult issues are addressed, the ex-member reaches a saturation point. He gets to the point of saying "They're not going to take the rest of my life!" and starts making plans for the future.

Sometimes there are additional issues that need more extensive individual counseling. Sarah, a former ten-year member of the Church Universal and Triumphant, had been forcibly deprogrammed more than five years earlier, yet was still experiencing cult-related problems. I agreed to work with her for ten sessions. Her first homework assignment was to begin writing down her entire cult experience. *This is something I recommend for every ex-member as an exercise for gaining a complete perspective of the experience.* It was certainly something Sarah needed to do in order truly to regain herself.

I suggested that since she had been involved for such a long time, she should begin by making an outline. I told her to take ten folders and number them from 1973 to 1983, put twelve sheets of paper in each folder, and label them January through December. With that as a starting point I told her to begin writing down everything she could remember that was significant to her— positive and negative. I told her not to worry if there were huge gaps— eventually they would all be filled in.

In order to help her remember, I told her to think of specific places she had lived in or visited. For example, she had lived in several different states during her membership, and visited home a few times. I also told her to think about significant friends or people. Last, I told her to remember specific activities or events that were significant.

Step by step she was able to fill in her entire experience, to record how she came to be recruited, and identify her likes and dislikes. She was able to chart her ups and downs as a member and see that at many different points, she was very unhappy and disillusioned, but had no way out. At one point she had actually come home to her parents, complaining about her unhappiness, and they had taken her to a psychologist, who unfortunately did not recognize her problems as being cult related. After two months at home, Sarah had gone back to the group.

By writing down her entire experience, Sarah was able to process her experience and gain a greater perspective on it. She no longer had to carry a lot of swirling, seemingly contradictory feelings in her head. It was now all on paper.

As part of her therapy, I explained to her that the person whose story filled those ten folders no longer existed. I suggested that she think about that person as a younger Sarah, someone who was doing the very best she could. Back at the time of her recruitment, she didn't know about cults or mind control. If she had, she surely would never have gotten involved.

I had her imagine herself as a time traveler and instructed her to go back in time and teach the younger Sarah about mind control so she could avoid the group's recruiters. I asked her to imagine how differently her life would have turned out if she had never gotten into the group. This enabled her to see that with more information, she would have had more choice and could have averted the danger. This piece of work became very important for her later in her therapy.

I asked her to re-experience, one at a time, traumatic cult experiences. This time, however, she could correct her responses. She told off one of the leaders in front of the members and angrily walked out of the cult. Even though she knew that we were just doing an exercise, it provided her the opportunity to channel her emotions constructively and reclaim her personal power and dignity.

By standing up for herself and telling the cult leader to "Shove it!" she could walk out of the group on her own and avoid the trauma of the forcible deprogramming. Sarah knows that in reality, her parents did need to rescue her. However, through this process she was able to regain personal control over the experience. This was extremely important in order to enable Sarah to go on with her life.

Like everyone else in her position, she needed to take all the things she had learned, and all the people she met and come to care for, and integrate them into a new sense of identity. Integrating the old into the new allows former members to be unusually strong. They are survivors. They have suffered hardship and abuse, and through information and self-reflection they are able to overcome adversity.

Like all former members I have counseled, Sarah suffered from lack of trust in herself and others, and fear of commitment to a job or a relationship. By helping her to reprocess her cult experience, I was able to show her that she now has resources that the younger Sarah didn't have, and that she is no longer the same person who was tricked and indoctrinated into a cult.

She is older, smarter, and wiser now. She knows on a very deep personal level that she can identify and avoid any situation in which she is being manipulated or used. She can rely more completely on herself, and if she needs assistance, she will be able to get what she needs. Likewise, she need not fear making commitments. She knows now to ask questions and keep on asking questions, and to distrust any job or relationship which asks for anything that violates her sense of ethics or values.

Like anyone who has been molested or abused, former members need to learn to rebuild their trust in themselves and others step by step. In their own good time, they can learn to take little risks and test the waters. They don't have to jump in any faster than is comfortable for them.

FACILITIES FOR FORMER CULT MEMBERS

For those people who need extensive, short-term care, there are only three facilities currently operating in the United States. Participation in all three is completely voluntary and normally involves two to four weeks. The largest and oldest is a place called Unbound, in Iowa City, Iowa. Run by Kevin Crawley and Diana Paulina for seven years, Unbound offers a house stocked with an excellent library of books, videotapes, and audiotapes, and a paid full-time staff of former members.

Wellspring Retreat, run by Paul and Barbara Martin, is a private farm house in Ohio which is being converted to a rehabilitation facility. Paul is a licensed psychologist and former eight-year member of the Great Commission International, a Bible cult.[13] A relatively new facility, Wellspring is now building a substantial library of resources.

The Cook Home, Inc., in Enid, Oklahoma, is run by Betty and Jack Cook and also has an extensive library. The Cooks rescued their daughter Sheryl from The Way International several years ago and are very much involved in helping others. Betty has a master's degree in counseling.

All these places are privately funded. Fees can can run into the thousands of dollars, but vary somewhat, depending on need. In considering the cost of facilities such as these, it's important to remember that for some people, the opportunity to have a place to go for a few weeks to get support and counseling is invaluable. Clearly there is a need for additional financial support to allow more former members access to these facilities. In addition, it is important that other rehabilitation centers are established around the country.

When working with former cult members it is most important to take a constructive approach. Remember, people who have come out of cults need to take all their positive experiences with them—extensive travel, sales experience, foreign language acquisition, self-discipline, public speaking skills, and others—and integrate them into their lives. By doing so they can become strong people, perhaps stronger than most. They have had an unusual life experience which, with a healthy sense of perspective, will surely foster a deeper appreciation for freedom. Former members of destructive cults are *survivors*. They should acknowledge their own strength and power. If they can come through their cult experiences, then they can make it through just about anything.

Chapter 11

The Next Step

THE unethical use of mind control, in my opinion, has reached the point where it is a major social problem, not only in the United States but in many other countries as well. Some destructive cults have grown to have considerable political influence, as we have shown in the case of the Unification Church.[1] Others prefer to exercise influence on society by "training" business people in key positions in corporate America. Cults are also gaining ground among the new wave of Asian and Hispanic immigrants to the United States, moving beyond their traditional recruitment of the white middle class. Most remarkable of all, some cult groups have become so skilled at their public relations work that they have gained a high degree of social acceptance even among prominent professionals. Whenever respected professionals attend cult-sponsored conferences (for scientists, lawyers, politicians, clergy, and academicians) they give the cult an air of legitimacy. Even though such people do not know or do not care about the cult involvement in such conferences, their mere presence gives an indirect approval to cult activities.

My concern about cults is very specific. Their activities, if unchecked, will continue to wreak untold psychological and sometimes even physical damage on many thousands (if not millions) of people who have no idea of what constitutes unethical mind control. Unless legislative action is taken to make destructive cults accountable to society for their violations of the rights of their members, these groups will continue to deceive the general public into believing that they are doing nothing out of the ordinary at all.

From a practical point of view, we are all understandably reluctant to accept one more subject as a matter of serious concern. Every day that we read a newspaper or watch the news on television we are reminded of the threat of nuclear war, massive destruction of the earth's natural resources, starvation in Africa, widespread political corruption, AIDS, and other concerns. Why add another subject of concern to that list?

Although literally hundreds of stories about cults have been printed or aired in the media in the past few years, few address the issue of mind control directly. Cult stories tend to be presented as "religious" stories rather than stories about people under mind control. In addition, ever since the abatement of media attention after the Jonestown massacre, it may seem to the public at large that there are fewer cults because there has been relatively less cult coverage. I will be the first to admit that there have been no national polls to provide as a measuring stick for public attitudes about cults; they are very expensive, and the Cult Awareness Network struggles to find enough money to continue operating. Yet, many people with whom I come into casual conversation on the subject of destructive cults express surprise when approached with the idea that such groups are still a major problem in American society. I believe that many people simply assume that cult recruiting activities attracted a lot of "mixed up young people" in the 1960s and 1970s, and then died out as the counterculture was absorbed into society at large.

This perception of cults as a "passing phase" is no accident. Many cults have exercised their influence at very crucial places and times in the past few years in order to prevent public scrutiny of their affairs. Let me give you a few examples.

CULTS AND THE UNITED STATES GOVERNMENT

Public reaction to what became known as "the Jonestown massacre" was shock and disbelief, and a growing concern with the influence of destructive cults. In particular, the murder of a United States Congressman by cultists showed that some people in cults would stop at nothing to keep anyone, especially someone in a legitimate position of authority, from exposing them to public scrutiny.

I was deeply saddened by the news of Congressman Ryan's murder. I knew that Leo Ryan had been highly knowledgeable and concerned about destructive cults, for he had been an important force in the Congressional Subcommittee Investigation of Korean-American Relations headed by Congressman Donald Fraser. Released on October 31, just a few short weeks before the mass suicide at Jonestown, the Fraser Report (as it came to be known) recommended that an Executive branch inter-agency task force be set up to pursue any illegal activities of the Moon organization.

No action was taken on that recommendation.

Of course, some people might have thought something was being done about the cult problem because of all the activity on Capitol Hill. There was an inquiry into Jonestown, and in 1979, the House Foreign Affairs Committee issued its report on the People's Temple massacre. In it, the brainwashing tactics of Jim Jones were described in detail. It recommended that the National Institute of Mental Health be funded to further research mind control and destructive cult groups.

Nothing was ever done to follow up that recommendation, either.

However, Senator Bob Dole did put together a hearing on cults after Jonestown, and I was invited to speak. On the morning of the hearing, however, I was suddenly told that all former cult members would no longer be permitted to speak. We were told that the reason was to avoid having to allow cult members equal time to speak. However, at the hearing room, the people were holding up signs that read "Elect Bob Dole President, Repeal the First Amendment." Even though all ex-members had been forbidden to speak, the committee did grant permission to Neil Salonen, the spokesperson for the Moonies, to deliver a statement. I was beginning to realize the political clout of the cults.

Something was very wrong. Nothing was being done about the Korean-American investigation. Nothing was being done about the People's Temple investigation.

However, important developments in other areas began to throw new light on the problems of the use of unethical mind control.

In 1979, a book called *The Search for the Manchurian Candidate,* by John Marks, was published to the accompaniment of a fair amount of national publicity. In it, the author detailed CIA mind control research performed in the 1950s and early 1960s. Code-named MK-ULTRA, this research included experimentation with LSD, hypnosis, and electroshock therapy. A few months later, ABC did a television special based on the book. Among the many people interviewed was the former top psychologist for the CIA, John Gittinger. He admitted that such mind control research did take place at one time, but that hypnosis, a central subject of the research, was of no use "in any operationally feasible way." Sidney Gottlieb, another agency official who was engaged in mind control research, said that all research had been abandoned in 1963. He retired in 1973 and destroyed his records.[2]

I knew that techniques for mind control were indeed real. I had lived in a mind control environment and practiced it on others. I had researched the subject of mind control with top experts on the subject, such as Robert Jay Lifton. I knew that no self-respecting psychologist would deny that there was anything "useful" in mind control research. The statements of Gittinger and Gottlieb forced me to confront a number of questions that needed answers.

Why wasn't our federal government informing the American people about the dangers of mind control? Why was the issue continually shuffled into a discussion of religious liberty and the First Amendment? There had to be a reason. According to John Marks, some of the government's research into mind control has resulted in the abuse of people who served as test subjects. No doubt an admission of responsibility by the government in such cases would not only be embarrassing but costly.

Perhaps there are political reasons why the government does not admit to any knowledge of mind control techniques. Whatever the reasons, though, there is now little doubt that the American people have been spending millions of dollars for decades on mind control research.

My point here is not one against research into mind control. As a mental health professional, I am heartily in favor of ethically conducted research which increases our knowledge of ourselves and the workings of the mind. Nor, for that matter, am I opposed to the classification of some information in the interest of maintaining national security. However, if the government has indeed been conducting research into mind control, then it has a responsibility to inform the American public that mind control exists. There are no laws on the books, however, which recognize that mind control exists much less prohibit the unethical use of mind control as it is now being applied by groups like the Unification Church.[3] In the absence of recognition by the government that mind control exists and that unethical mind control is wrong, then *the government's silence indirectly condones the practice of unethical mind control in the rest of society.* In a practical sense, one only need look around to see the effects of government silence and inaction: mind control groups are proliferating at an unprecedented pace.

The principles of freedom and democracy in our country demand that the reality of mind control be exposed to full public scrutiny.

DESTRUCTIVE CULTS AND MENTAL HEALTH

Although progress against destructive cults in the political arena is painfully slow, there have been some very favorable developments in the mental health community. Among them is the fact that the diagnostic book used by psychologists, the *DSM*-III,[4] now includes a category that mentions victims of cults.

That category is called "Atypical Dissociative Disorder 300.15." As a definition of the pathological effects of mind control, it reads in part: "Examples include trance-like states, derealization unaccompanied by depersonalization, and those more prolonged dissociated states that may occur in persons who have been subjected to periods of prolonged and intense coercive persuasion (brainwashing, thought reform, and indoctrination while the captive of terrorists or cultists)."

There is still a need, however, for more mental health professionals who are trained to identify and help people who have been victims of mind control. Unfortunately, too, there have been several cult "researchers," who appear to be well-financed and are waging a silent war to try to dispel any concern about mind control or cults. One has to wonder about the validity of any research that relies solely on the cooperation of cult leaders for data collection and analysis. When I was in the Moonies, we would make sure to tell such academicians what *we* wanted them to know and show them only what *we* wanted to show.

Despite the problems of such questionable forms of research, there have been legitimate inquiries into the problems associated with mind control techniques. Dr. Flavil Yeakley, a respected psychologist from Abilene Christian University, has done considerable research into the psychological profiles of cult members.[5] Dr. Yeakley administered the Meyers-Briggs Type Indicator (MBTI), a personality profile research device, to hundreds of members of different religious groups, both mainline and cultic. He asked members to fill out the questionnaire three times. The first time, they were asked to answer the questions from the frame of mind in which they were presently living. The second time, they were asked to answer the questions from the state of mind they were in prior to joining the group. Last, Dr. Yeakley asked his test subjects to respond to the questions as they thought they would answer in five years' time.

He administered this test to members of the Boston Church of Christ, the Church of Scientology, the Hare Krishnas, Maranatha, the Children of God, the Moonies, and The Way International. The results showed a high level of change toward certain standard personality types as defined by the test. In other words, people in certain cults appeared to be all moving toward having the same kinds of personalities, regardless of the original personalities they brought with them into the group. I see this test result as offering interesting support for my idea that cults actually give new personalities to their members (he refers to it as "cloning") as they suppress their original identities. As Dr. Yeakley explained in a letter to me:

"In the Boston Church of Christ and in three of the cults, the shifting was toward the ESFJ (extrovert, sensing, feeling, judging) personality type. Two of the cults were shifting toward ESTJ (extrovert, sensing, thinking, judging) and one toward ENTJ (extrovert, intuitive, thinking, judging). There is nothing wrong with any of these three types. The problem is with the pressure to conform to any type. It is the shifting which is negative, not the type toward which the shifting takes place."

In comparison, this test was given to members of the Baptist, Catholic, Lutheran, Methodist, and Presbyterian churches and "mainline" Churches of Christ. There were no significant changes in psychological type scores over time. In other words, there was no indication of any pressure to conform to any certain type of personality. People's fundamental personality types remained intact.

STUDY AND APPLICATION OF MIND CONTROL RESEARCH

Much more research of this kind, of course, needs to be done and will be done before too long, it is hoped. Top mental health professionals who are experts on cult mind control such as Dr. Margaret Singer (UC- Berkeley), Dr. Louis Jolyon West (UCLA Neuro-Psychiatric Institute), Dr. John Clark (Harvard Medical school), and Dr. Michael Langone (American Family Foundation) are joining ranks with many other scholars to form a research society to study the social impact of coercive persuasion.

The use of mind control technology is not inherently evil. Like any technology, it can be used to serve or to destroy. It can be used to empower people or to enslave them.

Severe depression affects millions of Americans and robs them of their strength and their ability to enjoy being alive. It is not Orwellian to consider a useful application of a mind control technique if the person *freely chooses to use it* and *if the person is doing it on himself,* to give him the freedom to imagine and create a better future. This is very different from taking the locus of power away from the individual and placing it with another.

To a certain degree, destructive cults are performing impermissible social psychology experiments. Their practices are impermissible because ethical standards used for research would never allow such behavior. However, much can be learned by studying the people who have been through a mind control experience. I am convinced that much good can come out of research in this area.

For example, I believe mind control techniques can be ethically used to help those currently stuck in the criminal justice system. There is a great need for massive reform of our correction system. Prisoners need to be taught more effective ways to break their negative cycles of low self-esteem and law-breaking behavior. Perhaps new models can be instituted for their rehabilitation.

In addition, *people who know how mind control operates will have a distinct advantage over those who do not.* For those people of principle, their knowledge of mind control will be reserved exclusively for ethical uses. In addition, they can use their knowledge to protect themselves from others' unethical use of mind control on them.

Still, morality and wisdom require a measured approach to using any powerful tool for altering the human mind. We can hope that all the issues will be debated at length and protections built in to prevent any abuses of this technology.

These considerations represent just the beginning of an approach to coming to terms socially with cult mind control. Much more must be done to educate mental health professionals and empower them to help the people who are still suffering from its ill effects.

CULTS AND THE LAW

Another area to be addressed is the law. Current laws do not recognize that mind control exists unless there is use of force or threat of force. There are no laws against covert hypnotic inductions or secret use of mind control techniques for unscrupulous purposes.

In fact, the law tends to protect destructive cults more than its unwitting victims. No group should violate the civil rights of its members, yet people are being deprived of life, liberty, and the pursuit of happiness by recruitment into destructive cults. Many cult members cannot read what they please, speak freely, choose their own jobs, or in some cases, even chose whom they may marry.

The enormous wealth of cult groups has allowed them to hire the best attorneys and file harassment lawsuits (unwinnable but troublesome to the person sued) against critics and former members. Even some of the leaders of the American Civil Liberties Union (ACLU) have historically sided with cults, invoking the First Amendment and ignoring any evidence of mind control research. To my knowledge, any attempts to legislate against deceptive recruitment or even deceptive cult fundraising tactics have so far been struck down.

Part of the problem facing lawmaking against cult activities which violate individual rights has been the manner in which cults have sought to hide behind the constitutional guarantee of religious freedom. In this country, people's right to *believe* whatever they want is absolute, and it should be. What is *not* absolute is a group's right to *do* anything it wants. For example, a sect may believe that it is a sacred act to handle poisonous snakes, but the law prohibits snake-handling rituals because too many people have died. Cult lawyers do their best to ignore this difference and try to turn legal issues into issues of belief rather than issues of behavior.

The recruitment and "conversion" experience has been particularly difficult to analyze. Does a group really have the right to deceive a potential convert because he would stay away if he knew the truth? Likewise, does a group have the right to manipulate a person's thoughts, feelings, and environment in order to create a "conversion" experience? If so, where should the line be drawn between legal and illegal manipulation?

For years, it has been scientifically impossible to determine whether a person is under mind control. Any evaluation has had to be subjective. But with each year that passes, science is moving toward being able to provide concrete proof that there is a measurable dysfunction. Before the turn of the century, I am certain, there will be measurable proof that a person's brainwave pattern is changed as a result of the process of mind control. Right now, some of the technology which may be able to determine the effects of mind control is being used to confirm the diagnostic status of people believed to be suffering from multiple personality disorder. These people are shown to have different brainwave patterns when they are "in" each of their distinct personalities. Any attempt by a person to merely give a good "acting performance" can be easily detected. I think it is only a matter of time before research will be able to pinpoint and prove in a court of law that an individual's ability to function is impaired by mind control.

In the meanwhile, there has been some positive progress in the area of law. Former members of many different cults are beginning to initiate civil law suits. They charge fraud, negligence, involuntary servitude, and harassment. They also sue for lost wages, for money and property turned over to the cult, and for psychological damages caused by the group's programs. Right now, 550 former Scientologists have a $1 billion class action suit against Scientology.[6] TM-Ex, a support and information group of former meditators, has a number of former members filing suit against Transcendental Meditation.[7] People are suing Werner Erhard and his "Forum"[8] and John Hanley and his "Lifespring,"[9] as well as other large group awareness programs.

The London *Daily Mail* newspaper was sued for libel by the Moonies for two articles it published in 1983. In the longest libel suit in England's history, the court found that Moonies did "brainwash their members and did try to cut people off from their families" so the lawsuit was lost, and the group was forced to pay $2 million in expenses.[10]

In England, the libel laws are such that whoever loses the suit is responsible for the expenses of both sides. So in this case, the legal expenses of the London *Daily Mail* were paid by the Moonies. I believe this system should be adopted in the United States. It would certainly reduce the number of nuisance libel suits brought by cults and create a more free and fair journalistic atmosphere.

I have personally seen the fear of cults at work in the media. In early 1988, the editor of a popular magazine saw me on television and asked me to write a book review of *L. Ron Hubbard—Messiah or Madman?* by Bent Corydon, a former 22-year Scientologist. As it happened, I had just finished the book the week before, and happily agreed. However, the review was never published. Even though everything in the review was true, the publisher told me she was afraid of being sued by the Church of Scientology. She told me that they regretted not being able to print it, but that it just didn't make good "business" sense for them to do so.

There is little doubt, as well, that if the American economy becomes more shaky, cult-owned businesses will continue to grow, and new employees will be expected to attend all company-sponsored "workshops" and "seminars." (Even now, business executives are flocking to programs that can teach them how to better influence and control people. In some cases, cults have actually taken over the running of a company in this way.) Many cult-owned businesses are able to undercut competition because they have free labor. They can also avoid paying taxes because their bookkeeping systems show payment of full salaries, yet those paychecks are in reality turned over to the tax-exempt organization. It therefore appears the business is making a marginal profit in comparison with the monies it is actually taking in.

DANGERS OF CULTISM IN THE NEW AGE MOVEMENT

The New Age movement has gathered a tremendous amount of momentum. Channeling, a new word for "mediumship" (presumably a psychic form of communication with the dead or disembodied spirits) has become a multi-million-dollar business. Despite the lack of verifiable evidence from channeled spirits, many people are extremely interested in the phenomenon, and many books and courses are now on the market which claim to teach people how to become a trance channel.

What people get for their hundred-dollar seminars in channeling may well be only entertainment coupled with an experience of mass hypnosis. Whenever someone is hypnotized, there is a pleasant sense of relaxation, time distortion (you don't know if it is 2 o'clock or 5 o'clock, Tuesday or Sunday) and most importantly, a side-stepping of the critical mental faculties. People lose the ability to consciously and critically evaluate the experience.

Hypnosis, an important component of mind control technology, is a fantastic tool for self-exploration and development, but the locus of control should always remain within the individual and not be shifted to some external authority.

If people come to believe that someone else knows better than they what is best to do, they can be in real danger. I am very concerned that people are being encouraged to abandon their critical thinking abilities and "surrender." What are they supposed to surrender to? Moreover, in this belief system there is apparently no such thing as chance or accident. If something happens to you, it was meant to occur to teach you something. That belief, by extension, applies to all kinds of violence, including unethical mind control. Does this mean that people should permit themselves to be subjected to cult mind control just because it happens to cross their paths? We have free will and should never abandon our personal responsibility for making good choices. In my opinion, *there can be no true spiritual growth when one abdicates personal integrity and responsibility.*

Too many charlatans and hucksters eager for power and money have suddenly appeared in the last few years. Spirituality is too precious and too personal to be reduced to a collection of formulas and truisms or to be given a monetary value.

Another recent development has been an increased public re-awakening of interest in UFOs, which is now connected with the channeling movement. The tremendous interest shown in Whitley Strieber's *Communion* is a good indicator of how "hot" this subject has again become. Though some of his readers might not have expected it of him, Strieber has made numerous comments critical of the channeling movement and social tendencies toward UFO cultism. Various investigators besides Festinger (notably Jacques Vallee, author of *Messengers of Deception,* a 1979 study of UFO cults) have been warning the public for years about the dangers of cult activities centering on the UFO phenomenon, and there is no lack of similar examples.

While there may be some validity to the UFO phenomenon (all the reports can't be explained by conventional means), we still have not definitely established what it is. In the absence of certain knowledge, though, plenty of people will tell us what they think it is. In the 1980s, we have seen the development of a type of UFO-related channeler who may claim to be contacting "space brothers" from the stars. I believe that these varieties of channeling are just as suspect as more conventional ones, and have the potential for developing into new UFO cult activities. A word of caution is in order.

The ideals of creating a new age for mankind on the planet Earth are certainly worthy ones, for the most part. I believe that a new age of priorities must be established, wherein greed, naked power, and crass materialism are not rewarded or celebrated. Creativity, compassion, and wisdom should be qualities that everyone aspires to develop. Unquestionably, a new, positive vision needs to be adopted by people all over the world. A revolution in consciousness might usher in a new age of peace, goodness, and responsibility.

I remain leery, though, of anyone or anything that professes to have arrived at absolute answers or only one absolute method for attaining enlightenment. As the poet and visionary William Blake wrote: "I must Create a system, or be enslav'd by another Man's."

CULTS AND RELIGIOUS FREEDOM

It is very important to me that people's religious freedoms not be impinged upon. The Constitution's guarantee that people be free to choose to worship and follow their own religious principles should be enforced at all times. Nothing would grieve me more than to learn that this book has caused anyone to become religiously intolerant.

Discrimination toward anyone who merely has different beliefs is sad as well as illegal. I remember how I felt being spit upon, kicked, punched, and verbally abused because I was a Moonie. Such treatment, always uncalled for, only served to reinforce my feelings that I was being persecuted for my faith in God.

In principle, I am against banning cults from college campuses unless they expressly violate rules of conduct that every student organization is expected to follow. I believe that these groups have the right to exist, and I would not like to see legislation banning them. However, I would like to see programs sponsored by colleges to teach people about the specifics about mind control and the recruitment techniques commonly used by destructive cults.

THE FUTURE

Why are destructive cults thriving? Why is it that people are so ripe to take part in the activities of cultic organizations? These are questions that I feel must be addressed in looking to the future.

While the development of more sophisticated techniques of mind control has helped lead to increased group membership, the proliferation of destructive cults can also be attributed to the diminished sense of community that characterizes life in our present age. We no longer live and die within the same forty-mile radius; it is indeed common for an individual to move several times and many miles during his lifetime.

This transience undermines the sense of community that I think human beings need in order to feel whole. I hear over and over that a person is initially attracted because he or she enjoys being around a group of people acting like one big family; more than anything else, former members miss that sense of being part of a tight-knit community.

Reliance on television for entertainment and information is also a factor in predisposing one to cult membership. Unfortunately, most television viewing does not stimulate our intellect, imagination, or higher aspirations. Instead, television encourages conformity and creates a distorted perception of reality. Where else can all problems be resolved in a one-hour episode? In addition, while it is certainly important to know what is happening in the world, incessant news reports on drug problems, sex scandals, corruption and violence take their toll on the American psyche. We become desensitized to our own values and lose the powers of creativity and discrimination.

Much can be done to stop the spread of cults in our society. Through responsible leadership, spiritual and social organizations can make vigorous efforts toward addressing the needs of the community and utilizing its resources. These efforts will result in a cohesive group of people working toward a constructive purpose, thus satisfying the need so many people feel to be part of a genuine community.

The other answer to the spread of cults in society is massive public education. Federal funds should be appropriated for research and treatment of mind control victims. Reform within public education must be made toward encouraging people to think for themselves and scrutinize the information and choices available to them. I would love to see every high school and college teach its students about mind control and destructive cults. The course needn't mention any particular group by name; it should discuss the psychological principles of mind control and teach students to be suspicious of any environment that discourages them from asking critical questions. In order to make democracy work, people must be willing to take responsibility for making change. It will be necessary to re-examine our principles and our priorities, and ensure the free flow of information.

FINAL THOUGHTS

Writing this book marks the fulfillment of my long-standing desire to contribute a practical, informative guide to the problems people deal with in encountering the influence of destructive cults. It has been a long hard road.

After all the threats, harassment, and fear, I can now look back and say it was all worth it, if my work and this book enable others to understand more clearly how mind control operates within destructive cult groups. It was important, I think, to tell the whole story, including my methods for exit-counseling even though I feared it might make the cults more sophisticated in their programming. By demystifying exit-counseling, I hope to enable countless numbers of people, who didn't want to employ forcible deprogramming, to start working to help their loved ones.

I also hope that this book will create a new and powerful public consumer awareness about mind control and destructive cults. I hope that the government will acknowledge the problem and do something about it. In the meantime, I hope readers of this book will join the Cult Awareness Network and the American Family Foundation and subscribe to their newsletters and journals. Furthermore, I encourage those people who have been through a cult mind control experience to get involved and make a stand. We need your help!

As destructive cults and mind control come to be better understood, the social stigma attached to being a former cult member will begin to dissolve. Former members will come to realize that we were not to blame for our involvement. People will see that we have a lot to give back to society, if we have a chance. Many of my former clients and friends have gone on with their lives and become happy, productive citizens. They are doctors, lawyers, dentists, chiropractors, psychologists, architects, artists, teachers, mothers, fathers, and social activists. FOCUS can help a lot, but it requires participation. Whether you are in need, or have something to give, or both, I urge you to take a positive step. You do make a difference.

In the words of Edmund Burke: "All it takes for evil to triumph is for enough good men to do nothing."

Appendix

LIFTON'S EIGHT CRITERIA OF MIND CONTROL

The following excerpt from Robert J. Lifton's *The Future of Immortality and Other Essays for a Nuclear Age* (New York, Basic Books, 1987) is a concise explanation of Lifton's eight criteria for defining mind control. Although they are mentioned in quotation marks in the text, I will list them here for ease of identification:

1. "milieu control"
2. "mystical manipulation" (or "planned spontaneity")
3. "the demand for purity"
4. "the cult of confession"
5. "sacred science"
6. "loading of the language"
7. "doctrine over person"
8. "dispensing of existence"

The essay from which this selection is taken is entitled "Cults: Religious Totalism and Civil Liberties." In it, Lifton frames his comments in relation to what he called "ideological totalism," or the environment in which Chinese thought reform was practiced, as he came to know of it from the Korean War and afterwards.

Ideological Totalism

The phenomenology I used when writing about ideological totalism in the past still seems useful to me, even though I wrote that book in 1960. The first characteristic is "milieu control," which is essentially the control of communication within an environment. If the control is extremely intense, it becomes an internalized control—an attempt to manage an individual's inner communication. This can never be fully achieved, but it can go rather far. It is what sometimes has been called a "God's-eye view"—a conviction that reality is the group's exclusive possession. Clearly this kind of process creates conflicts in respect to individual autonomy: if sought or realized in such an environment, autonomy becomes a threat to milieu control. Milieu control within cults tends to be maintained and expressed in several ways: group process, isolation from other people, psychological pressure, geographical distance or unavailability of transportation, and sometimes physical pressure. There is often a sequence of events, such as seminars, lectures, and group encounters, which become increasingly intense and increasingly isolated, making it extremely difficult—both physically and psychologically—for one to leave.

These cults differ from patterns of totalism in other societies. For instance, the centers that were used for reform in China were more or less in keeping with the ethos of the society as it was evolving at the time: and therefore when one was leaving them or moving in and out of them, one would still find reinforcement from without. Cults, in contrast, tend to become islands of totalism within a larger society that is on the whole antagonistic to these islands. This situation can create a dynamic of its own; and insofar as milieu control is to be maintained, the requirements are magnified by that structural situation. Cult leaders must often deepen their control and manage the environment more systematically, and sometimes with greater intensity, in order to maintain that island of totalism within the antagonistic outer world.

The imposition of intense milieu control is closely connected to the process of change. (This partly explains why there can be a sudden lifting of the cult identity when a young person who has been in a cult for some time is abruptly exposed to outside, alternative influences.) One can almost observe the process in some young people who undergo a dramatic change in their prior identity, whatever it was, to an intense embrace of a cult's belief system and group structure. I consider this a form of doubling: a second self is formed that lives side by side with the prior self, somewhat autonomously from it. Obviously there must be some connecting element to integrate oneself with the other—otherwise, the overall person could not function; but the autonomy of each is impressive. When the milieu control is lifted by removing, by whatever means, the recruit from the totalistic environment, something of the earlier self reasserts itself. This leavetaking may occur voluntarily or through force (or simply, as in one court case, by the cult member moving across to the other side of the table, away from other members). The two selves can exist simultaneously and confusedly for a considerable time, and it may be that the transition periods are the most intense and psychologically painful as well as the most potentially harmful.

A second general characteristic of totalistic environments is what I call "mystical manipulation" or "planned spontaneity." It is a systematic process that is planned and managed from above (by the leadership) but appears to have arisen spontaneously within the environment. The process need not feel like manipulation, which raises important philosophical questions. Some aspects— such as fasting, chanting, and limited sleep—have a certain tradition and have been practiced by religious groups over the centuries. There is a cult pattern now in which a particular "chosen" human being is seen as a savior or a source of salvation. Mystical manipulation can take on a special quality in these cults because the leaders become mediators for God. The God-centered principles can be put forcibly and claimed exclusively, so that the cult and its beliefs become the only true path to salvation. This can give intensity to the mystical manipulation and justify those involved with promulgating it and, in many cases, those who are its recipients from below.

Insofar as there is a specific individual, a leader, who becomes the center of the mystical manipulation (or the person in whose name it is done), there is a twofold process at work. The leader can sometimes be more real than an abstract god and therefore attractive to cult members. On the other hand, that person can also be a source of disillusionment. If one believes, as has been charged, that Sun Myung Moon (founder of the Unification Church, whose members are consequently referred to frequently as "Moonies") has associations with the Korean Central Intelligence Agency and this information is made available to people in the Unification Church, their relationship to the church can be threatened by disillusionment toward a leader. It is never quite that simple a pattern of cause and effect—but I am suggesting that this style of leadership has both advantages and disadvantages in terms of cult loyalty.

While mystical manipulation leads (in cult members) to what I have called the psychology of the pawn, it can also include a legitimation of deception (of outsiders)—the "heavenly deception" of the Unification Church, although there are analogous patterns in other cult environments. If one has not seen the light, and it is not in the realm of the cult, one is in the realm of evil and therefore can be justifiably deceived for the higher purpose. For instance, when members of certain cults have collected funds, it has sometimes been considered right for them to deny their affiliation when asked. Young people have been at centers of a particular cult for some time without being told that these were indeed run by it. The totalistic ideology can and often does justify such deception.

The next two characteristics of totalism, the "demand for purity" and the "cult of confession," are familiar. The demand for purity can create a Manichean quality in cults, as in some other religious and political groups. Such a demand calls for radical separation of pure and impure, of good and evil, within an environment and within oneself. Absolute purification is a continuing process. It is often institutionalized; and, as a source of stimulation of guilt and shame, it ties in with the confession process. Ideological movements, at whatever level of intensity, take hold of an individual's guilt and shame mechanisms to achieve intense influence over the changes he or she undergoes. This is done within a confession process that has its own structure. Sessions in which one confesses to one's sins are accompanied by patterns of criticism and self-criticism, generally transpiring within small groups and with an active and dynamic thrust toward personal change.

One could say more about the ambiguity and complexity of this process, and Camus has observed that "authors of confessions write especially to avoid confession, to tell nothing of what they know." Camus may have exaggerated, but he is correct in suggesting that confessions contain varying mixtures of revelation and concealment. A young person confessing to various sins of pre-cultic or pre-institutional existence can both believe in those sins and be covering over other ideas and feelings that he or she is either unaware of or reluctant to discuss. In some cases, these sins include a continuing identification with one's prior existence if such identification has not been successfully dishonored by the confession process. Repetitious confession, then, is often an expression of extreme arrogance in the name of apparent humility. Again Camus: "I practice the profession of penitence, to be able to end up as a judge," and "the more I accuse myself, the more I have a right to judge you." That is a central theme in any continual confessional process, particularly where it is required in an enclosed group process.

The next three patterns I describe in regard to ideological totalism are "the sacred science," the "loading of the language," and the principle of "doctrine over person." The phrases are almost self-explanatory. I would emphasize especially sacred science, for in our age something must be scientific as well as spiritual to have a substantial effect on people. Sacred science can offer considerable security to young people because it greatly simplifies the world. The Unification Church is a good example, but not the only one, of a contemporary need to combine a sacred set of dogmatic principles with a claim to a science embodying the truth about human behavior and human psychology. In the case of the Unification Church, this claim to a comprehensive human science is furthered by inviting prominent scholars (who are paid unusually high honoraria) to large symposia that stress unification of thought; participants express their views freely but nonetheless contribute to the desired aura of intellectual legitimacy.

The term "loading the language" refers to a literalization of language—

and to words or images becoming God. A greatly simplified language may seem cliché-ridden but can have enormous appeal and psychological power in its very simplification. Because every issue in one's life—and these are often very complicated young lives—can be reduced to a single set of principles that have an inner coherence, one can claim the experience of truth and feel it. Answers are available. Lionel Trilling has called this the "language of non-thought" because there is a cliché and a simple slogan to which the most complex and otherwise difficult questions can be reduced.

The pattern of doctrine over person occurs when there is a conflict between what one feels oneself experiencing and what the doctrine or dogma says one should experience. The internalized message in totalistic environments is that one must find the truth of the dogma and subject one's experiences to that truth. Often the experience of contradiction, or the admission of that experience, can be immediately associated with guilt; or else (in order to hold one to that doctrine) condemned by others in a way that leads quickly to that guilty association. One is made to feel that doubts are reflections of one's own evil. Yet doubts can arise; and when conflicts become intense, people can leave. This is the most frequent difficulty of many of the cults: membership may represent more of a problem than money.

Finally, the eighth, and perhaps the most general and significant of these characteristics, is what I call the "dispensing of existence." This principle is usually metaphorical. But if one has an absolute or totalistic vision of truth, then those who have not seen the light—have not embraced that truth, are in some way in the shadows—are bound up with evil, tainted, and do not have the right to exist. There is a "being versus nothingness" dichotomy at work here. Impediments to legitimate being must be pushed away or destroyed. One placed in the second category of not having the right to exist can experience psychologically a tremendous fear of inner extinction or collapse. However, when one is accepted, there can be great satisfaction of feeling oneself a part of the élite. Under more malignant conditions, the dispensing of existence, the absence of the right to exist, can be literalized; people can be put to death because of their alleged doctrinal shortcomings, as has happened in all too many places, including the Soviet Union and Nazi Germany. In the People's Temple mass suicide-murder in Guyana, a single cult leader could preside over the literal dispensing of existence—or more precisely, nonexistence—by means of a suicidal mystique he himself had made a part of the group's ideology. (Subsequent reports based on the results of autopsies reveal that there were probably as many murders as suicides.) The totalistic impulse to draw a sharp line between those who have a right to live and those who do not—though occurring in varying degrees—can become a deadly approach to resolving fundamental human problems. And all such approaches involving totalism or fundamentalism are doubly dangerous in a nuclear age.

I should say that, despite these problems, none of these processes is airtight. One of my purposes in writing about them is to counter the tendency in the culture to deny that such things exist; another purpose is to demystify them, to see them as comprehensible in terms of our understanding of human behavior.

RESOURCE ORGANIZATIONS

Cult Awareness Network (C.A.N.—affiliates nationwide)
National Office
2421 West Pratt Blvd., Suite 1173
Chicago, IL 60645
(312) 267-7777

FOCUS (Former member support network)
Contact Cult Awareness Network (C.A.N.) for information.

American Family Foundation (A.F.F.—research, information, publications)
P.O. Box 336
Weston, MA 02193
(617) 893-0930

International Cult Education Program (I.C.E.P.)
P.O. Box 1232, Gracie Station
New York, NY 10028
(212) 439-1550

Interfaith Coalition of Concern about Cults
111 West 40 St.
New York, NY 10018
(212) 983-4977

Task Force on Missionaries and Cults
Jewish Community Relations Council of New York
711 Third Ave., 12th floor
New York, NY 10014
(212) 983-4800

Jewish Board of Family and Children's Services
Cult Clinic Service
1651 Third Avenue
New York, NY 10028
(212) 860-8533

Commission on Cults and Missionaries/
Community Relations Committee, Suite 802
Jewish Family Services Cult Clinic, Suite 608
Jewish Federation Council of Greater Los Angeles, Suite 802
6505 Wilshire Blvd.
Los Angeles, CA 90048
(213) 852-1234

Committee on Cults and Missionaries
Greater Miami Jewish Federation
 4200 Biscayne Blvd.
 Miami, FL 33137
 (305) 576-4000

Christian Research Institute (C.R.I.)
 Box 500
 San Juan Capistrano, CA 92693
 (714) 855-9926

Personal Freedom Outreach
 P.O. Box 26062
 St. Louis, MO 63136
 (314) 388-2648

Watchman Fellowship
 P.O. Box 74091
 Birmingham, AL 35253
 (205) 871-3366

Restrictive Group Recovery
Michael Lisman, M.S.W.
 P.O. Box 8443
 Berkeley, CA 94707–8443

PACT (People Against Cultic Therapies)
 P.O. Box 4011, Grand Central Station
 New York, NY 10160
 (212) 316-1560

Stop Abuse by Counselors
 P.O. Box 68292
 Seattle, WA 98168
 (206) 243-2723

TM-EX (ex-members of transcendental meditation)
Patrick Ryan
 P.O. Box 2520
 Philadelphia, PA 19147
 (215) 467-4939

Ex-COG (ex-Children of God)
Karen Meyer
 1409 Kuehner Drive #202
 Simi Valley, CA 93063
 (213) 522-8401

F.A.I.R. (ex-Scientologists)
P.O. Box 11136
Burbank, CA 91510
(213) 413-3267

Bethel Ministries (ex-Jehovah's Witnesses)
Randall Waters
P.O. Box 3818
Manhattan Beach, CA 90266
(213) 545-7831

Comments From the Friends (ex-Jehovah's Witnesses)
P.O. Box 840
Stoughton, MA 02072

Network of Friends (ex-Church Universal and Triumphant)
P.O. Box 1093
Livingston, MT 59047

Jews for Judaism
1054 S. Robertson Blvd., Suite 205
Los Angeles, CA 90035

Ambassador Report (ex-Worldwide Church of God)
P.O. Box 60068
Pasadena, CA 91106

Fundamentalists Anonymous
P.O. Box 20324
Greeley Square Station
New York, NY 10001
(212) 696-0420

Rehabilitation Facilities for Former Members

Unbound (Research, re-entry, and education)
P.O. Box 1963
Iowa City, IA 52244
(319) 337-3723

Wellspring Retreat and Resource Center
Paul R. Martin, Ph.D., Director
P.O. Box 67
Albany, OH 45710
(614) 698-6277

The Cook Home, Inc.
    Route 5, Box 49 C
    Enid, OK 73701
    (405) 446-5406

Canadian Resources

Saskatchewan Citizens Against Mind Control (SCAMC)
    Meadow Lake Chapter, Box 358
    Meadow Lake, Saskatchewan SCM 1V0
    Canada

Alberta Cult Education
    0136-100 St., Suite 502
    Edmonton, Alberta T5P 4C1
    Canada
    (403) 476-9601

Council on Mind Abuse (COMA)
    Box 575, Station Z
    Toronto, Ontario
    Canada M5N 2Z6
    (416) 484-1112

Cult Project
    3460 Stanley Street
    Montreal, Quebec H3A 1R8
    Canada
    (514) 845-6756

Centre d'Information sur les Nouvelles Religions
    8010 St. Denis Street
    Montreal, Quebec H2R 2G1
    Canada
    (514) 382-9641

Overseas

FAIR (Family Action Information and Rescue)
    BCM Box 3535,
    P.O. Box 12
    London WC1N 3XX
    England
    Tel: (44) 1-539-3940

Irish Family Foundation
    Box 1628
    Balls Bridge
    Dublin 4, Ireland

Association Pour La Defense de la Famille et L'individu (ADFI)
    4 Rue Flechier
    75009 Paris, France
    Tel: (33) 1-42-85-15-52

Pastor Friedrich-W. Haack
Bavarian Lutheran Church
    Bunzlauer Str. 28,
    D-8000 Munchen 50
    West Germany
    Tel: (49) 89-141-2841

Elterninitiative gegen psychische Abhangigkeit und religiosen Extremismus
    Postfach 30 33 25
    1000 Berlin 30, B.R.D.
    West Germany

Dialog Center International
    Katrinebjergve 46,
    DK-8200 Aarhus N, Denmark
    Tel: (45) 6-10-54-11

Okumenische Arbeitsgrubbe "Neue religiose Bewegungen in der Schweiz"
    9403 Goldach, Switzerland
    Tel: (71) 41-22-65

Concerned Parents
    Box 1806
    Haifa, Israel
    Tel: (972) 4-71-85-22

The Jewish Center
    Box 34,
    Balaclava, Victoria 3183
    Australia
    Tel: (61) 3-527-5069

CCG Ministries
    176 Albert Street
    Osborne Park
    West Australia 6017
    Tel: (61) 9-344-2200

Pro Juventud
    Aribau 226,
    08006 Barcelona, Spain
    Tel: (34) 3-42-85-15-52

Notes

Chapter 1

1. Report of the Subcommittee on International Relations, U.S. House of Representatives, Oct 31, 1978 (also known as Fraser Report), 338–348.

2. Ibid., 316.

3. Steve Kemperman, *Lord of the Second Advent* (Ventura, California: Regal Books, 1982), 13.

4. Gary Scharff, "Autobiography of a Former Moonie," *Cultic Studies Journal* (Vol. 2, No. 2, 1986), 252.

5. Moon's original name is Yung Myung Moon, which means "Thy Shining Dragon." Cited in "Honor Thy Father Moon," *Psychology Today* (Jan 1976).

6. "Jury Finds Rev. Moon Guilty of Conspiracy To Evade Income Tax," *The Wall Street Journal* (May 19, 1982).

Lyda Phillips (UPI), "Rev. Moon free after year in prison for tax evasion," *The Boston Globe* (July 5, 1985).

7. Frank Greve, in "Seeking Influence, Rev. Moon Spends Big on New Right," *Philadelphia Inquirer* (Dec 20, 1987), states the numbers to be even lower.

8. "On Witnessing," Master Speaks (Jan 3, 1972).

James and Marcia Rudin, Prison or Paradise, (Philadelphia: Fortress Press, 1980), 25.

Robert Boettcher, *Gifts of Deceit—Sun Myung Moon, Tongsun Park and the Korean Scandal* (New York: Holt, Rinehart and Winston, 1980), 175–176.

Gary Scharff, "Autobiography of a Former Moonie," *Cultic Studies Journal* (Vol. 2, No. 2, 1986), 252.

9. Michael Warder, "Bribemasters," *Chronicles* (June 1988).

Gary Scharff, "Autobiography of a Former Moonie," *Cultic Studies Journal* (Vol. 2, No. 2, 1986).

Douglas Lenz, "Twenty-two Months As a Moonie," Lutheran Church of America Partners (Feb 1982).

Barbara Dole, "Former Member's Story," *The Advisor* (Feb/March 1981).

Michael Lisman, statement about his membership, 1981.

10. "Completion of Our Responsibility," *Master Speaks* (Oct 28, 1974), 8.

11. "Relationship Between Men and Women," *Master Speaks* (May 20, 1973).

12. "Moon Tells How He Regulates Sex," *San Jose Mercury* (May 27, 1982).

13. Fraser Report, 338–348.

Fred Clarkson, "The New Righteous Plan a Third Party," *The Washington Herald* (Feb 8, 1988).

14. Laura Knickerbocker, "Mind Control: How The Cults Work," *Harper's Bazaar* (May 1980).

James and Marcia Rudin, *Prison or Paradise* (Philadelphia: Fortress Press, 1980), 28, 45.

15. Fraser Report, 311–390.

16. Ibid., 354.

17. Fred Clarkson, "Moon's Law: God is Phasing Out Democracy," *Covert Action Information Bulletin* (Spring 1987).

18. Ibid., 36.

19. Douglas Lenz, "Twenty-two Months as a Moonie," *Lutheran Church of America Partners* (Feb 1982), 13–15.

Josh Freed, *Moonwebs* (Toronto: Dorset Publishing, Inc., 1980), 191.

20. Fraser Report, 326, 366.

21. (UPI) "Ousted Editor Says Church Controls *Washington Times*," *The Boston Globe* (July 18, 1984).

22. Fred Clarkson, "Behind the Times: Who Pulls the Strings at Washington's #2 Daily," *Extra!* (Aug/Sept 1987).

23. "The Significance of the Training Session," *Master Speaks* (May 17, 1973).

24. Frank Greve, *Knight-Ridder Newspapers* (Dec 20, 1987).

"Moon/Mormon Conference for Legislators," *City Paper* (Washington D.C.: July 25–31, 1986).

25. Fred Clarkson, "Behind the Times: Who Pulls the Strings at Washington's #2 Daily," *Extra!* (Aug/Sept 1987).

26. Andrew Ferguson, "Can Buy Me Love: The Mooning of Conservative Washington," *The American Spectator* (Sept 1987).

27. Frank Greve, *Knight-Ridder Newspapers* (Dec 20, 1987).

28. David Shaw, "Washington Times Fights for Its Niche: Paper Tainted by Ties to Right Wing, Moon Church," *Los Angeles Times* (April 26, 1987).

Chapter 2

1. Douglas Lenz, "Twenty-two Months as a Moonie," *Lutheran Church of America Partners* (Feb 1982), 13–15.

Josh Freed, *Moonwebs* (Toronto: Dorset Publishing Inc., 1980), 191.

2. "Jacob's Course and our Life in Faith," (May 27, 1973), 3.

Robert Boettcher, *Gifts of Deceit—Sun Myung Moon, Tongsun Park and the Korean Scandal* (New York: Holt, Rinehart and Winston, 1980), 343–344.

3. Kamiyama was co-convicted with Moon for conspiracy to defraud the U.S. government of tax revenues.

U.S. vs. Sun Myung Moon and Takeru Kamiyama: Kamiyama accused of aiding and abetting filing of false returns, obstruction of justice, and perjury.

4. Michael Warder, "Bribemasters," *Chronicles* (June 1988).

Frazer Report, 313.

5. "The Seven Day Fast," *Master Speaks* (Oct 20, 1974), 19.

6. "Children's Day," *Master Speaks* (Aug 4, 1974), 12.

7. Moon and Hak Ja Han, his third wife, were regarded by members to be the perfect Adam and Eve. Moon's theology says that the original Eve was tempted into sexual intercourse by Satan before she had grown to perfection, and then she seduced Adam. Therefore, all mankind were the offspring of tainted blood. The kingdom of heaven will be established when God sends a perfect man again in order to establish the "pure" lineage. Jesus was killed before he had a chance to marry and have perfect children. Therefore, Moon (being 'perfect' himself) can spiritually "adopt" members into his "true family" and assign them marriage partners in order to redo their spiritual lineage. Moon married more than 2,000 such couples in Madison Square Garden in 1984.

8. Vernon Scott, "Controversy Shrouds Obscure Movie 'Inchon,' " *Santa Barbara News—Press* (Oct 10, 1982).

"Times Kills Review," *Washington Post* (Sept 18, 1982), C1.

"Stars Tricked into Making Cult Movie," *Globe* (June 8, 1982).

9. Fred Clarkson. "The Messiah Who Bilked IRS," *The Sacramento Bee* (Sept 15, 1985).

Herbert Rosedale, "Moon's Conviction Justified by the Record," *The Cult Observer* (Nov 1984).

10. Douglas Lenz, "Twenty-two Months as a Moonie," *Lutheran Church of America Partners* (Feb 1982), 12.

Steve Kemperman, *Lord of the Second Advent* (Ventura, California: Regal Books, 1982), 14.

11. Christopher Edwards, *Crazy for God* (Englewood Cliffs, New Jersey: Prentice-Hall, Inc., 1979), 144–145.

12. Douglas Lenz, "Twenty-two Months as a Moonie," *Lutheran Church of America Partners* (Feb 1982), 12.

Jerry Carroll and Bernard Bauer, "Suicide Training in the Moon Cult," *New West* (Jan 29, 1979), 62.

13. "God's Plan for America," Sun Myung Moon (Dec 18, 1975).

14. Marcia R. Rudin, "The Cult Phenomenon: Fad or Fact?" *New York University Review of Law and Social Change* (Vol. IX, No. 1), 31.

15. Fraser Report, 311–392.

Chapter 3

1. Glenn Collins, "The Psychology of the Cult Experience," *The New York Times* (March 15, 1982).

2. Fraser Report, 326, 351–53, 368.

"The Outline of Rev. Moon's Hand in Central America: The Unification Church, the World Anti-Communist League, CAUSA and John Singlaub," Ford Greene, 1987, 13–17.

"Moonie Interests Said to Choose Mentevideo as Centre," *Latin America Regional Reports* (Oct 14, 1983).

Tim Cain, "Moonie Recruiting Groups Have Ties to Contras in Central America," *Sandpaper* (Oct 16, 1987).

Jean Francois Boyer and Alejandro Alem, "Moon in Latin America: Building Bases of a World Organization," *Manchester Guardian Weekly* (March 3, 1985).

3. Fraser Report, 345.

"The Way International," Anti-Defamation League Report (Spring 1982).

"Government probe of The Way Disclosed Political Activism, 'pattern' of Harassment of Witnesses," *CAN News* (July–July 1987), from "Religious Group's Political Activities Subject of Probe," *Bangor Daily News* (Nov 21, 1986).

4. Louis Trager, "Evidence Points Toward North Tie to Rev. Moon," *San Francisco Examiner* (July 20, 1987).

5. "Moonie Interests on the Rise: The Empire Consolidates" *Latin America Regional Reports* (April 1984).

6. "Significance of the Training Session," *Master Speaks* (May 17, 1973).

7. John Marks, *The Search for the Manchurian Candidate* (New York: Times Books, 1979), 72, 133, 182–192.

8. Patricia C. Hearst with Alvin Moscow, *Patty Hearst: Her Own Story* (New York: Avon Books, 1982).

9. Ted Patrick with Tom Dulack, *Let Our Children Go* (New York: E. P. Dutton and Company, Inc., 1976).

10. Allan Maraynes, producer, "Scientology," *60 Minutes* (Volume XII, Number 51), aired Aug 31, 1980.

Eugene H. Methvin, "Scientology: Anatomy of a Frightening Cult," *Reader's Digest* (May 1980), and "Scientology: The Sickness Spreads," *Reader's Digest* (Sept 1981).

Bent Corydon and L. Ron Hubbard, Jr., *L. Ron Hubbard: Messiah or Madman?* (Secaucus, New Jersey: Lyle Stuart, 1987).

Russell Miller, *Bare Faced Messiah: The True Story of L. Ron Hubbard* (Great Britain: Penguin Books Ltd., 1987).

11. Patricia Ward Biederman, "$1.5 Million Award to Former C.U.T. Member," *Los Angeles Times* (April 3, 1986).

Karen Kenney, "Church Universal and Triumphant: Of Church business, Public and Private," *The Valley News* (Feb 1, 1980).

"Fear of Church Grips Montana Town," *Daily News* (Feb 4, 1982).

Mark Reiter, "One Man's Story: Why Would a Man in His 50s Join a Cult? Listen to Gregory Mull's Tale," *50 Plus* (Oct 1981).

Kerry Webster, "Her Will Be Done: Elizabeth Claire Prophet and the Church Universal and Triumphant," *Herald Examiner* (Jan 27, 1985) (six-part series).

Jim Robbins, "A Question of Good Neighbors," *Boston Globe Magazine* (Aug 9, 1987).

12. Wendy B. Ford, "Way Seduction 'Invisible,' " *The Journal Herald* (Jan 13, 1981).

Jan Pogue, "The Mysterious Ways of the Way: Victor Paul Wierwille has quietly built a huge religious following. He believes that if people would just listen to what God told him 40 years ago, he could 'remake the world.' Some who know him well are afraid he's right." *Today, The Philadelphia Inquirer* (Aug 1, 1981).

Anne Cocroft Cole, "Janney Lost Career Dreams as Follower of 'The Way,' " *Loudoun Times-Mirror* (Dec 10, 1981), and "Janney's Life in the Way: Sacrifice and Obedience," (Dec 17, 1981), and "Now Out of 'The Way' Janney Warns Others," (Dec 24, 1981).

13. Win McCormack, "Bhagwan's Bottom Line: Rajneesh's Far-flung Empire is More Material than Spiritual," *Oregon Magazine Collector's Edition/The Rajneesh Files 1981–86*, 97.

14. "The LaRouche Network—A Political Cult," *ADL/Civil Rights Report* (Spring 1982, Vol. 27, No. 2).

Howard Blum and Paul Montgomery, "U.S. Labor Party: Cult Surrounded by Controversy," *The New York Times* (Oct 7, 1979), and "One Man Leads U.S. Labor Party on its Erratic Path," (Oct 8, 1979).

John Mintz, "Lyndon LaRouche: From Marxist Left to Well-Connected Right," *The Washington Post National Weekly Edition* (Feb 25, 1985).

15. "MOVE Leader Wanted 'Absolute Control,' " *The Boston Globe* (May 15, 1985) and (May 16, 1985).

"New Life for 'Move' Child in Wake of Philadelphia Disaster," *The Cult Observer* (Jan/Feb 1986), from the *Wall Street Journal* (Nov 1, 1985).

16. Chip Berlet, "White, Right, and Looking for a Fight: Has Chicago Been Targeted by a New Alliance of White Supremacists?" *Reader* (June 27, 1986, Vol. 15, No. 39).

"Idaho Bombings Part of Race War Planned by Neo-Nazi Splinter Group," *CAN News* (Oct 1986), from Couer d'Alene Press, Idaho.

Press Oct 8, 1986, and the *Spokane Spokesman-Review* Oct 9, 1986.

"Racist Groups Meet," *The New York Times* (July 14, 1986).

"Two Neo-Nazis Convicted in Slaying," *The Cult Observer* (Jan/Feb 1988) from "Two Convicted in Radio Host's Death," *The Fort Wayne News-Sentinel* (Nov 18, 1987).

17. Peter Siegel, Nancy Strohl, Laura Ingram, David Roche, and Jean Taylor, "Leninism as Cult: The Democratic Workers Party," *Socialist Review*, 58–85.

18. Marcia R. Rudin, "The Cult Phenomenon: Fad or Fact?" *New York University Review of Law and Social Change* (Vol. IX, No. 1), 18–19.

19. For more information on treatment of phobias, contact the Anxiety Disorders Association of America, 600 Executive Blvd., Suite 200, Rockville, MD 20852-3801, (301) 231-9350.

20. James and Marcia Rudin, *Prison or Paradise* (Philadelphia: Fortress Press, 1980), 103.

Lorraine Ahearn, "Mind Control Called the Way of The Way," *The Capital* (Annapolis, April 2, 1986), 12.

21. Diane Salvatore, "The New Victims of Cults," *Ladies Home Journal* (Aug 1987).

Andree Brooks, "Cults and the Aged: A New Family Issue," *The New York Times* (April 26, 1986).

22. "Public Hearing on the Treatment of Children by Cults," The Assembly of the State of New York (Aug 9–10, 1979).

Shirley Landa, "Hidden Terror: Child Abuse in 'Religious Sects and Cults,' " *Justice for Children* (Fall 1985, Vol. 1, No. 5).

Chapter 4

1. Robert Jay Lifton, *Thought Reform and the Psychology of Totalism* (New York: W.W. Norton & Company, 1961).

2. "Jury Indicts 9 Linked to Synanon," *The Cult Observer* (Oct 1985), from *The New York Times* (Oct 2, 1985).

"Point Reyes Light Wins $100,000 settlement from Synanon," *The Cult Observer* (March/April 1987).

Steve Allen, *Beloved Son* (Indianapolis, New York: The Bobbs-Merrill Company, Inc., 1982), 187–194.

Myrna Oliver, "Two Synanon Members Get Year in Jail," *Los Angeles Times* (November 22, 1980).

3. Moon made this speech to an audience of several hundred people during the summer of 1975 in upstate New York.

4. See Adorno, Frenkel-Brunswik, Levinson, Sanford, *The Authoritarian Personality* (New York: Harper & Brothers, 1950).

5. Solomon Asch, "Effects of Group Pressure Upon the Modification and Distortion of Judgement," in *Groups, Leadership, and Men*, ed. M.H. Guetzkow, (Pittsburgh: Carnegie, 1951).

Solomon Asch, "Studies of Independence and Conformity: A Minority of One Against a Unanimous Majority," *Psychological Monographs*, 70 (1956).

6. Stanley Milgram, *Obedience to Authority* (New York: Harper & Row, 1974), xii.

7. Leon Festinger, Henry W. Riecken, and Stanley Schachter, *When Prophecy Fails* (Harper & Row, 1964).

8. Ibid.

9. Michael Mahoney and Carl Thoreson, *Self-Control: Power to the Person* (Monterey, California: Brooks/Cole, 1974).

10. Fred Clarkson, "Moon's Law: 'God is Phasing Out Democracy,' " *Covert Action Information Bulletin No. 27* (Spring 1987), 38.

11. Kurt Lewin, "Frontiers in Group Dynamics: Concept, Method, and Reality in Social Science," Human Relations, 1947.

12. Edgar H. Schein, *Coercive Persuasion, 1961* (The Massachusetts Institute of Technology, W.W. Norton, 1971).

13. One of the best books I've read on linguistic double binds is Milton Erickson's *Hypnotic Realities* (New York: Irvington Publishers, 1976).

Chapter 5

1. Eric Hoffer, *The True Believer* (New York: Harper & Row, 1951), 77.

2. Michael Warder, "Bribemasters," *Chronicles* (June 1988), 31.

3. "Central Figure," *Master Speaks* (Feb 13, 1974), 6.

"Untitled," *Master Speaks* (Jan 3, 1972).

"Parents Day," *Master Speaks* (March 24, 1974).

4. Mark Brewer, "We're Gonna Tear You Down and Put You Back Together," *Psychology Today* (Aug 1975).

Willa Appel, *Cults in America* (New York: Holt, Rinehart & Winston, Inc., 1983), 19–20.

5. Flo Conway and Jim Siegelman, *Snapping* (New York: Dell Publishing Co., Inc., 1978), 22–27.

Susan C. Orlean, "Est Puts Itself in Charge of Tomorrow," *Boston Phoenix* (Jan 18, 1983), Section 2, 4.

6. See R.E. Ornstein, *The Mind Field* (England: Octagon Press, 1983), 97–98.

7. Mark Brewer, "We're Gonna Tear You Down and Put You Back Together," *Psychology Today* (Aug 1975).

Flo Conway and Jim Siegelman, *Snapping* (New York: Dell Publishing Co., 1978).

Karen Lee Ziner, "Encounters Suit: Jack Slee's Family Sues est," *The Norwich Bulletin* (August 19).

8. Mark Brewer, "We're Gonna Tear You Down and Put You Back Together," *Psychology Today* (Aug 1975), 36.

Snapping, 180.

9. Jude Dratt, producer, "West 57th Street, CBS News Magazine" (Oct 10, 1987).

10. Ibid.

11. Ibid.

12. John Mintz, "LaRouche Intelligence Organization Has Contacts in High Places," *The Washington Post* (Jan 15, 1985), A5.

13. The story given here is taken from the "West 57th Street, CBS News Magazine" program. At the time this program was aired, Elizabeth Rose was still an active member of the LaRouche organization.

14. " 'Psychological Damage' from TM Found Worth $137,890," *The Washington Times Metro* (Jan 14, 1987), 5B.

Snapping, 174, 176.

15. Darrel Sifford, "A Psychiatrist Probes Effects of Transcendental Meditation," *Philadelphia Inquirer* (June 19, 1988), 2F.

16. Michael A. Persinger, Normand J. Carrey, and Lynn A. Seuss, *TM and Cult Mania* (Massachusetts: The Christopher Publishing House, 1980), 155–56.

17. Ibid., 60–65.

18. Doug Johnson, "Former Truth Station Member Tells of Secret Practices," *Victor Valley Daily Press* (March 5, 1981), A1.

"TV Producer Charges Kin Abused by Religious Cult," *Oxnard Press Courier* (March 5, 1981), 2.

19. Michael Kelly, "A Couple Still Hearing the Chant," *Cult Awareness Network News* (Jan-Feb 1985), 3.

20. Toby Smith, "Where The Way Goes Controversy Follows," *Impact/Albuquerque Journal Magazine* (July 14, 1981), 4.

Lorraine Ahearn, "The Way," *The Capital* (Annapolis, April 1, 1986), 7.

21. "The Way International," *ADL Research Report* (Spring 1982), 1.

Lorraine Ahearn, "Mind Control Called the Way of The Way," *The Capital* (Annapolis, April 2, 1986), 1, 12.

Snapping, 16.

22. See Arthur Lyons, *Satan Wants You* (New York: Mysterious Press, 1988), 135.

23. Jerry Adler, "The Second Beast of Revelation," *Newsweek* (Nov 16, 1987), 73.

24. *Satan Wants You,* 135.

25. Ibid.

Chapter 6

1. Andrea Estes, "Cult Attracts Trouble in Travels: The Ex-Carnival Barker Turned Church Apostate," *The Boston Herald* (June 23, 1984).

Mark Starr, "The Kingdom at Island Pond," *Newsweek* (Nov 29, 1982).

Joan Guberman, "Another Jonestown: The Kingdom at Island Pond," *The Advisor* (Feb/ March 1983).

Josh Freed, *Moonwebs* (Toronto: Dorset Publishing, Inc., 1980), 50.

2. Mark Brewer, "We're Gonna Tear You Down and Put You Back Together," *Psychology Today* (Aug 1975), 82.

Richard Behar and Ralph King, Jr., "The Winds of Werner: The IRS, The Order of Malta and a Swiss Banker Have a Problem: A Onetime Used Car Salesman from Philadelphia," *Forbes* (Nov 18, 1985).

3. Dianne Dumanoski, "The Gospel According to Stevens: Evangelist Carl Stevens Started Out as a Bakery Driver. Now he's a shepherd in the Berkshires, with a flock of born-again Christians—and newly acquired fields," *Boston Phoenix* (May 24, 1977).

4. Robert Lindsey, "L. Ron Hubbard Dies of Stroke; Founder of Church of Scientology," *The New York Times* (Jan 29, 1986).

5. Phil Garber, "The Way: Religious Sect a Center of Controversy," *Daily Record* (March 30, 1986).

Wendy B. Ford, "Way Seduction 'Invisible,' " *The Journal Herald* (Jan 13, 1981).

"The Way International," Anti-Defamation League Report, Spring 1982.

6. Robert Boettcher, *Gifts of Deceit—Sun Myung Moon, Tongsun Park and the Korean Scandal* (New York: Holt, Rinehart and Winston, 1980), 35.

Moonwebs, 50.

7. Lyda Phillips (UPI), "Rev. Moon Free After Year in Prison for Tax Evasion," *The Boston Globe* (July 5, 1985).

8. Bent Corydon and L. Ron Hubbard, Jr., *L. Ron Hubbard: Messiah or Mad-Man?* (Secaucus, New Jersey: Lyle Stuart, 1987).

Russell Miller, *Bare Faced Messiah: The True Story of L. Ron Hubbard* (Great Britain: Penguin Books, 1987).

Richard Behar, "The Prophet and Profits of Scientology," *Forbes 400* (Oct 27, 1986), 314–315.

"Penthouse Interview: L. Ron Hubbard, Jr." *Penthouse* (June 1983), 111, 174–175.

9. Fraser Report, 387.

10. Ibid., 313, 316, 333–334.

11. Eugene H. Methvin, "Scientology: The Sickness Spreads," *Reader's Digest* (Sept 1981), 5.

"Penthouse Interview: L. Ron Hubbard, Jr." *Penthouse* (June 1983), 113.

12. Richard Behar, "The Prophet and Profits of Scientology," *Forbes 400* (Oct 27, 1986), 316.

13. Rachel Martin, *Escape: The True Story of a Young Woman Caught in the Clutches of a Religious Cult* (Denver, Colorado: Accent Books, 1979).

14. Deborah Berg Davis, *The Children of God: The Inside Story* (Grand Rapids, Missouri: The Zondervan Publishing House, 1984).

Herbert J. Wallerstein, Final Report on the Activities of the Children of God to Honorable Louis J. Lefkowitz, Attorney General of the State of New York. Charity Frauds Bureau, Sept 30, 1974.

Una McManus, *Not for a Million Dollars* (Impact Books, 1980).

15. Steve Allen, *Beloved Son: A Story of the Jesus Cults* (New York: Bobbs-Merrill Company, Inc., 1982), 192–193.

16. Lindsey Gruson, "2 Hare Krishna Aides Accused of Child Molesting," *The New York Times* (Feb 18, 1987).

"Murders, Drug and Abuse Charges Shake Krishnas," *Akron Beacon Journal* (June 22, 1986).

Eric Harrison, "Crimes Among the Krishnas: The world wouldn't listen to Stephen

Bryant's charges against his religion's leaders, until he was murdered," *The Philadelphia Inquirer Magazine* (April 15, 1987).

John Hubner and Lindsay Gruson, "Dial Om for Murder: The Hare Krishna church, once brimming with youthful idealism, has become a haven for drug traffickers, suspected child molesters—and killers," *The Rolling Stone* (April 9, 1987), 53.

"Krishna Killer Ordered Extradited," *CAN News* (Sept-Oct 1987) from "Dreschner Ordered Extradited," *The Intelligencer* (Aug 14, 1987).

"Hare Krishna Leader Reported to be Linked to Murder of His Critic," *The New York Times* (June 17, 1987), 9.

17. "Scientology's 'Campaign of Harassment,' " *The Cult Observer* (Nov/Dec 1987) from "Scientologists in Dirty Campaign to Stop Book," *The Sunday Times* (London, Oct 18, 1987).

"Scientologists Try to Block Hubbard Biography," *The Cult Observer* (July/Aug 1987), from "New Hassle over Scientology Book," *The New York Post* (Aug 4, 1987) and "Lawsuits Surround Book on L. Ron Hubbard," *Publishers Weekly* (Aug 1987).

18. Robert Lindsey, "2 Defectors from People's Temple Slain in California," *The New York Times* (Feb 28, 1980), A 16.

19. Peter Siegel, Nancy Strohl, Laura Ingram, David Roche, and Jean Taylor, "Leninism as Cult: The Democratic Workers Party," *Socialist Review,* 58–85.

20. "Center for Feeling Therapy Founder Fights to Keep License," *The Cult Observer* (Jan/Feb 1987) from the *Los Angeles Times* (Sept 21, 1986).

"Center for Feeling Therapy Psychologists Lose Licenses," *The Cult Observer* (Nov/Dec 1987) from "Psychologists in Feeling Therapy Lose Licenses," *The Los Angeles Times* (Sept 29, 1987).

21. Darrell Sifford, "Psychiatrist Probes the Effects of Transcendental Meditation," *Philadelphia Inquirer* (June 19, 1988).

The Various Implications Arising from the Practice of Transcendental Meditation (Bensheim, Germany: Institute for Youth and Society), 80.

22. Marc Fisher, "I Cried Enough to Fill a Glass," *The Washington Post Magazine* (Oct 25, 1987), 20.

Alfrieda Slee, Administratrix to the Estate of Jack Andrew Slee, vs. Werner Erhard, et al. Civil Action #N-84-497-JAC, United States District Court for the District of Connecticut.

Evangeline Bojorquez vs. Werner Erhard, et al, Civil Action #449177, Superior Court of the State of California in and for the County of Santa Clara.

Nancy Urgell vs. Werner Erhard and Werner Erhard Associates, Civil Action #H-85-1025 PCD, United States District Court, District of Connecticut.

23. Teresa Ramirez Boulette and Susan M. Anderson, "Mind Control and the Battering of Women," *Community Mental Health Journal* (Summer 1985, Vol. 21, No. 2).

Chapter 7

1. Alan MacRobert, "Uncovering the Cult Conspiracy," *Mother Jones* (Feb/March 1979, Vol. 4, No. 2), 8.

2. The names of the cult member and his family have been changed to protect their identities.

3. For a complete listing of all of the groups affiliated with the Boston Church of Christ, see the appendix of *The Discipling Dilemma* by Flavil Yeakley (Nashville, Tennessee: Gospel Advocates, 1988).

4. Buddy Martin has put together information packets on the Multiplying Ministries. Videotapes of his lectures are available through the Memorial Church of Christ in Houston, Texas.

5. Daniel Terris, "Come, All Ye Faithful," *Boston Globe Magazine* (June 6, 1986).

Linda Hervieux, "The Boston Church of Christ: Critics Call It a Cult, but Members Maintain Their Church's Legitimacy," *Muse Magazine,* Boston University (Feb 18, 1988).

Gregory L. Sharp, "Mind Control and 'Crossroadism,'" *Gospel Anchor* (March 1987), 23.

Jeanne Pugh, "Fundamentalist Church Gathers Campus Converts . . . and Critics," *St. Petersburg Times* (July 21, 1979), 1.

6. Letter published in the Crossroads bulletin, March 16, 1987.

7. Letter from Memorial Church of Christ elders, March 1977, firing McKean.

8. The names of the cult member and her family have been changed to protect their identities.

9. See Deborah Berg Davis, *The Children of God: The Inside Story* (Grand Rapids, Michigan: The Zondervan Publishing House, 1984).

10. Kathy Mehler, "Published Preachings: Even Prostitution Can Attract Converts to Cults," *The Daily Illini* (April 16, 1981).

11. The names of the cult member and his family have been changed to protect their identities.

12. Larry Woods, "The Masters Movement, Parts I and II," Turner Broadcasting Systems, CNN (Jan 13, 1986).

13. Ray Richmond, "Masters—A Healer in Bluejeans?" *Los Angeles Times* (Dec 1, 1985), 90.

Paul Taublieb, "Masters' Touch," *US Magazine* (April 23, 1984), 39–41.

Lauren Kessler, "Roy Masters: 'I Can Do No Wrong,'" *Northwest Magazine* (Sept 4, 1983).

Chapter 9

1. "Indemnity and Unification," *Master Speaks* (Feb 14, 1974), 11–12.

Christopher Edwards, *Crazy for God* (Englewood Cliffs, New Jersey: Prentice Hall, Inc., 1979), 173–174.

2. Douglas Lenz, "Twenty-two Months as a Moonie," *Lutheran Church of America Partners* (Feb 1982), 14.

3. Steve Kemperman, *Lord of the Second Advent* (Ventura, California: Regal Books, 1982), 87.

4. Ibid.

5. John Hubner and Lindsay Gruson, "Dial Om for Murder," *The Rolling Stone* (April 9, 1987), 53.

Chapter 10

1. Cf. "Relationship Between Men and Women," *Master Speaks* (May 20, 1973), 2.

Although this is a dramatic example of the things members are told by the Moonies, I have heard many similar tales from ex-members.

2. Gary Scharff, "Autobiography of a Former Moonie," *Cultic Studies Journal* (1986), Vol. 2, No. 2, 254.

3. See Marcia R. Rudin, "The Cult Phenomenon: Fad or Fact?" *New York University Review of Law and Social Change* (1979–80), Vol. IX, No. 1, 31–32.

4. See Steve Kemperman, *Lord of the Second Advent* (Ventura, California: Regal Books, 1981), 87.

5. Floating has also been linked to "Post Traumatic Stress Disorder," from which many Vietnam veterans suffer.

6. Geraldo Rivera, "Lifespring Part 2," ABC's "20/20" (Nov 6, 1980).

7. Decreeing is used by only one group that I am familiar with: Elizabeth Claire Prophet's Church Universal and Triumphant. It is a high-speed recitation of the group's "prayers." It is done so fast that anyone listening will not understand what a member is saying. In my opinion, it is a highly effective technique for trance induction and thought-stopping.

8. During my time in the Moonies, I had personally recruited fourteen people and influenced hundreds of people to join.

9. Francine Jeane Daner, *The American Children of Krishna: A Study of the Hare Krishna Movement* (New York: Holt, Rinehart, and Winston, 1976).

Hillary Johnson, "Children of a Harsh Bliss: In a West Virginia Commune, An Extraordinary Look at Life and Love Among the Krishnas," *Life Magazine* (April 1980).

Eric Harrison, "Crimes Among the Krishnas: The world wouldn't listen to Stephen Bryant's charges against his religion's leaders, until he was murdered," *The Philadelphia Inquirer Magazine* (April 5, 1987).

10. See 3HO/Sikh Dharma Publication, *Beads of Truth,* Preuss Road, Los Angeles, California.

11. Richard Behar, "The Prophet and Profits of Scientology."

12. Flo Conway and Jim Siegelman, *Snapping* (New York: Dell Publishing Co., 1978), 249.
"Penthouse Interview: L. Ron Hubbard, Jr." *Penthouse* (June 1983), 112.

13. Jim Healey, Sharry Ricchiardi, and D. Vance Hawthorne, "ISU Bible Study Group: Wonderful or a Cult?" *Desmoines Sunday Register* (March 9, 1980), 1B.

Michelle M. Bell, "I think I was Brainwashed: Religious Group Criticized as Cult-like is now at KSU," *Daily Kent Stater* (Dec 3, 1982), 1.

Chapter 11

1. Fraser Report, 338–372.

2. John Marks, *The Search for the Manchurian Candidate* (New York: Times Books, 1979), 186–192, 208, 212.

Paul Altmeyer, "Mission: Mind Control—ABC News Close-up," (Jan 30, 1979).

3. Douglas Lenz, "Twenty-two Months as a Moonie," *Lutheran Church of America Partners* (Feb 1982), 13–15.

Josh Freed, *Moonwebs* (Toronto: Dorset Publishing, Inc., 1980), 191.

4. American Psychiatric Association, DSM-III: *Diagnostic and Statistical Manual of Mental Disorders* (Washington, D.C., 3rd edition), 1980.

5. Flavil R. Yeakley, *The Discipling Dilemma* (Nashville: Gospel Advocate Press, 1982).

6. F.A.I.R. (listed in resources section) is pursuing this suit, case #CA001012, County of Los Angeles, Superior Court.

7. Attorney Gerald Ragland currently represents more than twenty former members of TM in litigation. His client Robert Kropinsky won an award of more than $100,000 in 1987 against TM for fraud and negligence.

8. Alfrieda Slee, Administratrix to the Estate of Jack Andrew Slee, vs. Werner Erhard, et al. Civil Action #N-84-497-JAC, United States District Court for the District of Connecticut.

Evangeline Bojorquez vs. Werner Erhard, et al. Civil Action #449177, Superior Court of the State of California in and for the County of Santa Clara.

Nancy Urgell vs. Werner Erhard and Werner Erhard Associates. Civil Action #H-85-1025 PCD, United States District Court, District of Connecticut.

9. Marc Fisher, "I Cried Enough to Fill a Glass," *The Washington Post Magazine* (Oct 25, 1987), 20.

10. William Borders, "Moon's Church Loses a Libel Suit in London over Recruiting Tactics," *The New York Times* (April 1, 1981).

Gordon Greig and Ted Oliver, "Daily Mail Wins Historic Libel Action: The Damning Verdict on the Moonies," *Daily Mail* (April 1, 1981), London.

Otto Friedrich, "Om . . . The New Age, Starring Shirley Maclaine, Faith Healers, Channelers, Space Travelers and Crystals Galore," *Time* (Dec 7, 1987).

Bibliography

General

Allen, Steve. *Beloved Son: A Story of the Jesus Cults.* Indianapolis: Bobbs-Merrill, 1982.

* Andres, Rachel, and Lane, James R., eds. *Cults and Consequences: The Definitive Handbook.* Los Angeles: Jewish Federation of Greater Los Angeles, 1988.

Appel, Willa. *Cults in America: Programmed for Paradise.* New York: Holt, Rinehart & Winston, 1983.

* Conway, Flo, and Siegelman, Jim. *Snapping: America's Epidemic of Sudden Personality Change.* New York: J. B. Lippincott, 1978.

———. *Holy Terror.* New York: Doubleday, 1982.

Diamond, Sara. *Spiritual Warfare: The Politics of the Christian Right.* Boston: South End Press, 1989.

Hearst, Patricia Campbell, with Moscow, Alvin. *Every Secret Thing.* New York: Pinnacle, 1982.

Huxley, Aldous. *Brave New World Revisited.* New York: Harper & Brothers, 1958.

* Orwell, George. *Nineteen Eighty-Four.* Middlesex, England: Penguin, 1954.

Mehta, Gita. *Karma Cola: Marketing the Mystic East.* New York: Simon & Schuster, 1979.

Patrick, Ted, with Dulack, Tom. *Let Our Children Go!* New York: E.P. Dutton, 1976.

Randi, James. *The Faith Healers.* Buffalo, NY: Prometheus Books, 1989.

Ross, Joan and Langone, Michael. *Cults: What Parents Should Know.* Secaucus, NJ: Lyle Stuart, 1989.

Rudin, James, and Rudin, Marcia. *Prison or Paradise? The New Religious Cults.* Philadelphia, Fortress Press, 1980.

Schecter, Robert E., and Noyes, Wendy L. *Cultism on Campus: Commentaries and Guidelines for College and University Administrators.* Weston, Mass.: American Family Foundation, 1987.

Shirer, William L. *The Rise and Fall of the Third Reich.* Greenwich, Conn.: Fawcett, 1960.

Sklar, Dusty. *Gods and Beasts: The Nazis and the Occult.* New York: Thomas Y. Crowell, 1977.

Stoner, Carroll, and Parke, Jo Anne. *All God's Children: The Cult Experience— Salvation and Slavery?* New York: Penguin, 1979.

Psychology

Addis, M., et al. "The Cult Clinic Helps Families in Crisis." *Social Casework: The Journal of Contemporary Social Work,* 1984.

---

* Indicates material of special interest.

Adorno, T.W.; Frenkel-Brunswik, E.SE; Levinson, D.J.; and Sanford, R.N. *The Authoritarian Personality*. The American Jewish Committee, New York: Harper, 1950; Norton Library, 1969.

Anderson, S.M. "Identifying coercion and deception in social systems." In *Scientific Research and the New Religions: Divergent Perspectives,* edited by B. Kilbourne. San Francisco: Pacific Division of the American Association for the Advancement of Science, 1985.

Anderson, S.M., and Zimbardo, Phillip G. "Resisting Mind Control." *USA Today,* November 1980.

Asch, S.E. "The Doctrine of suggestion, prestige, and imitation in social psychology." *Psychological Review* 55, 1948.

––––––. "Effects of group pressure upon the modification and distortion of judgments." In *Groups, Leadership, and Men,* edited by H. Guetzkow. Pittsburgh: Carnegie Press, 1951.

––––––. *Social Psychology.* New York: Prentice-Hall, 1952.

Bandler, R., and Grinder, J. *Patterns of the Hypnotic Techniques of Milton H. Erickson, M.D.* Cupertino, Calif.: Meta Publications, 1975.

Bandura, A. *Principles of Behavior Modification.* New York: Holt, Rinehart & Winston, 1969.

Bateson, G. *Steps to an Ecology of Mind.* New York: Ballantine, 1972.

Brown, J.A.C. *Techniques of Persuasion.* Middlesex, England: Pelican, 1963.

Brownfield, Charles A. *The Brain Benders.* New York: Exposition Press, 1972.

* Cialdini, Robert B. *Influence: The New Psychology of Modern Persuasion.* New York: William Morrow, 1984.

Clark, John G. "We Are All Cultists at Heart." *Newsday,* November 30, 1978.

––––––. Statement during Informational Meeting on the Cult Phenomenon in the U.S. Washington, D.C.: Senate Hearing Room, February 5, 1978.

––––––. "The Manipulation of Madness." Unpublished paper.

––––––. "Cults." *Journal of the American Medical Association,* Vol. 242, No. 3., July 20, 1979.

* Clark, J.G.; Langone, M.D.; Schecter, R.E.; and Daly, R.C.B. *Destructive Cult Conversion: Theory, Research, and Treatment.* Weston, Mass.: American Family Foundation, 1981.

Conway, Flo, and Siegelman, Jim. "Information Disease: Have Cults Created a New Mental Illness?" *Science Digest,* January 1982, 86ff.

––––––. "Information Disease: Effects of Covert Induction and Deprogramming." *Update,* Vol. 10, No. 2, June 1986.

––––––. "University study concludes mind control can cause lasting and damaging alterations of thought: University of Oregon researchers studied 400 former members of 48 cults." *Cult Awareness Newsletter,* December 1985.

Cushman, Philip. "The Self Besieged: Recruitment, Indoctrination Processes in Restrictive Groups." *The Journal for the Theory of Social Behavior,* March 1986.

* Dellinger, R. *Cults and Kids: A Study of Coercion*. Nebraska: Boys Town, 1985.

Dilts, Robert; Grinder, John; Bandler, Richard; Bandler, Leslie C.; and Delozier, Judith. *Neuro-Linguistic Programming: The Structure of Subjective Experience*. Vol. 1. Cupertino, Calif.: Meta Publications, 1980.

* Ellul, Jacques. *Propaganda: The Formation of Men's Attitudes*. New York: Alfred A. Knopf, 1965.

Erickson, M.H., and Rossi, Ernest, eds. *The Collected Papers of Milton H. Erickson on Hypnosis*. New York: Irvington, 1980. Vol. 1, *The Nature of Hypnosis and Suggestion;* Vol. 2, *Hypnotic Alteration of Sensory, Perceptual and Psychophysiological Processes;* Vol. 3, *Hypnotic Investigation of Psychodynamic Processes;* Vol. 4, *Innovative Hypnotherapy*.

Erickson, Milton H.; Rossi, Ernest L.; and Rossi, Sheila I. *Hypnotic Realities: The Induction of Clinical Hypnosis and Forms of Indirect Suggestion*. New York: Irvington, 1976.

Farber, I.E.; Harlow, Harry F.; and West, Louis Jolyon. "Brainwashing, Conditioning, and DDD." *Sociometry*, Vol. 20, No. 4, December 1957.

Festinger, Leon; Riecken, Henry W.; and Schachter, Stanley. *When Prophecy Fails: A Social and Psychological Study of a Modern Group That Predicted the Destruction of the World*. New York: Harper & Row, 1956.

Frank, Jerome D. *Persuasion and Healing*. New York: Schocken, 1961.

Freud, Sigmund. *Group Psychology and the Analysis of the Ego*. New York: W.W. Norton, 1959.

Fromm, Erich. *Escape from Freedom*. New York: Avon, 1965.

Glass, Leonard L.; Kirsch, Michael A.; and Parris, Frederick N. "Psychiatric Disturbances Associated with Erhard Seminars Training: A Report of Cases; Additional Cases and Theoretical Considerations." *American Journal of Psychiatry;* March 1977 and November 1977.

* Goldberg, Lorna, and Goldberg, William. "Group Work with Former Cultists." *Social Work*, Vol. 27, No. 2, March 1982.

Goldfried, Marvin R., and Merbaum, Michael, eds. *Behavior Change Through Self-Control*. New York: Holt, Rinehart & Winston, 1973.

* Gordon, David, and Meyers-Anderson, Maribeth. *Phoenix: Therapeutic Patterns of Milton H. Erickson*. Cupertino, Calif.: Meta Publications, 1981.

Greek, Adrian, and Greek, Anne. *Mind Abuse by Cults and Others*. Portland, Ore.: Positive Action Center, 1985.

Haley, J. *Uncommon Therapy: The Psychiatric Techniques of Milton H. Erickson, M.D.* New York: Norton, 1973.

* Halperin, David, ed. *Psychodynamic Perspectives on Religion, Sect and Cult*. New York: John Wright, 1983.

Heller, Randy K. *Deprogramming for Do It Yourselfers: A Cure for the Common Cult*. Medina, Oh.: Gentle Press, 1982.

Hersh, Tom. "The Phenomenology of Belief Systems." *Journal of Humanistic Psychology,* Vol. 20, No. 2, Spring 1980.

Hochman, John. "Iatrogenic Symptoms Associated with a Therapy Cult: Examination of an Extinct 'New Psychotherapy' with Respect to Psychiatric Deterioration and 'Brainwashing'." *Psychiatry,* Vol. 47, November 1984.

* Hoffer, Eric. *The True Believer.* New York: Harper & Row, 1951.

———. *The Ordeal of Change.* New York: Harper & Row, 1963.

* Hoyt, Karen C. "The Use of Thought Reform in Large Group Awareness Training with Specific Focus on est." Master's thesis, John F. Kennedy University, June 1985. Available through Spiritual Counterfeits Project (see Resource Organizations in Appendix).

Jung, C.G. *Psychology and Religion.* New Haven: Yale University Press, 1938.

Key, Wilson Bryan. *Subliminal Seduction.* New York: Signet, 1973.

Kaslow, Florence, and Sussman, Marvin. "Cults and the Family." *Marriage and Family Review,* Vol. 4, Nos. 3 and 4. New York: Haworth, 1982.

Kilbourne, Brock, ed. *Scientific Research and New Religions: Divergent Perspectives.* San Francisco: Pacific Division of the American Association for the Advancement of Science, 1985.

Kilpatrick, William Kirk. *Psychological Seduction: The Failure of Modern Psychology.* New York: Thomas Nelson, 1983.

La Barre, Weston. *They Shall Take Up Serpents: The Psychology of the Southern Snake-Handling Cult.* New York: Schocken, 1969.

* Lankton, Stephen R., and Lankton, Carol H. *The Answer Within: A Clinical Framework of Ericksonian Hypnotherapy.* New York: Brunner/Mazel, 1983.

Leary, Timothy. *Neuropolitique.* Las Vegas: Falcon Press, 1988.

Lewin, Kurt. *Frontiers in Group Dynamics: Concept, Method, and Reality in Social Science.* Human Relations, Vol. 1, 1947.

* Lifton, Robert Jay. *Thought Reform and the Psychology of Totalism.* New York: W.W. Norton, 1961.

———. *The Future of Immortality and Other Essays for a Nuclear Age.* New York: Basic Books, 1987.

Lisman, Michael, and Tanenhaus, Sara. *Cults as Restrictive Groups: Assessing Individuals During Recruitment, Indoctrination and Departure.* Unpublished manuscript, California State University, Sacramento, 1988.

MacHovec, Frank J. *Cults and Personality.* Springfield, Ill.: Charles C. Thomas, 1989.

Mahoney, Michael J., and Thoreson, Carl E. *Self-Control: Power to the Person.* Monterey, Calif.: Brooks/Cole, 1974.

* Marks, John. *The Search for the Manchurian Candidate: The CIA and Mind Control.* New York: Times Books, 1979.

* Meerloo, Joost A. *Rape of the Mind.* New York: Grosset & Dunlap, 1961.

Milgram, Stanley. *Obedience to Authority.* New York: Harper & Row, 1974.

————. "Behavioral Study of Obedience." *The Journal of Abnormal and Social Psychology,* Vol. 67, No. 4, 1963.

* Miller, Jesse S. "The Utilization of Hypnotic Techniques in Religious Cult Conversion." Weston, Mass.: *The Cultic Studies Journal,* Vol. 3, No. 2, 1986.

* Morse, Edwin L., and Morse, Julia C. "Toward a Theory of Therapy with Cultic Victims." *American Journal of Psychotherapy,* Vol. 41, No. 4, October 1987.

Mostache, Harriet. *Searching: Practices and Beliefs of the Religious Cults and Human Potential Groups.* New York: Stravon Educational Press, 1983.

Northrup, Bowen. "Treating the Mind—Psychotherapy Faces a Stubborn Problem: Abuses by Therapists; Role Imparts Power That is Easy to Misuse, and Field is Tricky One to Regulate; The Damage a Victim Suffers." *The Wall Street Journal,* Vol. 208, No. 85.

* Ofshe, Richard, and Singer, Margaret. "Attacks on Peripheral versus Central Elements of Self and the Impact of Thought Reforming Techniques." *The Cultic Studies Journal,* Vol. 3, No. 1, 1986.

Packard, Vance. *The Hidden Persuaders.* New York: David McKay, 1965.

Randi, James. *Flim Flam! Psychics, ESP, Unicorns and Other Delusions.* Buffalo, NY: Prometheus Books, 1986.

Reich, Wilhelm. *The Mass Psychology of Fascism.* New York: Pocket Books, 1976.

Rose, Steven. *The Conscious Brain.* New York: Vintage Books, 1976.

Rosen, R.D. *Psychobabble.* New York: Avon, 1975.

* Sargant, William. *Battle for the Mind.* London: Pan Books, 1951, 1959.

————. *The Unquiet Mind.* London: Pan Books, 1967.

————. *The Mind Possessed.* New York: Penguin, 1975.

* Satir, Virginia. *Conjoint Family Therapy.* Palo Alto: Science and Behavior Books, 1964.

————. *Helping Families to Change.* Hays, Kansas: The High Plains Comprehensive Community Mental Health Center, 1972.

————. *Peoplemaking.* Palo Alto: Science and Behavior Books, 1972.

* Schein, Edgar, with Schneier, Inge, and Barker, Curtis. *Coercive Persuasion.* New York: W.W. Norton, 1971.

Shapiro, E. "Destructive Cultism." *American Family Physician,* February 1977.

* Singer, Margaret. "Coming Out of the Cults." *Psychology Today,* January 1979.

————. "Cults: What Are They? Why Now? *Forecast for Home Economics,* May/June 1979.

————. "Consultation With Families of Cultists." In Wynne, L.C.; McDaniel, S.H.; and Weber, T.T. *Systems Consultation: A New Perspective for Family Therapy.* New York: Guilford Press, 1986.

————. "Group Psychodynamics." In *The Merck Manual of Diagnosis and Therapy,* edited by R. Berkow. Rahway, N.J.: Merck Sharp & Dohme Research Laboratories, 1987.

* Singer, Margaret, and West, Louis J. "Cults, Quacks and Non-Professional Psychotherapies," *Comprehensive Textbook of Psychiatry, III.* Baltimore: Williams & Wilkins, 1980.

Spero, M.H. "Psychotherapeutic procedure with religious cult devotees." *The Journal of Nervous and Mental Disease,* 1982.

Sprecher, Paul. "The Cult as a Total Institution: Perceptual Distortion, Consensual Validation, and Independent Decision Making" delivered to the panel "Taking the Cult to Court," Conference on Law and Society, Washington, D.C., June 13, 1987.

Skinner, B.F. *Beyond Freedom and Dignity.* New York: Alfred A. Knopf, 1971.

* Temerlin, M.K., and Temerlin, J.W. "Psychotherapy Cults: An Iatrogenic Perversion." *Psychotherapy: Theory, Research and Practice,* Vol. 19, No. 2, Summer 1982.

Verdier, Paul A. *Brainwashing and the Cults.* Calif.: The Institute of Behavioral Conditioning, 1977.

Watzlawick, P.; Weakland, J.; and Fisch, R. *Change.* New York: W.W. Norton, 1974.

West, Louis Jolyon. "Contemporary Cults—Utopian Image, Infernal Reality." *The Center Magazine,* March/April 1982.

West, L. J., and Delgado, Richard. "Psyching Out the Cults' Collective Mania." *Los Angeles Times,* October 26, 1978.

* Zeig, J.K. *Ericksonian Approaches to Hypnosis and Psychotherapy.* New York: Brunner/Mazel, 1982.

Zeitlin, Hilly. "Hypnosis and Cultic Induction Analyzed." *CAN News,* August 1986.

Zimbardo, Phillip. "Now That Cognitive Science Has Put the Head Back on the Body of Psychology, We Might Consider Implanting a Little Soul." *Psychology Today,* May 1982.

* Zimbardo, Phillip, and Ebbesen, Ebbe B. *Influencing Attitudes and Changing Behavior.* Reading, Mass.: Addison-Wesley, 1970.

Religious Orientation

Bjornstad, James. *The Moon Is Not the Son.* Minneapolis, Minn.: Bethany Fellowship, Dimension Books, 1976.

* Bussell, Harold. *Unholy Devotion: Why Cults Lure Christians.* Grand Rapids, Mich.: Zondervan, 1983.

Cohen, Daniel. *The New Believers: Young Religion in America.* New York: Ballantine, 1975.

Eisenberg, Gary D. *Smashing the Idols: A Jewish Inquiry into the Cult Phenomenon.* Northvale, NJ: Jason Aronson, 1988.

* Enroth, Ronald. *Youth, Brainwashing and the Extremist Cults.* Grand Rapids, Mich.: Zondervan, 1977.

Groothius, Douglas R. *Unmasking the New Age: Is there a New Religious Movement Trying to Transform Society?* Downers Grove, Ill.: InterVarsity Press, 1986.

Hunt, Dave. *The Cult Explosion.* Irvine, Calif.: Harvest House, 1980.

James, William. *Varieties of Religious Experience.* Britain: Fontana, 1960.

Jones, Jerry. *What Does the Boston Movement Teach?* Bridgeton, Mo.: Mid-America Book and Tape Sales, 1990.

Langford, Harris. *Traps: A Probe of Those Strange New Cults.* Decatur, Ga.: Presbyterian Church of America, 1977.

Larson, Bob. *Larson's Book of Cults.* Wheaton, Ill.: Tyndale House, 1982.

LeBar, Rev. James J. *Cults, Sects, and the New Age.* Huntington, In.: Our Sunday Visitor, 1989.

Levitt, Zola. *The Spirit of Sun Myung Moon.* Irvine, Calif.: Harvest House, 1976.

Martin, Rachel. *Escape: The True Story of a Young Woman Caught in the Clutches of a Religious Cult.* Denver, Colo.: Accent Books, 1979.

Martin, Walter. *The New Cults.* Santa Ana, Calif.: Vision House, 1980.

———. *Kingdom of the Cults.* Minneapolis: Bethany House, 1985.

MacCollam, Joel A. *Carnival of Souls.* New York: Seabury, 1978.

May, Rollo. *Man's Search for Himself.* New York: Delta Books, 1978.

Needleman, Jacob, and Baker, George, eds. *Understanding the New Religions.* New York: Seabury, 1978.

Yamamoto, J. Isamu. *The Puppet Master: A Biblical Perspective and Inquiry into Sun Myung Moon.* Downers Grove, Ill.: InterVarsity Press, 1977.

* Yeakley, Flavil R., ed. *The Discipling Dilemma.* Nashville, Tenn., Gospel Advocate Press, 1988.

Legal

Aronin, Douglas. "Cults, Deprogramming, and Guardianship: A Model Legislative Proposal." *Columbia Journal of Law and Social Problems,* 17, 1982.

Brandon, Thomas S. *New Religions, Conversions, and Deprogramming: New Frontiers of Religious Liberty.* The Center for Law and Religious Freedom, January 1982.

* Delgado, Richard. "Religious Totalism: Gentle and Ungentle Persuasion Under the First Amendment." *Southern California Law Review,* Vol. 51, No. 1, 1977.

———. "Ascription of criminal states of mind: Toward a defense theory for the coercively persuaded ('brainwashed') defendant." *Minnesota Law Review,* 1978.

———. "Religious totalism as slavery." *New York University Review of Law and Social Change,* 1979–80.

————. "Cults and Conversion: The Case for Informed Consent." *Georgia Law Review,* Vol. 16, No. 3, Spring 1982.

* ————. "When Religious Exercise is Not Free: Deprogramming and the Constitutional Status of Coercively Induced Belief." *Vanderbilt Law Review,* 1984.

————. "A Response to Professor Dressler." *Minnesota Law Review.*

Dressler, Joshua. "Professor Delgado's 'Brainwashing' Defense: Courting a Determinist Legal System." *Minnesota Law Review.*

* Greene, Ford. "Appellant Molko's Response to Briefs by Amicus Curiae National Council of Churches of Christ, Christian Legal Society, and the American Psychological Association." Supreme Court of the State of California, March 18, 1987.

Greene, Robert H. "People v. Religious Cults: Legal Guidelines for Criminal Activities, Tort Liability, and Parental Remedies." *Suffolk University Law Review.*

Lemoult, John E. "Deprogramming Members of Religious Sects." *Fordham Law Review,* 1978.

Lucksted, Orlin D., and Martell, Dale F. "Cults: A Conflict Between Religious Liberty and Involuntary Servitude?" *FBI Law Enforcement Bulletin,* 1982.

Robbins, Thomas. *"Cults, Brainwashing and Deprogramming: The View from the Law Journals."* Unpublished manuscript.

Rosedale, Herbert L. *"Letter to Mr. Ira Glasser."* American Civil Liberties Union, 1984.

Rudin, Marcia. "The Cult Phenomenon: Fad or Fact?" *New York University Review of Law and Social Change,* Vol. 9, No. 3, 1979–80.

Shapiro, Robert N. " 'Mind Control' or Intensity of Faith: The Constitutional Protection of Religious Beliefs." Harvard Civil Liberties Law Review, 1978.

————. "Of Robots, Persons, and the Protection of Religious Beliefs." *Southern California Law Review,* 1983.

Shepherd, William C. "The Prosecutor's Reach: Legal Issues Stemming from the New Religious Movements." *Journal of the American Academy of Religion.*

(author unavailable) "Cults, Deprogrammers, and the Necessity Defense." *Michigan Law Review,* Vol. 80.

Zoning Board of Appeals, Town of New Castle, New York; Society of Neighbors. Petition to Deny Application of the Moon Organization to Operate an Indoctrination Center; Legal Decision, Appendix, and footnotes. 1981.

* The Assembly of the State of New York. "Public Hearing on the Treatment of Children by Cults." August 9–10, 1979.

The Moon Organization

Anderson, Scott, and Anderson, Jon Lee. *Inside the League.* New York: Dodd Mead, 1986.

* Boettcher, Robert. *Gifts of Deceit—Sun Myung Moon, Tongsun Park and the Korean Scandal.* New York: Holt, Rinehart & Winston, 1980.

Edwards, Christopher. *Crazy for God: The Nightmare of Cult Life.* Englewood Cliffs, N.J.: Prentice-Hall, 1979.

* Freed, Josh. *Moonwebs: Journey into the Mind of a Cult.* Toronto, Ont.: Dorset, 1980.

* Greene, Ford, esq. *The Outline of Rev. Moon's Hand in Central America: The Unification Church, the World Anti-Communist League, CAUSA and John Singlaub.* Unpublished manuscript, 1987.

Heftmann, Erica. *Dark Side of the Moonies.* Sydney, Australia: Penguin, 1982.

Horowitz, Irving Louis, ed. *Science, Sin and Scholarship: The Politics of Reverend Moon and the Unification Church.* Cambridge, Mass.: MIT Press, 1978.

Lofland, John. *The Doomsday Cult.* New York: Irvington, 1977.

* *Investigation of Korean-American Relations: Report of the Subcommittee on International Organizations.* Washington, D.C.: U.S. Government Printing Office. Stock number 052-070-04729-1, October 31, 1978.

* Kemperman, Steve. *Lord of the Second Advent.* Ventura, Calif.: Regal Books, 1981.

Moon, Sun Myung. *Divine Principle.* New York: Holy Spirit Association for the Unification of World Christianity, 1973.

Racer, David G. *Not for Sale: The Rev. Sun Myung Moon and One American's Freedom.* St. Paul: Tiny Press, 1989.

Underwood, Barbara, and Underwood, Betty. *Hostage to Heaven: Four Years in the Unification Church by an Ex-Moonie and the Mother Who Fought to Free Her.* New York: Clarkson N. Potter, 1979.

* U.S. v. Sun Myung Moon and Takeru Kamiyama (Moon conviction of conspiracy and filing false tax returns, Kamiyama of aiding and abetting filing of false returns, obstruction of justice and perjury). 718 Federal Reporter, 2nd Series, Nos. 755, 765, 766 and 1153, Dockets 82-1275, 82-1279, 82-1277, 82-1357 and 82-1387. United States Court of Appeals, Second Circuit. Argued March 23, 1983. Decided September 13, 1983.

Wood, Allen Tate with Vitek, Jack. *Moonstruck: A Memoir of My Life in a Cult.* New York: William Morrow, 1979.

Transcendental Meditation

Lazarus, A. "Psychiatric Problems Precipitated by Transcendental Meditation." *Psychological Reports,* 1976.

* Persinger, Michael A.; Carrey, Normand J.; and Suess, Lynn A. *TM and Cult Mania.* North Quincy, Mass.: Christopher Publishing House, 1980.

Scott, R.D. *Transcendental Misconceptions.* San Diego: Bobbs-Merrill, 1978.

NSA (Nichirin Shoshu of America)

Tono, Reverend Kando. ". . . the Background, Meaning, Content and Spirit . . ." *Kando Tono,* P.O. Box 1868, Grand Central Station, New York, NY 10163, 1981.

Eckankar

* Lane, David Christopher. *The Making of a Spiritual Movement: The Untold Story of Paul Twitchell and Eckankar.* Del Mar, Calif.: Del Mar Press, 1983.

Scientology

Cooper, Paulette. *The Scandal of Scientology.* New York: Tower Publications, 1971.

* Corydon, Bent, and Hubbard, L. Ron, Jr. *L. Ron Hubbard: Messiah or Madman?* Secaucus, N.J.: Lyle Stuart, 1987.

Evans, Dr. Christopher. *Cults of Unreason.* New York: Delta, 1973.

Kaufman, Robert. *Inside Scientology.* New York: Olympia, 1972.

Lamont, Stewart. *Religion, Inc.* London: Harrap, 1986.

Malko, George. *Scientology—The Now Religion.* New York: Delacorte, 1970.

* Miller, Russell. *Bare Faced Messiah: The True Story of L. Ron Hubbard.* New York: Henry Holt, 1988.

Vosper, Cyril. *The Mind Benders: The Book They Tried to Ban.* London: Neville Spearman, Ltd. 1973.

Wallis, Roy. *The Road to Total Freedom: A Sociological Analysis of Scientology.* New York: Columbia University Press, 1977.

Krishna

Daner, Francine Jeane. *The American Children of Krishna: A Study of the Hare Krishna Movement.* New York: Holt, Rinehart & Winston, 1976.

Hubner, John and Gruson, Lindsey. *Monkey on a Stick: Murder, Madness and the Hari Krishnas.* New York: Harcourt, Brace & Jovanovich, 1988.

Levine, Faye. *The Strange World of Hare Krishna.* New York: Fawcett, 1973.

Yanoff, Morris. *Where is Joey? Lost Among the Hare Krishnas.* Chicago: Swallow, 1981.

The Children of God (Family of Love)

* Davis, Deborah Berg. *The Children of God: The Inside Story.* Grand Rapids, Mich.: Zondervan, 1984.

McManus, Una. *Not for a Million Dollars.* Nashville, Tenn.: Impact Books, 1980.

Wallerstein, Herbert J. *Final Report on the Activities of the Children of God to Honorable Louis J. Lefkowitz, Attorney General of the State of New York.* New York: Charity Frauds Bureau, September 30, 1974.

Satanic Cults

Kehaner, Larry. *Cults That Kill: Probing the Underworld of Occult Crime.* New York: Warner Books, 1988.

Lyons, Arthur. *Satan Wants You.* New York: Mysterious Press, 1988.

Scott, Gini G. *The Magicians: A Study of Power in a Black Magic Group.* Oakland, Calif.: Creative Communications Press.

Terry, Maury. *The Ultimate Evil.* New York: Doubleday, 1987.

Manson

Atkins, Susan, and Slosser, Bob. *Susan Atkins: Child of Satan—Child of God.* Plainfield, N.J.: Logos International, 1977.

Bugliosi, Vincent, and Gentry, Curt. *Helter Skelter: The True Story of the Manson Murders.* New York: Bantam, 1974.

The People's Temple (Jim Jones)

Kilduff, Marshall, and Javers, Ron. *The Suicide Cult: The Inside Story of the Peoples Temple Sect and the Massacre in Guyana.* New York: Bantam, 1978.

* Mills, Jeannie. *Six Years with God.* New York: A & W, 1979.

* Reiterman, Tim, and Jacobs, John. *Raven: The Untold Story of the Rev. Jim Jones and His People.* New York: Dutton, 1982.

White, Mel. *Deceived: The Jonestown Tragedy.* Old Tappan, N.J.: Fleming H. Revel, Spire Books, 1979.

Wooden, Kenneth. *The Children of Jonestown.* New York: McGraw-Hill, 1981.

Yee, Min S., and Layton, Thomas N. *In My Father's House: The Story of the Layton Family and the Reverend Jim Jones.* New York: Holt, Rinehart & Winston, 1981.

The LaRouche Organization

King, Dennis. *Lyndon LaRouche and the New American Fascism.* New York: Doubleday, 1989.

The Way International

Morton, Douglas V., and Juedes, John P. *The Integrity and the Accuracy of The Way's Word.* St. Louis: Personal Freedom Outreach, 1980.

Williams, J. L. *Victor P. Wierwille and The Way International.* Chicago: Moody Press, 1979.

Synanon

Gerstel, David U. *Paradise Incorporated: Synanon.* Novata, Calif.: Presidio Press, 1982.

* Mitchell, Dave; Mitchell, Cathy; and Ofshe, Richard. *The Light on Synanon.* Point Reyes, Calif.: Seaview Books, 1980.

Jehovah's Witnesses

* Franz, Raymond. *Crisis of Conscience.* Atlanta: Commentary Press, 1983.

Harrison, Barbara Grizzuti. *Visions of Glory: A History and a Memory of Jehovah's Witnesses.* New York: Simon & Schuster, 1978.

* Magnani, Duane, and Barrett, Arthur. *Dialogue with Jehovah's Witnesses,* Vols. 1 and 2. Clayton, Calif.: Witness Inc., 1983.

Penton, James A. *Apocalypse Delayed: The Story of the Jehovah's Witnesses.* Toronto: University of Toronto Press, 1985.

* Reed, David A. *Jehovah's Witnesses: Answered Verse by Verse.* Grand Rapids, Mich.: Baker Book House, 1986.

Rajneesh

Belfrage, Sally. *Flowers of Emptiness: Reflections on an Ashram.* New York: Seaview Books, 1980.

Gordon, James S. *The Golden Guru.* Lexington, Mass.: The Stephen Greene Press, 1987.

Milne, Hugh. *Bhagwan: The God That Failed.* New York: St. Martin's Press, 1987.

Strelley, Kate. *The Ultimate Game: The Rise and Fall of Bhagwan Shree Rajneesh.* New York: Harper & Row, 1987.

Index

About the Author

Raised in a middle-class Jewish family, Steven Hassan was recruited into the Moon organization at the age of nineteen while a student at Queens College. During his twenty-seven-month membership, he was involved in a wide range of activities including recruiting and indoctrinating new members, fundraising, political campaigning, and personally meeting with Sun Myung Moon during numerous leadership sessions. He ultimately rose to the rank of Assistant Director of the Unification Church at National Headquarters. Following a serious automobile accident, Mr. Hassan was deprogrammed by several former members at his parents' request.

In the fourteen years since he left the Moon cult, Steven Hassan has been involved in educating the public about destructive cults in America. He holds a master's degree in counseling psychology from Cambridge College, and his understanding and expertise in the area of cult mind control have been acknowledged internationally. During his years of work he has helped hundreds of persons victimized by cult-related mind control. He has provided numerous training workshops and seminars for mental health professionals, educators, and law enforcement officers. Mr. Hassan also served as the National Coordinator of FOCUS, a support and information network organized by and for former members of all destructive cult groups.

Steven Hassan has helped to pioneer a new approach to deprogramming called "non-coercive cult exit-counseling." Unlike the stressful and media sensationalized "kidnap deprogramming," the non-coercive approach is an effective and legal alternative for families to help cult victims. This approach utilizes family members and friends and teaches them how to strategically influence the individual involved in the group. He periodically holds training workshops for families of cult members around the country.

A major portion of Steven Hassan's time and energy is devoted to preventive education. He has addressed the Cardinal's Commission on Human Rights, the American Jewish Committee, the American Bar Association Conference on Religion and Tort; the Eastern Regional Conference on Multiple Personality and Dissociation; the American Association for Counseling and Development's International Counseling Conference in Hong Kong, as well as hundreds of campus, youth, and religious organizations throughout the country.

Mr. Hassan has appeared on numerous television and radio shows, including *The Today Show; Oprah Winfrey; Sally Jessy Raphael; Evening Magazine; Larry King Live;* and *Good Morning America.* His work has been referred to in *Newsweek; The Boston Globe; The Los Angeles Times; The Psychiatric Times; USA Today;* and the *Washington Post.*

For more information contact Steven Hassan, PO Box 686, New Town Branch, Boston MA 02258.

904 2345701

Zulma L Ibáñez